For Maggie

Contents

Acknowledgements

This book could not have been written without the advice, support and input of a number of people. Thanks are due in particular to the many people who took part in the research that formed the basis of this book, including the disabled people, individuals from disabled people's organisations, housing providers and financial services representatives who shared their thoughts and advice. I am especially grateful to the disabled people who generously gave me their time, shared accounts of their lives and histories, and welcomed me into their homes. I would also like to thank my colleagues at the Centre for Disability Studies and the School of Sociology and Social Policy at the University of Leeds for all their help over the years, and thanks go particularly to Malcolm Harrison and Colin Barnes for their continual advice and encouragement. Finally, I owe special thanks to my family, and especially to my partner, Steve, for all of the love and support they have provided during the writing of this book. I could not have completed it without them.

ONE

Introduction

This book examines housing issues, policies and practices relating to disabled people, and explores available choices, opportunities and barriers in the field. The focus is on disabled people's acquisition of, or *access* to, accommodation, and how individuals *experience* housing. We will see how housing options and pathways can be constrained, conditioned and assisted by a range of actors, institutions and practices. With regard to disabled people's experiences, the book will show how housing can be a place of independence, control and security, or (if inaccessible or unsuitable) how it can restrict an individual and their family, leading to dependency and negatively affecting lifestyle choices. While other variables are clearly significant for daily living – including financial position, household composition and available support – the dwelling itself plays a vital role in people's lives. As such, although housing circumstances are significant elements of life for everybody, for disabled people they can be especially crucial in the achievement of independent living.

In reviewing the roles of the home, we should not separate the dwelling from its socio-economic contexts. There has been a tendency for housing providers and professionals to concentrate on physical factors when considering disabled people's housing needs, and while these are extremely significant, such a focus may neglect social and financial issues, which may be just as important for some residents. One idea underpinning this book is the need to see the housing settings and needs of households in holistic ways. This theme is especially evident in the later chapters where we look at the various aspects of housing affecting disabled people's opportunities that can be identified from a broadly social approach to understanding disability. These include aspects of housing design and construction (especially the general accessibility and adaptability of the physical environment), the availability and presentation of information on housing options, the economic factors that affect access to housing (including general affordability and ability to secure housing finance) and the role of 'actors' involved in the process of building, selling and allocating housing. Thus, we see how disabled people's choices and opportunities within housing may be restricted by barriers that can be categorised as physical, attitudinal, financial and related to communication. It is hoped that such an approach will be more in line with the views and expectations of disabled people themselves.

It is intended that this book will help to fill an important gap in current literature by providing a general overview of housing issues for disabled people that is not readily available at present. It is hoped that the text will be of value to those involved in housing, whether in relation to building and constructing dwellings; planning, managing and allocating social or private rented housing; providing housing finance for owner-occupation; developing policy; or conducting research in the area. The book is also designed to be accessible and useful for both undergraduate and postgraduate students given the rise of disability issues within a wide range of fields in recent years (including sociology, social policy, geography, urban studies and health studies). This chapter begins by highlighting what we currently know about the housing circumstances of disabled people, as indicated in available data. This is followed by an outline of the intentions of the text, some brief notes on terminology and details of the book's contents.

Disabled people and housing

Although data are dependent on the definitions used, figures indicate that there are 11 million disabled adults in the UK and 770,000 disabled children (seven per cent of all children) (PMSU, 2005, p 27). While these figures are contentious, the PMSU report makes clear that they include some of those who may not identify themselves as disabled people. In addition, the Office for Disability Issues (ODI) (2010) points out that the prevalence of impairment increases with age, with one in two people over state pension age being a disabled person, compared with one in 20 children and one in seven working-age adults. With disabled people constituting such a large percentage of the population, and with an ever-increasing ageing population, ensuring that housing needs are met is crucial. The relationship between disability and housing has been of increasing interest in recent decades to the academic community, as well as to political audiences, policymakers and governments. The 1995 Disability Discrimination Act, for instance, has influenced a range of initiatives and policy changes that have affected disabled people's opportunities within housing. Official commitment is particularly evidenced in Part M of the 1999 English Building Regulations (and the equivalent regulations in Northern Ireland and Scotland), in discussions around Lifetime Homes standards and in the 2006 Disability Equality Duty, which have all aimed to tackle specific housing issues for disabled people (see Chapter Two for further detail).

Despite the data limitations, some useful statistics illuminate the current relationship between disabled people and housing. Recent data from a study for the ODI indicate that 31 per cent of disabled people live in social rented housing compared with 20 per cent of the population as a whole (Williams et al, 2008, p 166). In addition, figures obtained from the Survey of English Housing show that the number of households in the social rented sector containing a disabled person increased '... from 38 per cent in 1994-95 to 43 per cent in 2003-04. By then, more than twice the proportion of social tenant households contained such a member as in owner-occupier or private rented households' (Hills, 2007, p 47). Although such statistics may not be ideal, the data do indicate reliance on social renting for disabled people, which is in keeping with claims made in literature on the subject (Morris, 1990; Laurie, 1991; Oliver and Barnes, 1998; Stewart, 2004; Wood, 2004). Families with a disabled child are also more likely than families with a non-disabled child to live in social rented accommodation (Beresford and Rhodes, 2008). Furthermore, the Greater London Authority (GLA) (2006) report found that those defined as 'special needs' households were half as likely to live in private renting as all London households (using 412,378 households). Moreover:

> A high proportion of 'frail elderly', 'severe sensory disability', and multiple special needs households as well as households with more than one special needs member, are owner-occupiers without mortgages, reflecting the high proportions of older people in these categories. (GLA, 2006, p 17)

This is likely to be because some impairments are associated disproportionately with older age and older people are more likely to have purchased their dwellings. As we shall see later, it is often more difficult for people who have impairments prior to purchasing their property to become home owners.

In addition to the main housing tenures, various forms of residential and what tend to be referred to as 'supported' housing options are also available. These include residential care homes, nursing homes, sheltered housing and 'very sheltered housing' (with the latter two tending to provide for older residents), as well as shared housing and hostels or self-contained clustered housing. (It is important to note that 'supported housing' can also refer to options within the mainstream tenures.) It is estimated that 129,548 people are in residential placements in the UK (Mansell et al, 2007), with 48,781 living in large institutions (30 people or more), 33,530 living in small institutions and 47,237 unclassified (although, again, data are problematic). It seems that particular groups are more represented than others within this form of housing, especially people labelled with learning difficulties and mental health service users. Age is also a factor here, with most people residing in institutions being classified as adults (Mansell et al, 2007). Some people may be forced to live in residential care accommodation because there are limited options available to them, or, as some have suggested, because such arrangements are more financially viable for local authorities than supporting people to live independently (Clements, 2007). One local authority area highlighted in the PMSU (2005, p 79) report, for instance, was shown to use only four per cent of 'learning disability revenue funding' to support people labelled with learning difficulties to live in their own home. The other 96 per cent was being used on residential care services, 60 per cent of which paid for large residential settings.

National data suggest that disabled people are more likely to have experienced homelessness than non-disabled people (see Hamer, 2006). How homelessness is defined in secondary statistics is important, as these figures are unlikely to include 'hidden homelessness'. This tends to involve people who may not have independent housing options available to them, or who experience limited social networks and support, such as people labelled with learning difficulties residing in the family home or in residential care accommodation (Harrison with Davis, 2001). Although being in residential care or staying with family is not directly homelessness, it reflects a severe lack of choice and limited opportunities to establish a 'home' that may induce feelings of a lack of control. It therefore needs to be treated alongside homelessness as an extension of the same issue. There may also be problems for people living in insecure, temporary and/or unsuitable accommodation. As Shelter (2006) has noted, even if a property does become available, certain factors may limit a person's ability to accept it. The time period in which the prospective tenant is expected to move in, for instance, is often relatively short, which could present difficulties where adaptations or support packages are needed before moving into a property. There may be particular impairment-specific issues too, for, as the Mental Health Foundation (MHF) (2006) points out, homelessness both creates or exacerbates mental illness and is precipitated by it. Such claims are supported by a recent report relating to London's street homeless that found that 85 per cent had 'mental health problems' (Roof News, 2009, p 4) and by research showing that people with '... schizophrenia and other major psychiatric disorders have a much higher risk of homelessness and housing instability' (Padgett, 2007, p 1926). The links between disability, health and homelessness are therefore complex. People may become homeless due to problems associated with ill health, but poor health and disablement may be exacerbated by homelessness. Unfortunately, we lack information on these processes.

Looking at the conditions in which disabled people live and the suitability of housing, an ODI study by Williams and colleagues (2008, p 167) found that those most likely to report the unsuitability of their dwellings were young people, people with visual impairments, those on lower incomes and people with three or more impairments. Unsuitability was often associated with structural limitations within the property, inability to afford adaptations, and being refused adaptations. It has also been shown that families with a disabled child are more likely to live in unsuitable housing than families with a non-disabled child, with overcrowding, lack of space, safety concerns, accessibility issues with stairs, poor repairs and wiring, and draughts and damp being noted (Beresford and Rhodes, 2008). There is some evidence, too, that black and minority ethnic disabled households are especially likely to experience poor housing conditions (Begum, 1992; Beresford and Rhodes, 2008), particularly Pakistani and Bangladeshi households with a disabled child (Chamba et al, 1999). Furthermore, there is a link between the perceived suitability of housing and tenure. The PMSU (2005) found that disabled people who were most likely to live in housing that did not suit their needs lived in privately rented accommodation. Those in owner-occupied housing were most likely to feel that their housing was suited to their needs. Finally, in relation to housing conditions, research on health and housing has shown that poor housing can affect health, just as health can affect housing opportunities. There have been, for instance, various studies that explore the relationship between health and residential environments (see *Housing Studies* special issue, May 2000). It is difficult in practice, however, to prove causation in situations where housing is allied with poor health or illness, as it may be that health affects housing circumstances.

There are, then, some useful data that highlight the housing situations of disabled people, and there has been some recognition of the need to address problems within recent policy and legislation. Nonetheless, despite the evidence available, and the recognised importance of housing, many disabled people continue to live in unsuitable, inaccessible or undesirable accommodation that may compromise their everyday lives. In particular, the level of choice available to disabled people within housing may be limited. These issues have taken on increased salience in the era of credit constraint and in the light of recent cuts in public expenditure, and are addressed in detail within this book.

About the book

There are three key objectives underpinning this book, the first of which is to demonstrate the importance of utilising a social approach to disability within housing policy, practice and research. For many who are familiar with disability model debates, this might at first seem outdated. Indeed, for people from the disabled people's movement or for academics involved in disability studies, the argument for the acceptance of social model ideas has been around for many years. What the current author suggests, however, is that the social approach to disability retains its value for exploring the many interlocking elements of disablement within housing, its administration and provision. While social model ideas have been developed theoretically within the disabled people's movement, these have yet to fully infiltrate housing policy and practice for disabled people, the attitudes of practitioners and society in general. We have seen a move towards some of the principles underpinning this model in recent years, notably in the PMSU (2005) report *Improving the Life Chances of Disabled People*, yet understanding and actual practice of these principles remain somewhat limited, and disabled people still encounter a range of physical, communication, financial and attitudinal barriers to participation in society (and specifically within housing).

The individual or 'medical' model of disability has tended to dominate policy and provision for disabled people, and locates the 'cause' of disadvantage in the impairment or condition that an individual has. Thus, it is a person's impairment that is seen to 'disable' them. As a result, housing provision for disabled people has tended to involve separate, segregated and 'special needs' solutions to housing problems. In the 1970s, this individual view of disability began to be challenged, with disabled activists arguing that it is in fact society that creates disability (UPIAS, 1976). This led to a redefinition of disability and the introduction of the social model of disability (Oliver, 1983, 1990a). A social model emphasises the structural factors that can affect, and shape, people's lives, rather than assuming that disadvantage results from individual restriction. Here, 'impairment' is the functional attribute of the individual (whether physical, sensory or cognitive) and disability is that which is socially created – a result of social, environmental and attitudinal barriers experienced by the individual. It has taken some time for these ideas to gain recognition, and it is only within the past decade that the UK government has begun to adopt at least the terminology of the social model. The model has also been challenged, with debates arising through claims that it does not fully explain experiences of impairment or differences between disabled people (see Chapter Three). It is significant to note at the outset, however, the importance of the social model as a tool for action and for targeting barriers (Oliver, 2004) rather than as a theory about society. The social model usefully highlights the holistic nature of disability experiences, identifying oppressive practices that are linked to a range of structural factors. It is this social understanding of disability that forms the focus of the current book and is used to underline the importance of structural factors, institutional discrimination and 'barriers'. It is also suggested that the social model can be extended, through exploring specific actions and processes that highlight differential experiences.

The second objective of the book is to synthesise previous findings in the field, while also introducing insights from the author's own research to address key gaps in knowledge and chart some new issues. In addition, the book documents historical and current trends in housing policy and provision for disabled people, emphasising key changes, as well as continuities. The book focuses mainly on access to, and experiences within, the three main tenures (social renting, private renting and owner-occupation). Other significant matters are addressed, however, such as homelessness, residential care and student housing. Looking at *access* to housing involves considering the available housing stock (see Chapter Four, which addresses mainly physical considerations), access to information (see also Chapter Four), financial resources (Chapter Five), and finally, the attitudes, assumptions and practices of 'gatekeepers' and organisations or institutions (Chapter Six). These factors will ultimately affect *experiences* of the dwelling too, and the *meanings* that individuals apply to their 'home' (see Chapter Seven). This comprehensive overview of the topic is important for policymakers and practitioners, as well as researchers, for an improved understanding of the opportunities and barriers facing disabled people within housing. It is particularly important that the constraints that prevent disabled people from exercising the right to live in suitable housing and to live in the housing tenure of their choice are made known. There are aspects of the disability and housing relationship that fall beyond the scope of this book but that are no less important for not being addressed here. These include the provision of allied support services within housing, relationships with formal and informal carers, and a more detailed analysis of homelessness and institutionalised forms of housing. For more information on these issues, see the website listings at the end of the book.

As noted above, the book draws on insights from the current author's own research. This explored several elements of the housing and disability relationship, including the housing circumstances of disabled people, relationships with different tenures (principally social renting, private renting and home ownership), issues related to meanings of 'home' and any barriers experienced during access to housing (particularly in the owner-occupied sector) (see Hemingway, 2008). Within disability research, the approach adopted for design, implementation and dissemination is an important consideration, as previous research paradigms have been held to be non-inclusive and oppressive (Oliver, 1992; Beazley et al, 1997; Moore et al, 1998). There is increasing pressure to apply an emancipatory framework to disability research (see Oliver, 1992; Shakespeare, 1996; Barnes, 2003), which, in short, is controlled by disabled people, is based on disabling experiences and embraces the social model of disability; for more detail, see the seven core principles put forward by the United Kingdom's Disabled Person's Council (UKDPC, 2005a). The research conducted by the current author was not emancipatory, but it aimed more modestly to provide evidence that might help to improve disabled people's housing situations and to do this in part through disabled people's own voices and perspectives. It therefore adopted a 'dual approach', with an experiential or 'grass-roots' perspective (gathering and putting forward disabled people's voices and experiences), complemented by mortgage and housing industry insights. These included the views of independent financial advisers, lender representatives, mortgage brokers, underwriters and estate agents. The latter were used, in particular, to provide a detailed illustration of industry practices, notions of risk and access to owner-occupation.

Investigating aspects of the lives of disabled people in a direct way was seen as fundamental to the study, and so experiences and opinions were gathered as far as possible in disabled people's own words. The study drew on informants from disabled people's organisations, including six organisations *of* disabled people and four organisations *for* disabled people, as well as 20 disabled individuals. Individual informants contacted the researcher in response to advertisements placed on various websites or via contacts made through disabled people's organisations. There was some diversity within the group, and informants lived in various forms of housing tenure (social and private renting, and owner-occupation). A variety of impairment groups were included in the sample, with self-defined categories of visual, hearing, mobility, cognitive and progressive impairments, as well as one mental health service user. A good set of insights was thus achieved in these terms, although there were inevitable limitations in the range. The material from these investigations informs parts of the following chapters. Some of the examples shown in this book also derive from six pilot interviews conducted with disabled people prior to the larger research project (see Hemingway, 2004a, 2004b). The names of all disabled informants have been changed for anonymity.

The final aim of the book is to draw attention to significant aspects of housing need in relation to disabled people. Notions of housing need are central to housing provision and allocation, particularly in the public sector. The type and level of support and assistance a disabled person receives has been previously described as a 'living options lottery', being determined by chance rather than by need (Fiedler, 1988). Classifications of 'priority' or 'deserving' have been deemed necessary for distributing available resources, and housing provision for disabled people has largely focused on targeting specific or individual access needs, often under the label of 'special needs' provision. While this form of housing is important for providing accessible living environments, it is often argued that a more appropriate solution might be to tackle inaccessible housing in general and meet need more effectively for the population as a whole. Even so, housing need is about more than physical accessibility, making consideration of social, cultural and financial factors a necessity. Difference in terms of age, ethnicity, religion, sexuality, culture, gender or impairment may also affect the use of the dwelling and consequent housing needs. Furthermore, housing need is about more than pathways; it entails what the 'home' means, or concerns feeling at 'home' in a dwelling.

While the concepts of house and home are often conflated, they are distinctive. For many, 'home' symbolises more than a shelter, or physical space, and instead relates to emotions, relationships and aspects of identity. In contrast, the 'house' is more commonly perceived as the physical 'container' (Tomas and Dittmar, 1995). This is not to suggest, however, that every house becomes a home or that interpretations of home will be the same across different cultures, nor that the house can be so neatly separated from home. Much of the literature on the meanings of home draws attention to the emotional significance of home; a place often associated with family, intimate relationships and memories, and especially with rearing children (Rakoff, 1977; Dupuis and Thorns, 1996; Bowlby et al, 1997; Lewin, 2001). Over time, the roles and presence of family members in the home may alter, but the significance of these relationships are, for some, retained in memories and nostalgia (Dupuis and Thorns, 1996; Walsh, 2004). While the family or household often signifies a positive association with home, it can also convey conflict and violence, psychologically or physically (Tomas and Dittmar, 1995; Bowlby et al, 1997) or hold negative associations resulting from relationship breakdown (Gurney and Means, 1993). As such, rather than a retreat or 'haven', home may be a point of conflict, making it '... not only a place we can escape *to,* but ... also ... a place we want to escape *from*' (Tomas and Dittmar, 1995, p 496; emphasis in original). 'Home' is a place associated with identity and self-expression, possessions, autonomy, control, comfort, security and privacy (especially through its distinction from the workplace and wider public domain), and the literature has discussed these factors in detail. Understanding such associations with home is important, but as Imrie (2004) points out, they tell us little about '... the cross-cutting variables that imbue domestic space with meaning' (p 747).

In the 1980s and 1990s, work in various fields began to emerge exploring the different variables and contexts that may affect experiences and meanings of home for different people. These have been categorised by several different authors (Rakoff, 1977; Gurney, 1990; Somerville, 1997; Harrison, 2004a; Mallet, 2004; Heywood, 2005; Nygren et al, 2007), and while the resulting categories have included a range of different factors, they have tended to cover similar variables. Thus, feelings of 'home' may be affected by households, families and relationships, tenure, work, responsibilities, time, place and culture. It is important, for instance, to be aware of historical and cultural variations in the meanings applied to home (Altman, 1993; Tamm, 1999). Furthermore, experiences relating to '... the composition and features of households' (Harrison, 2004b, p 61) or ascribed categories (such as age, gender, socio-economic position, sexual orientation, ethnicity and impairment) may play a significant role in the meanings attributed to home. Meanings may be affected, for example, by generational experiences and different life stages (Saunders and Williams, 1988; Saunders, 1989; Dupuis and Thorns, 1996; Lewin, 2001), by perceptions of sexuality (Smailes, 1994; Mallett, 2004), by gender distinctions relating to household roles, functions or income distribution (see Madigan et al, 1990; Bowlby et al, 1997; Kearns et al, 2000) or by ethnicity. In relation to the latter, the home may represent a place of increased security in which cultural preferences can be pursued in a less restricted environment than outside of it (Harrison with Davis, 2001), although such preferences may affect members of the household differently (for instance, in terms of age and gender). It is therefore important to take into account the various associations and influential variables in the meanings of home when considering housing need, and we return to some of these issues (as they relate to disabled people) in the concluding chapter. As we have seen, then, issues of housing need are complex, and housing practitioners, providers and policymakers should avoid simple associations between need and specific impairment.

Language and terminology

The language used to define and classify individuals and groups is an important consideration in discussions of disability, and is arguably influential in the construction of negative attitudes and perceptions within different cultures, which can have a detrimental impact on the people to whom it is directed (see Brisenden, 1986; Clark and Marsh, 2002). These issues have been well raised in relation to women and minority ethnic groups, but for disabled people only recently has more acceptable terminology started to emerge within society, shifting away from language that individualises disability. As mentioned earlier, in adopting a social understanding of disability, two distinct terms are identified within this book. 'Impairment' is the biological, functional attribute or condition of the individual, and 'disability' is social disadvantage or the experience of barriers and constraints of a social, economic and environmental nature (UPIAS, 1976; DPI, 1981). A person has an 'impairment' (either physical, sensory, intellectual or cognitive) and may then become 'disabled' by society's perception of, and reaction to, their impairment. Thus, the term 'people with disabilities' is avoided, for although once considered positive for the placing of 'people' first (and is still used in the US for this reason), it inaccurately labels the 'disability' as the functional condition of the person and the social 'disability' is overlooked. Where direct quotations from sources are included, however, alternative terminology may be used that is not considered appropriate by the author.

Although disabled people are not a homogeneous group, the book uses the term 'disabled people' to reflect the point that people with a range of impairments '... face social oppression and discrimination' (Beresford and Wallcraft, 1997, p 67). The term as a marker of 'difference' can also represent a '... source of identity and pride' (Swain and French, 2008a, p 2). The label 'people with learning difficulties' is also a contentious phrase and so within this book 'people labelled with learning difficulties' is used to illustrate an awareness of the controversies surrounding it. As noted by Barnes (2005), while the use of the term 'impairment' is problematic – commonly referring to 'weakened' bodies – it is inclusive of all conditions and recognises that '... labels are generally imposed rather than chosen, and, therefore, socially and politically divisive' (p 8).'Impairment label' and 'impairment group' are sometimes used within the book to highlight specific differences of experience between people with different types of impairment. It is important to distinguish here between impairment and 'chronic illness', which is a term often used by medical sociologists and perceived as the cause of disability. Although impairment may affect functioning or well-being, it becomes disabling because of the environment and may only be disabling in certain situations or societies. Chronic illness is a medical condition that comes upon a person and is perceived differently. The PMSU (2005) report distinguishes between impairment and ill health, with impairment being related to long-term individual functioning and ill health '... the short-term or long-term effect of disease or sickness' (p 26). 'Chronic illness' or 'ill health' can also be disabling, however, through people's reaction to it. The distinction is therefore related to society's perception, but there is an overlap.

Simultaneous oppression is another significant term requiring explanation and refers to the ways in which discrimination or oppression related to various elements of a person's identity might overlap and have simultaneous effects (so different oppressions interact, such as disablism, sexism and racism). The words of Begum (1993, p 51) illustrate this effectively:

> As a black disabled woman I cannot separate different aspects of my identity into separate neat compartments. My experience, concerns and requirements are shaped by my collective experience of race, disability and gender. Of course there are times when certain things seem more important than others, i.e. when another disabled person tells me I would be lucky to get home help in the country I come from, then I know it is racism that is my concern at that point in time.

It is important to be aware of the complex relationships between aspects of identities, difference and diversity, in order to highlight the difficulties associated with classifying and measuring individuals.

The concept of 'independent living' has been an important development for the disabled people's movement. It does not necessarily mean people doing everything for themselves, but rather can be defined as disabled people having '... the same choice, control and freedom as any other citizen, with access to the practical assistance people need to exercise this right' (DRC, 2005a, 3.1.2). As Morris (1993a, p 7) states, the concept embraces '... the full range of human and civil rights. This means the right to have personal relationships, to be a parent, the right to equal access to education, training, employment and leisure activities and the right to participate in the life of the community'. These may be aspects of life that non-disabled people take for granted. The importance of independent living can perhaps be illustrated by the ODI (2010), which found that 'Over a fifth of disabled people say that they do not frequently have choice and control over their daily lives' (p 1). In the early 1980s, Ken Davis of the Derbyshire Coalition for Inclusive Living (DCIL) put together an operational framework for the social model of disability, presenting the seven needs necessary for the achievement of independent living. Appropriate housing constitutes the third most important essential need (which in logical order include information, peer counselling, housing, technical aids, personal assistance, transport and access) (Davis, 1990; Crosby and Jackson, 2000). The disabled people's movement has now extended this list to include 12 needs for independent living, which, as Morris (2004, pp 428-429) points out, cover: full access to the environment, an accessible transport system, technical aids and equipment, accessible adapted housing, personal assistance, inclusive education and training, adequate income, equal opportunities for employment, appropriate and accessible information, advocacy, counselling and appropriate and accessible healthcare. While this book focuses on the housing aspect of independent living, various chapters touch on both information and access needs.

Aside from some important terminology relating to disability and impairment, specific terms used throughout the book reference housing issues that would benefit from clarification. Tenure, for example, refers to '... the legal status of and the rights associated with different forms of housing ownership and occupancy' (Mullins and Murie, 2006, p 2). This can be further broken down into four key tenures, including owner-occupation, private renting, and social renting, either from the council/local authority, or from a housing association. Social renting includes housing provided by Registered Social Landlords, which are housing associations, trusts, cooperatives and companies who do not trade for profit. They are also registered with the Housing Corporation (now the Homes and Communities Agency), which is sponsored by Communities and Local Government. It is important to note that within these tenure labels there are vast differences in experience (Mullins and Murie, 2006). These might relate, for instance, to level of ownership within owner-occupation, whether outright or with a mortgage (see Gurney, 1990), or to type, size, quality and location of dwelling. Reference is sometimes made to 'housing pathways', which have been defined by Clapham (2005) as '... the household forms in which individuals participate and the routes they take over time in their experience of housing' (p 2). Households make choices and decisions along this pathway, according to the opportunities that are available to them, although some '... have more opportunities than others, depending on decisions they have already made, as well as many other factors including their employment situation and income' (Clapham, 2005, p 2). As we will see in later chapters, however, disabled people's housing pathways can be restricted by more than financial barriers. Finally, it is worth noting here that the term 'institution' is used in two ways throughout the book. First, it is used as a general term that denotes established organisations within society. Second, it refers to those forms of accommodation used commonly in the past to house disabled people. For the latter, it is '... features of "institutional culture" (depersonalisation, rigidity of routine, block treatment, social distance, paternalism)' (EC, 2009, p 5) that tend to define them as such. As the term is applied in these two ways, care is taken to make clear which use is being applied.

Key themes and structure of the book

Subsequent chapters are separated into different but related aspects of the disability and housing relationship from a social perspective. Chapter Two offers a review of developments in housing policy, regulation and official advice as it relates to disabled people, with the aim of highlighting the extent of progress towards better practices. The chapter is broken down into different periods, starting from the 1900s through to the present day, spanning workhouses, institutionalisation, community care and special needs provision. It goes further than previous historical overviews by offering some prediction of future patterns resulting from the change of government in the UK in 2010, and an overview of international good practice. Importantly, it also sets up the need for a social (rather than individual or medical) understanding of disability within housing by evaluating the approaches taken towards disabled people within housing provision. The introduction of social model ideas has led to some positive progress, and UK examples are used to emphasise innovations and improvements. The principal argument is that housing policy and practice has been largely influenced by an individual approach to disability that regards impairment as a disadvantage and 'personal tragedy' for the individual, rather than looking to the 'disabling' role of environments, attitudes and institutional practices. This has meant that disabled people's needs within housing have either been neglected or have focused on specific, specialised provision, which has been useful in some individual cases, but has on the whole been exclusionary. The chapter ends by highlighting the significance of a social approach to disability, demonstrating to the practitioner the importance of understanding what the model is and what it involves.

Chapter Three offers an overview of key debates in discussions around approaches to understanding disability. It points to the shift in thinking about what constitutes 'disability', from an individual approach to a social understanding of disability, and the developments we have seen in relation to these. This summary includes the more traditional, or individualistic, understanding of disability and impairment, sometimes referred to as the 'medical' model, which has been strongly criticised in recent years (although it has not disappeared), and the social model of disability that has become increasingly recognised as a more appropriate explanation for the disadvantage encountered by people with impairments. The criticisms that have been raised in relation to the social model – and the responses to these – are then discussed to emphasise ongoing developments. It is argued that despite the critique, the social model continues to offer a valuable tool for housing policy and practice, when extended to include important elements of structural constraints. Here, we look at how institutional outlooks and practices may involve some differentiation of assumptions or treatment related to specific impairments. One example is the evaluation of individuals during access to owner-occupation (through mortgage application), which can have more of a disabling effect for some disabled people than for others. Thus, differentiated disablement may be considered as an outcome of regularised practices of institutional power. The essential claim in the chapter is that while debates are ongoing about the social model, the core elements of the model remain central to looking at housing for disabled people. An investigation into housing choices, opportunities and barriers for disabled people therefore requires a broad approach that considers a range of different variables. These can include several overlapping or mutually reinforcing factors, including physical, financial, attitudinal and communication constraints. While these may overlap or work together, and thus some care is needed when categorising them in these ways, they are discussed separately for clarity within this book.

In Chapter Four we look at various physical (or access) barriers that can arise within housing for disabled people. These represent aspects of the environment that do not cater for a variety of bodily forms, largely relating therefore to inaccessible environments. The physical environment is an extremely significant component in the creation of barriers for people with impairments, and can be 'disabling' in a variety of ways. Accessible properties, for instance, that cater for a diversity of bodies tend to be lacking within the general stock of housing. This may cause difficulties when trying to find a property to either rent or buy, or when visiting family and friends. It is also important to consider communal areas and the local neighbourhood in relation to both their accessibility and safety (particularly for people with mobility or visual impairments). Disabled people may encounter additional difficulties when viewing potential properties, or have to contend with the inaccessible premises of housing providers, estate agents, solicitors and lending institutions. Most research into physical matters focuses on the experiences of people with mobility impairments, but this book shows that barriers need not be restricted to a particular impairment type, as people with various impairments may face constraints of a physical nature. The chapter then addresses communication (or information) barriers that disabled people may encounter within housing. These relate to the lack of information on housing options, the inaccessible nature of much information on offer and the limited availability of equipment or support to assist communication (for instance, the use of hearing loops or sign language interpreters). There have been significant developments in this area but difficulties still remain for many disabled people. The chapter ends by identifying ways forward for addressing some of these barriers.

Financial factors are extremely significant in the housing and disability relationship, yet these have been relatively overlooked in UK research. These form the focus of Chapter Five and range from factors arising from wider social disadvantage, such as income and employment (which affect access to all housing options) to lender perceptions of benefits in mortgage applications (which specifically affect access to owner-occupation). The chapter begins by looking at the income and employment situations of disabled people, as evidenced in existing literature. It is well known, for example, that disabled people experience disadvantage in the labour market, and this may have a negative impact on opportunities for exercising choice within housing. The next section looks closer at financial considerations that have not been examined in detail in previous research, focusing more specifically on access to the owner-occupied sector. Here, we look at how the mortgage industry might play a role in creating and reinforcing the barriers encountered by disabled people through risk assessment practices for mortgage application. It is shown, for instance, that when risk is assessed, disabled people's circumstances in relation to employment and income might be viewed negatively. The next chapter (Chapter Six) looks further at risk assessment in relation to how distinctions between impairments can be made by institutions or intermediaries. Chapter Five then moves on to look at the recent economic crisis and the possible implications for disabled people in the light of this. It provides an overview of the events in the US that led to the sub-prime market 'collapse', and its impact on the UK, including how lenders have become even more risk averse, withdrawing numerous mortgage products and reducing loan amounts. While this has meant that many people have been left unable to access the owner-occupied sector, for disabled people this can be even more difficult. The chapter concludes by offering some suggestions for tackling financial barriers.

The attitudes, assumptions and practices of various housing providers, organisations, institutions and 'gate keepers' can be just as 'disabling' as the physical and financial environment, and it is these that are documented in Chapter Six. The chapter shows, for instance, that the assumptions held by the building industry, the values underpinning renting allocation processes and the assessment procedures used in mortgage provision may affect disabled people's access to particular housing. We begin by looking at some of the assumptions made by the building industry about disabled people, and the effects that these can have on the availability of accessible housing. The chapter then examines the roles played by assumptions and practices within the rented sector in disabled people's housing opportunities. These include the ways in which allocation processes and additional duties placed on social landlords (with regard to antisocial behaviour) may affect disabled people's opportunities within social renting, as well as how private landlords may restrict disabled people's access to privately rented accommodation. In terms of the owner-occupied sector, and taking further the discussion of risk assessment (started in Chapter Five), we look at how people with particular impairments may be classified as 'higher risk' and hence experience further disadvantage. It may be, then, that assumptions and preconceptions about disabled people present a considerable obstacle to their ability to exercise choice within housing, whichever tenure is preferred. While such barriers might at first appear to relate to the individual prejudice of housing providers, it is important to remember that such assumptions are likely to be institutionalised and thus also represent a 'structural' constraint. The chapter ends by considering potential strategies for addressing various attitudinal barriers. It is hoped that the issues raised throughout will help encourage housing providers and practitioners to question their own practices towards, and treatment of, disabled people.

Chapter Seven offers a summary of key insights presented in the book, returning to some of the issues initially raised in Chapter Three and continued throughout the book, in relation to the social model of disability. It aims to show how the housing case can act as a reminder of some wider and important gaps in knowledge about the assumptions and mechanisms that contribute to opportunities and constraints. In addition, it highlights how the various types of barrier discussed in previous chapters come together to affect disabled people's sense of 'home'. The intention is to demonstrate the impact that the issues raised in the previous chapters may have on disabled people, not just in terms of housing choices, opportunities and pathways, but also in relation to *experiences* of housing or *meanings* of home. The chapter therefore highlights how – when considering housing options, provision and need – it is important not to neglect the meanings that a 'home' provides for its inhabitants, since these may be central to their experiences of the dwelling. The chapter ends by providing a list of the main issues presented throughout the book to underline key messages for policy, practitioner and researcher audiences.

TWO

Housing policy and disabled people: from past to present

Housing for disabled people has historically been provided via a variety of institutional forms of accommodation. Since the 1960s, however, coinciding with the emergence of the American Independent Living Movement (ILM), it has been argued that if inclusion and 'independent living' are to be achieved, disabled people must have the right to self-managed accessible housing. There have been several pieces of legislation that have had an impact on housing rights, entitlements and provision for disabled people in some way, whether for home support services for everyday living, for physical needs such as adaptations, or more broadly for housing tenure options. There have also been various providers of housing, including local authorities, social services departments, housing associations and private sector developers. This chapter offers an overview of some of the main developments in housing policy, regulation and official advice as it relates to disabled people, with the aim of highlighting the extent of progress towards better practices. This is not a definitive guide to policy and legislation; there is not the space here to offer the kind of detail that such an account would entail. The aim, instead, is to highlight important markers in housing policy history for disabled people.

We look back over the past century, from the 1900s to the present day, before providing a timeline of key events. We then consider future possibilities in light of the change of government in 2010, before reviewing some examples of international good practice. A key objective of the chapter is to underline the importance of understandings of disability for policymakers and service providers. Housing policy and provision for disabled people are affected by the availability and distribution of resources; the management of allocation processes and agencies responsible for provision; and the perceptions of disability held at both individual and institutional levels. This chapter aims to emphasise the significance of the latter. At a broad level, for instance, associations of disability with ideas of dependency, suffering or medical concerns have been built into the operations and regulations of institutions and agencies. This, in turn, has had implications for the actions of housing provider employees, and the subsequent provisions made within housing for disabled people. Given this, it is important to be aware of the approaches to disability and impairment that most commonly influence housing provision for disabled people.

From 'institutional' living to 'community care'

Historical accounts tend to suggest that the rise of industrialisation saw disabled people more frequently housed in 'institutions', including workhouses, that worked on the principle of less eligibility. That is, the conditions for the inhabitants should be less desirable than those for people living outside the workhouse (Finkelstein, 1980; Lund, 1996). Prior to this, in feudal societies, and with production often being based on collective rather than individual units, people with impairments participated in social and working life. During industrialisation, however, '... collectivist notions of production were eroded ... [and the] ... isolated individual thus became a competitive economic unit' (Allen, 1999, p 51). The incarceration of people with impairments and other people labelled as 'deviants' therefore became increasingly common. The 1845 Lunacy Act and the amendment in 1862 made it possible for a person to be detained against their will on the basis of medical diagnosis, often of 'mental illness' (Oliver and Barnes, 1998). This resulted in large numbers of people being moved from workhouses into asylums (Myers, 1998), and therefore, for some, 1845 marks the beginning of the dominance of medical professionals in disabled people's lives (Oliver and Barnes, 1998).

Asylums were alternative, yet still segregated, institutions intended to 'cure' patients, while supporting the notion that disabled people should be separated off from the rest of the population. Hence, the provision of a 'therapeutic environment' (Picking, 2000) was balanced against practices of concealment and potential risks posed to society. This 'asylum movement' excluded people labelled with 'mental illness' and other conditions from society, providing accommodation often characterised by '... long corridors for easy surveillance, locked wards and uniformed staff', making them more like '... prisons than homes' (Picking, 2000, p 12). By the mid-1900s, institutions were increasingly criticised for the poor living conditions, low standards of care and instances of abuse that were becoming apparent (and these poor conditions were not restricted to UK institutions; see EC, 2009). Additionally, this system of segregation, incarceration or 'containment', further influenced by the 1913 Mental Deficiency Act, was argued to be heavily based on professional interpretations of need and increased disabled people's dependency on others. Thus, there was an acknowledgement among reformers of the need to offer alternative forms of accommodation outside of institutional living arrangements. (For some of the critique of institutions, see Barnes, 1990; Ravetz with Turkington, 1995; Imrie and Kumar, 1998; Hawtin, 2005; Race, 2005.)

Rising expectations in the 1940s following the Second World War, and promises of a better life for citizens, led to a review of housing policy and standards. The 1944 Dudley Report and the 1944 official Housing Manual required that '... all local authority housing [should] comply with minimum room sizes and circulation space prescribed in the guidelines' (Milner, 2005, p 178). This led to a period between 1946 and 1951 in which local authority housing received a considerable amount of outlay, although this was later reduced under the Conservative government (Milner, 2005). This period was also the beginning of the post-war focus on owner-occupation as the preferred tenure. At the same time, there was a growing recognition of the need for improved services for disabled people. Part of this recognition is demonstrated in the Acts implemented subsequent to the Beveridge Report. In 1942, this report proposed a welfare state in which all citizens would contribute to, and be the recipients of, state support. This would include a National Health Service, free education to those under 16 years of age, family and child support and a comprehensive National Insurance scheme (see Mercer and Barnes, 2004). Following this report, the 1944 Disabled Persons (Employment) Act, the 1944 Education Act, the 1946 National Health Service Act and the 1948 National Assistance Act (NAA) were introduced. The 1948 NAA provided a definition of disability (later criticised and amended) that informed subsequent legislation. Disabled people were defined as those '... who are blind, deaf, or dumb, and other persons who are substantially and permanently handicapped by illness, injury or congenital deformity' (cited in Drake, 1999, p 58). While the stated intention was that '... people should live in their own homes and not institutions' (Oliver and Barnes, 1998, p 6), Part III of the NAA reinforced the tradition of institutional care through setting out the need for residential accommodation. Following this Act, Leonard Cheshire Homes was established and '... became the largest single voluntary provider of residential accommodation for people with physical impairments in the UK' (Mercer and Barnes, 2004, p 4).

'Community care' was a phrase first in official use in the mid-1950s, in the report of the Royal Commission on Mental Illness and Mental Deficiency of 1954-57, but it was in 1961 when it became more readily used as a policy objective (Barnes, 1990). Although such support had existed for years previously, proposals for provision were made more explicit in a range of legislation from this date. In the 1968 Seebohm

Report, for example, 'care' within the community was regarded as the remedy to the problems associated with segregation, and the report's proposals were later incorporated into the 1970 Chronically Sick and Disabled Persons Act (CSDPA). This Act, and the 1972 CSDP (Scotland) Act, required local authorities to cater for the housing needs of people registered as disabled in their areas (using the 1948 NAA definition) (Imrie, 2003; Milner, 2005). The services offered as an alternative to residential care aimed to support people to stay in their own homes and included assistance with arranging adaptations, home support and meals at home. Local authorities also had a duty to make disabled people aware of the services available (Heywood with Smart, 1996). At the same time, integrated social services departments were being formed for service provision, rather than various smaller local authority departments (Means, 1997) and so, following the CSDPA (as well as the 1970 Local Authority Social Services Act and the 1968 Social Work [Scotland] Act), social services departments became responsible for providing housing adaptations in all sectors of housing (Bull and Watts, 1998).

Specifically within housing policy, the Parker Morris standards were then introduced, which had an impact on public housing between 1967 and 1982, with improved standards for space and heating. The focus was on nuclear family households, however, with smaller dwellings being recommended for certain groups such as single couples with no children and older people (Milner, 2005). In the late 1960s, the Cullingworth Report (Cullingworth, 1969) provided guidelines for the allocation of council housing and '... singled out "the disabled", "the elderly", "the single", "students", "the large family" and "the homeless" as groups with "important" needs' (Milner, 2005, p 183). The consequence, as Milner and Madigan (2004) point out, was that 'general' and 'special' needs became officially separated, with people labelled under the latter being catered for through specially designed properties. Following this, the CDSPA made local authorities responsible for assessing the housing needs of disabled people and for ensuring that '... a small proportion (less than 5 per cent) of their stock was accessible' (Milner and Madigan, 2004, p 733). Furthermore, the 1974 Circular *Housing for People who are Physically Handicapped* (DoE and Welsh Office, 1974) emphasised a move away from accommodation being provided in hospitals and institutional environments, to community living. It highlighted the need for specially designed housing for people with physical impairments, with specific emphasis on 'special needs' housing (including 'mobility' and 'wheelchair housing') (Bull and Watts, 1998). This was intended for people considered both 'vulnerable' and 'deserving' and was often separated from mainstream housing (Milner, 2005; Lund, 2006). 'Mobility housing' is considered suitable for people with 'ambulant' impairments and *occasional* wheelchair users, whereas 'wheelchair housing' is suitable for permanent wheelchair users. The latter is characterised by increased space and specific design features (Barnes, 1991; Borsay, 1986) (for further discussion of 'special needs' housing, see Chapter Four).

Also at this time, and following the 1974 Housing Act, home improvement and intermediate grants were introduced to provide financial support for disabled people. Home improvement grants, awarded at the local authorities' discretion, could cater for adaptations, and the intermediate grant could be used to provide amenities that might be inaccessible or lacking in a disabled person's dwelling. It was not until 1980, however, that these grants were available within both private and social rented housing (Borsay, 1986). At this time, responsibility for provision also shifted from social services to housing authorities, resulting in the development of adaptations services and matching systems for tenants (Bull and Watts, 1998). In 1977, the Housing (Homeless Persons) Act provided homeless people with '... the right to a permanent home' (Birch, 2010, p 19), with priority need groups including families with dependent children, pregnant women, 'vulnerable' people without children and those who were homeless as a result of emergencies (such as fires) (Fitzpatrick and Stephens, 1999). In 1978, the British Standard 5619 was introduced, and this went further than 'mobility' and 'wheelchair housing' by providing accessibility standards that referred to private as well as social housing, and thus marked an important recognition of the role of private sector housing in providing accessible dwellings (Milner, 2005).

There were, then, some significant developments in housing and welfare provision for disabled people in the period leading up to the late 1970s, with a move away from institutional provision (in principle, if not wholly in practice); a recognition of the need for local authorities to meet disabled people's housing needs; the introduction of assistance for adaptations; and more accessible housing options for some. Furthermore, the move to 'community care' was supported by disabled people living in residential care (Dartington et al, 1981; Hunt, 1981; Finkelstein, 1991; Morris, 1999), with schemes such as Project 81 (HCIL, c1986), in which residents moved into their own homes with necessary support packages, and the Grove Road scheme (see Davis, 1981), a fully integrated scheme of accessible and non-accessible flats. These highlighted the independence that could be achieved through accessible housing as opposed to residential care. The focus on community care services for disabled people continued throughout the 1970s and 1980s (through political promotion) and in the 1990s (through legislation; see later).

Many aspects of the provisions made during this period have, however, come up against criticism. The motivations behind the move to community care, for example, are highly disputed, with assertions that it was actually driven by economic reasoning, rather than the interests of service users (cf Titmuss, 1968; Means, 1996; Hawtin, 2005), and that the additional personal and family costs – arising through informal care – have been overlooked (Borsay, 1986). It has also been shown that many people continued to have little option but to live in residential institutions (Oliver and Barnes, 1998) and that the provision of services under the CDSPA varied considerably among local authorities and other service providers (Imrie, 2003), as well as being '... underfunded, unplanned and insufficient' (Hawtin, 2005, p 35). Moreover, the allocation of housing has been criticised for largely relying on a medical interpretation of need (Borsay, 1986; Barnes, 1991). There was also some neglect of private housing developers within legislation, as governments believed that builders would meet the needs and wants of consumers without regulatory pressure (Imrie, 2003).

The Conservatives, the Disability Discrimination Act and independent living

When the Conservatives were in power during 1979-97, principles of competition, privatisation, marketisation, choice and individual responsibility were at the forefront of policy changes, alongside aims for a reduction in public spending. This was also a period in which housing providers used the term 'independent living' (identified in Chapter One as disabled people having appropriate support to exercise choice and control over their own lives) to describe many of the community care policies of the 1980s and 1990s. Unfortunately, as Morris (1993a) has argued, these initiatives failed to accurately reflect the actual principles of the independent living movement. Instead, as Clapham (2005) points out, 'The assumption seems to be that the very fact of living outside an institution, either at home or in a homely setting, is enough by itself to establish "independence"' (p 216). Nonetheless, many positive developments for disabled people were also introduced around this time.

Local authorities had been able to sell their council houses to tenants since 1952 (Lund, 2006), but it was following the 1980 Housing Act and the 'Right to Buy' (RTB) legislation, that this really took off. As part of the government's strategy for greater privatisation, the RTB and the 1980 Tenants' Rights (Scotland) Act granted council tenants the right to purchase their homes at discounted rates – ranging from 33 per cent to 50 per cent – depending on their length of residence at the property. This improved access to the owner-occupied sector for many who might previously have been unable to afford it, although only certain groups could benefit from such options. For some disabled people (living in accessible properties), for instance, their right to buy was limited until the 1988 Housing Act (Barnes, 1991), a move that, although it seemingly acknowledged the limited supply of accessible housing (Harrison with Davis, 2001), was essentially discriminatory. There is also some suggestion that such exclusion may still exist (see Chapter Five). The RTB also had some impact on the position of council housing, as its role as the provider for the poorer sectors of society became more pronounced. Council rents were raised and means-tested support via housing benefit, rather than keeping rents low, led to more targeting and priority provision (Harrison with Davis, 2001).

The 1986 Disabled Persons (Services, Consultation and Representation) Act reinforced the responsibilities set out for local authorities in the 1970 CDSPA, including assessing the needs of disabled people and informing people of the services available. Social services authorities became responsible for providing support to young adults leaving school as well as for considering the role of any carers in disabled people's lives (Bull and Watts, 1998). In 1987, Home Improvement Agencies (HIAs) were introduced; initially established under the national coordinating body Care and Repair (Harrison and Means, 1990; Bull and Watts, 1998) and still in operation today. These locally managed, not-for-profit organisations provide assistance to older and disabled people for adaptations, or for repairing and maintaining their properties, whether in owner-occupied or private rented tenancies (Garnett and Perry, 2005). There is some suggestion, however, that these agencies are '... not available universally and in Wales "Care and Repair" work only with homeowners' (Goodridge, 2004, p 10). The introduction of the Independent Living Fund (ILF) followed in 1988 and aimed to provide financial assistance to disabled people to choose to live in their own homes (rather than in residential care). New applicants were prevented from receiving payments from 1992, and the Independent Living (Extensions) Fund was set up to deal with existing claimants (Priestley, 1999). Following its success, however, the Independent Living Fund 1993 was established through the 1993 Disability Grants Act. The fund makes payments available to disabled people (rather than to service providers) who are already in receipt of support from social services or the higher rate of Disability Living Allowance (DLA) (Woodin et al, 2009). The payments can be used for a care agency or to employ someone to provide assistance in the home. It cannot be used, however, to pay for adaptations, equipment or a relative who lives with the claimant. (See later for more recent changes to the ILF.)

In 1988, we saw not only the establishment of the ILF, but also the publication of the Griffiths Report, *Community Care: An Agenda for Action* (Griffiths, 1988), which strongly advocated 'staying put' schemes (providing support for people to remain in their own homes for longer). Following this, in 1989 the Local Government and Housing Act (Part VIII) introduced Disabled Facilities Grants (DFGs) and assistance for repairs and maintenance or adaptations for older people. DFGs are administered by local authorities to provide assistance with payments for adaptations or facilities to make a dwelling (or communal area of a building) more 'accessible'. They can be used to improve access into and around a dwelling; ensure safety; improve accessibility of the toilet, washing facilities and kitchen; or improve heating systems and the positions of light fittings and power switches (Holmes, 2000). They are available to people in social and private rented properties (and to landlords on behalf of the tenant), as well as to owner-occupiers. It is the responsibility of the housing authority, under later changes in the 1996 Housing Grants, Construction and Regeneration Act, to assess whether adaptations are necessary (thus often requiring cooperation with occupational therapists and social services departments) (see Bull and Watts, 1998). Decisions are made on the basis that '... the work is necessary and appropriate and is reasonable and practicable' (Holmes, 2000, p 177) (see also Chapter Four).

The 1990 National Health Service (NHS) and Community Care Act, following the recommendations from the Griffiths Report and the White Paper *Caring for People, Community Care in the Next Decade and Beyond* (DH, 1989), made care for older and disabled people the responsibility of local authorities. The Act, effective from April 1993, has been especially important in the development of community care services, reflecting the trend for schemes that assist people to remain in their own homes. Within the Act, there was an emphasis on flexible care packages that would help move provision away from institutional living, as well as a recognition of the need for good-quality, suitable housing (including assistance with repairs and maintenance) and the contracting out of activities to various different agencies (Picking, 2000). The Act also required local authorities to consult service users '... at the collective level through community care planning and at the individual level through user-led assessment and care packaging' (Means and Smith, 1996, p 2). Of particular significance was the shift, at least in principle, from a service-led approach (where disabled people's needs are decided according to what is available) to a more needs-led approach (where needs are defined by disabled people) (Priestley, 1999).

Debate around accessibility standards also re-emerged around this time, as the necessity for suitable housing for the successful implementation of community care support became recognised. As Cooper and Walton (1995) state, 'This in part led to the joint DoE/ DoH Circular, *Mobility Housing Guidelines,* which contained a review of accessible housing criteria, followed in 1993 by the Housing Corporation adding accessibility into its *Scheme Development Standards'* (p 2). Furthermore, the concept of Lifetime Homes was given formal expression in 1989 by the Helen Hamlyn Trust, and later by Rowe (1990) and the Joseph Rowntree Foundation. The concept means that dwellings are designed with basic accessibility standards, offering the potential for future adaptations, making them flexible enough to meet the needs of the household throughout the life course (cf Donnison, 1967). Lifetime Homes are:

> ... ordinary homes, incorporating design standards across three design areas – access, inside the home, and fixtures/ fittings. These incorporate features such as level or sloping entrances, walls capable of taking handrails, space for turning wheelchairs, downstairs toilets with drainage and shower provision, and designs which incorporate provision for a future stairlift. (Crawford and Foord, 1997, p 99)

Thus, rather than providing specifically designed housing that is targeted at a population considered to have 'special needs', mainstream housing would itself be more accessible and flexible enough to cater for a wider, more diverse number of households, including those with disabled people, thus addressing general rather than just specific needs (see Chapter Four for more information).

This period also saw the introduction of the 1996 Housing Grants, Construction and Regeneration Act (Part I), which made changes to DFGs and replaced 'staying put' grants with Home Repair Assistance. The latter – which also supports people to remain in their own homes – involves the provision of a grant or materials from the local authority to the applicant (whether owner-occupier or private tenant) for essential but 'small-scale' improvements and repairs. These might include '... insulation, repairs to the drains or home security, a wheelchair ramp or grip rails' (Holmes, 2000, p 179). Grants are allocated according to local authorities' own criteria for priority need. Also in 1996, the Community Care (Direct Payments) Act introduced direct payments for any community care services, aids and adaptations that disabled people under 65 have been assessed as requiring (Bull and Watts, 1998). These payments are mandatory to recipients of community care assessments following the 2001 Health and Social Care Act. Direct payments provide disabled people with the choice of who to employ to provide the services they need. If desired, disabled people may use Centres for 'Independent', 'Integrated' or 'Inclusive' Living (CILs) (controlled and run by disabled people to support independent living), which can provide advice and assistance with this employment process. While some local authorities have been reluctant to implement direct payments (see Goodridge, 2004), and certain groups are under-represented (such as people labelled with learning difficulties, mental health service users, and older people), they have proved an important move towards greater user control of services.

Finally, building on previous legislation, the 1996 Housing Act restated the requirement to prioritise certain groups who were either homeless or at risk of homelessness. These groups include people with a physical impairment or a 'progressive' condition such as Multiple Sclerosis (MS), people labelled with learning difficulties, mental health service users and older people (as well as pregnant women and households with dependent children, among others). It also reduced the length of time housing should be provided to applicants to two years. The legislation changed again under New Labour (with apparently more generous arrangements emerging in Scotland). Also under this Act, social landlords were required to produce a single register for allocating housing and were made responsible for undertaking policies that reduce antisocial behaviour, which has been shown to have negative implications for some mental health service users (see Chapter Six).

The 1995 Disability Discrimination Act

The 1995 Disability Discrimination Act (DDA) requires more detailed discussion than can be offered for other policy developments covered in this chapter. There is also some overlap between the periods discussed, as the DDA was introduced by the Conservative government, with later amendments emerging under New Labour, and so greater continuity can be offered within this separate section. The DDA aimed to reduce discrimination against disabled people in several ways, but importantly for this book, by service providers. According to this Act, someone is defined as a disabled person if they have '... either a physical or a mental impairment which has a substantial and long-term adverse effect on a person's ability to carry out normal day-to-day activities' (Gooding, 1996, p 10). To ensure that the DDA was implemented and supported, the British government established the Disability Rights Commission (DRC). This has now been superseded by the Equality and Human Rights Commission (EHRC) (see later).

While the legislation is deficient in many ways (as this section will show), it is an important step in others. The DDA has ensured that some aspects of service provision have improved for disabled people, aiding the removal of discriminatory practices and demonstrating an acknowledgement of how social factors can 'disable' people with impairments. It states that it is *unlawful to treat a disabled person less favourably than a non-disabled person*, unless it can be justified. 'Less favourable' treatment would include a disabled person being refused a particular service, or the service being of a worse standard or provided on poorer terms (such as at higher costs). A service provider would be seen as discriminating if it treated someone less favourably for a reason that related to a person's impairment, or if it did not make reasonable adjustments without justification. This might include reducing the standard of service to all other customers, or affecting the health and safety of all customers, as a consequence of providing adjustments for a disabled person. In terms of housing, it would be '... unlawful to sell or let property in circumstances or on terms that discriminate against disabled people, including the maintenance of housing lists and priority allocation of housing' (Holmes, 2000, p 169). Since 2004, further 'reasonable adjustments' have to be made to physical features of the service provider's premises and services to ensure that they are accessible. There has been much debate as to what these reasonable adjustments might involve. One such adjustment might be to provide written information in a format that is accessible to a client (Shelter, 2007), the costs of which would not be charged to the client (Mind, 2006).

There were changes to the DDA in 2003 – known as the 2003 DDA (Amendment) Regulations – and again in 2005. The most recent changes to the DDA have meant not only that people with HIV, MS and all types of cancer are included in its provisions, but also that access to buildings is now a requirement, and disabled people have more rights in relation to private renting. This might include, for example, allowing a guide or assistant dog for a person with a visual impairment into the property, when there was previously a no-dogs policy (DRC, 2005b). Furthermore, as Cobb (2006) states:

Sections 22-24 of the DDA, which prohibit discrimination in housing provision, restrict the circumstances in which a landlord can take action to control anti-social behaviour 'related' to certain mental disorders. In particular, exclusion from social housing on grounds of such conduct, through either refusal to allocate property or eviction, will be discriminatory, and therefore illegal, unless it can be justified as necessary to protect the health or safety of other residents. (pp 238-9)

In addition, Part V of the DDA, the Disability Equality Duty (DED), was introduced in December 2006. Differing from its previous focus on discriminatory practices, this part of the DDA aimed to encourage public sector service providers to promote equality for disabled people, and to show how this would be achieved through the production of a Disability Equality Scheme and Action Plan. These schemes were to be regularly reviewed. In addition to promoting equality and positive attitudes towards disabled people, local authorities and Registered Social Landlords have a duty under these amendments to eliminate harassment related to a person's impairment and encourage the participation of disabled people in social life (Hunter et al, 2007). As the Office for the Deputy Prime Minister (ODPM, 2006) asserts, the DED '... marks a fundamental shift in disability discrimination law putting the onus for change on the public sector, rather than disabled individuals' (p 360). This was an important improvement, indicating a shift in thinking about disability, and at that moment seemed to mean that future policies would be '... scrutinised to ensure they promote rather than diminish, disabled people's housing opportunities' (PMSU, 2005, p 99).

The DDA has been subject to much debate for its medical model assumptions (Morris, 1999); neglect of mental health service users (Mind, 2006); limited impact made on private landlords (Aston et al, 2007); and questions around what constitutes 'reasonable'. Furthermore, while positive developments have been made in terms of ensuring that particular facilities (such as induction loops for people with hearing impairments) are installed within the premises of many service providers, the Office of Fair Trading (OFT, 1999) notes that there is no requirement for staff to be trained in how to use this equipment. This could have negative implications for disabled clients' experiences of such services (such as their privacy being compromised with the use of induction loops). A further possible restriction is highlighted by Monks (2005), who argues that because the DDA is a civil law, meaning that a case has to be brought by an individual or organisation, 'Only when the courts have heard a number of cases will there be a clear idea of what the law means in practice' (p 1).

Finance, owner-occupation and discrimination

We can also identify some concerns around the legislation that might affect access to home ownership. Within insurance provision (which may be necessary when trying to secure a mortgage for owner-occupation or shared ownership), there are certain circumstances in which refusal of a service could apparently be considered justified in accordance with the DDA. It seems that insurers are within their rights, for instance, to provide a less favourable service or decline a service to disabled people if the insurance is perceived to be offered at a higher 'risk' (Housing Options, 2004). This risk is often linked to certain impairments or conditions being associated with lower life expectancy. It appears, however, that there are problems with this rationalisation. The Office of Fair Trading (OFT, 1999) points out that justification must rest on statistical data or other 'reliable' information such as medical reports. Despite this, it found, in relation to life insurance, that classifications of impairments within financial institutions could prevent a disabled person from being provided with a service. As it asserts:

> One case brought to our attention concerned an individual with intermittent Multiple Sclerosis (MS) who had been offered unfavourable terms for life assurance, even though the condition did not affect the would-be policyholder's expected lifespan. The actuarial data used to justify these terms were more than 50 years old. The use of a blanket approach to various illnesses – such as cerebral palsy – is a cause for concern. We believe that, *while it is legitimate for insurers to discriminate on the basis of disability*, they should make every effort to distinguish between serious and less-serious conditions and apply relevant and up-to-date actuarial data when assessing the risk. (OFT, 1999, p 43, emphasis added)

As this quotation demonstrates, while in some cases it is regarded as reasonable to differentiate between disabled people and non-disabled people (and among disabled people), it is important that the grounds for this are well defined and accurate. It also draws attention to the issue of using 'blanket assumptions', which the DDA states must be avoided, so that people cannot be refused insurance on account of their impairment category alone (Mind, 2006). Indeed, the Association of British Insurers' (ABI, 2003, p 14) guidelines state that:

> You should never rely on assumptions, stereotypes or generalisations about disabled people. All your decisions must be based on relevant information or data available at the time which will form the basis of your underwriting manual.

Nonetheless, insurers have the ability to exercise choice as to whether people with certain impairments will be charged higher premiums or whether they want to request additional medical information from the client. Thus, practices can vary greatly between different institutions as to the treatment of various impairments (OFT, 1999; Youreable.com, 2006). Furthermore, it would seem that even if the judgement of the lender to reject an applicant on the basis of impairment proves to be ill founded, the service provider might not be seen as at fault. The OFT (1999, pp 45-46) states, for instance, in reference to the requirements of the DDA, that:

> If that opinion is wrong ... suppliers have been advised that they 'are not expected to be an expert on disability. The courts will accept your decision if you genuinely believed one of the reasons applied and it was reasonable for you to do so'. This could provide suppliers with the opportunity to dispute matters rather than complying with their obligations.

In addition, while 'blanket assumptions' are to be avoided within industry practices, it is uncertain whether organisations apply such anti-discriminatory practices, particularly in relation to 'credit scoring' (see also Chapter Five). For instance, the industry's *Guide to Credit Scoring* provides guidelines on avoiding discriminatory practices, stating that:

> Credit Scoring will not discriminate on the grounds of sex, race, religion, disability or colour. All scoring systems will be designed and used in a way that conforms to all relevant legislation. (Association for Payment Clearing Services et al, 2000, 2.4)

As Andreeva et al (2004, p 27) point out, however, these guidelines are not legally binding, and it is also '... not clear whether the statement covers direct or indirect discrimination or both'.

Overcoming such difficulties is not an easy task, for if certain characteristics are prohibited from being included in risk assessment, which would remove direct discrimination, it may be that these groups then experience *indirect* discrimination (Thomas, 2000; Andreeva et al, 2004). It may be difficult to prove discrimination in relation to a person having a particular impairment due to the existence of other variables that may have an effect and that may be more common for disabled people, such as disadvantaged employment and income situations. Furthermore, as Burns (2002, p 172) argues, it is difficult to label lender practices as discriminatory towards disabled people during application assessment due to '... the nature of the institution, which depends on discriminating at some level'. It seems, then, that while the DDA has facilitated significant advances, there is scope for further developments if disabled people are to have equal access to financial services. This may improve access to the owner-occupied sector through the removal of barriers created here.

New Labour: positive progress or repeating the past?

There were certain continuities from the Conservatives to the New Labour government, such as support for home ownership and the handling of social renting (where there has been a shift to housing associations and other providers rather than local authorities). In addition, the focus on conditionality (responsibilities with rights), the work ethic and belief in private investment and labour markets seem to be principles that remained intact throughout the New Labour period of government. Nevertheless, New Labour introduced several significant policies relating to disabled people and housing, such as changes to the 1995 DDA, access guidelines within building regulations and developments towards Lifetime Homes (LTH) standards. In general, during New Labour's period in government, we saw further moves, in principle, towards accommodating the social model of disability and a focus on choice, equality, independence and greater consultation with disabled people (even if such moves were not quite fully developed in practice).

Influenced by the DDA, Part M (Access to and Use of Buildings) of the English Building Regulations – sometimes referred to as 'visitability standards' – introduced basic accessibility guidelines for the construction of new properties in 1999 and apply to all developers. As Imrie (2003) points out, similar regulations can be found in Northern Ireland (Part R) and Scotland, with '... substantial references to access issues in Parts M, Q and S of the Scottish building regulations' (p 388). The accessibility criteria for Part M were drawn from the LTH standards (Lund, 2006) and include level access into the dwelling, provision of a downstairs toilet that is accessible for a wheelchair user, wider doorways and hallways, and plug sockets and light switches positioned at more accessible heights for various users. Thus, new housing is required to meet certain standards of accessibility (for more information, see Chapter Four).

In 2001, the government published the *Valuing People* White Paper (DH, 2001a), which acknowledged the problems facing people labelled with learning difficulties and their families within housing. It highlighted the lack of options available and asserted the need to improve information and advice on housing options, increase the choice and control that could be exercised and move people out of long-stay hospitals to more 'appropriate' accommodation by 2004. Not all local authorities managed to meet this deadline, however, and some people labelled with learning difficulties were moved into alternative institutional accommodation on a temporary basis, known as NHS residential campuses (Gillen, 2007), reflecting claims that resources for the proposals had been '... tied up in institutional provision' (Morris, 2004, p 430). Far from being considered community care-type options, there were plans to close these campuses by 2010. In relation to homelessness, in 2002, the Homelessness Act '... repealed the two-year time limit on the main homelessness duty introduced by the Housing Act 1996' (Fitzpatrick and Pawson, 2007, p 176), expanded the list of people deemed to have priority need to 16- and 17-year-olds and people considered vulnerable due to previously living in institutionalised accommodation, among others, and introduced the duty to address homelessness through preventative strategies (Fitzpatrick and Pawson, 2007).

The Supporting People programme was introduced in 2003 to provide support to people to find (or remain in) suitable accommodation and to live independently (Foord, 2005). It offers housing-related support to social tenants labelled as 'vulnerable' to enable them to continue living in their own homes. Older people, people with physical impairments, mental health service users and people labelled with learning difficulties are included in the list of those covered by the programme. It brought together the various different funding streams for housing-related support into one fund, to be used by local authorities in specific ways, and 'At its height of £1.8 billion, Supporting People represented the largest specific fund to the third sector in Europe' (Condie and Penney, 2009, p 23). An important objective of the programme was to provide more *locally controlled* housing-related support services, with the aim of meeting needs more appropriately (PMSU, 2005). The effectiveness of the programme has, however, been affected by gradual changes to the availability and allocation of resources. Foord (2005) draws similarities here with '... the implementation of community care in 1993 [which involved] a generous initial budget, followed by a radical paring back, leading to means-testing, the application of harsh eligibility criteria and year on year efficiency savings' (p 4). Indeed, recent changes to the allocation of Supporting People funding to councils '... as a non-ring-fenced area-based grant' (Condie and Penney, 2009, p 23) will have implications for the support provided. For a detailed overview of the impact of Supporting People on the housing and support needs of disabled people, see Foord and Simic (2005) and Fyson et al (2007).

Also in 2003, the introduction of the Homelessness etc (Scotland) Act led to an increase in the likelihood of disabled people's applications being accepted, or of more suitable, permanent accommodation being provided to those living in inaccessible housing (although lack of accessible temporary and social housing present some difficulties) (Doherty, 2006). The year 2005 saw the introduction of the report *Improving the Life Chances of Disabled People* (PMSU, 2005). This focused largely on the promotion of independent living for disabled people, with a clear acknowledgement of the importance of the social model of disability and an understanding of the discrimination that disabled people face. A key aim of the report is that by 2025 disabled people should be able to exercise choice in relation to all aspects of their lives and be equal citizens within society. With reference to housing in particular, the report identified concerns around lack of options within housing for disabled people (for some, leading to no option but to live in residential care homes), and problems with the DFG system (lack of resources, long waiting lists and administration procedures, and issues with means testing), and showed recognition of the value of LTH standards, particularly in terms of the long-term savings to be made. The Office for Disability Issues (ODI) was set up by the government to implement the *Life Chances* report's proposals. The report has been generally well received as one of the most positive developments to date for acknowledging the discrimination encountered by disabled people, although some recommendations and omissions from the report have been questioned (see the UKDPC, 2005b, the national umbrella organisation for organisations run and controlled by disabled people).

The 2005 Mental Capacity Act, implemented in England and Wales in 2007, was introduced to protect people who may not have the capacity to make decisions for themselves. The legislation states that it must be assumed that a person has the capacity to make decisions unless it can be proven otherwise. It also allows people to select a person to make decisions on their behalf. The Department for Constitutional Affairs (2007) developed a Code of Practice to offer guidance on the Act to a range of actors, including housing workers. The 2007 Mental Health Act introduced amendments to the 2005 Act, including the launch in 2008 of Community Treatment Orders (CTOs), which '... allow people detained in hospital to be discharged into the community with a requirement to comply with certain conditions, including medical treatment and restrictions on where they live and where they go, or face being returned to hospital against their will' (Mental Health Alliance, 2009, p 1). Also in 2007, the DRC was abolished and legal enforcement for disability issues is now a role of the EHRC. This brought together the responsibilities of the DRC, the Commission for Racial Equality and the Equal Opportunities Commission. The EHRC therefore has a broader human rights remit, addressing gender, disability and ethnicity rights, as well as equality in relation to religion and sexuality.

The ODI's independent living strategy was issued in 2008 and forms part of the delivery of the full and equal citizenship by 2025 proposed by the PMSU (2005) report. The key aims of the five-year strategy include providing disabled and older people with greater choice and control in the support services they use, improving access to housing, transport, health, employment, education and leisure, and ensuring greater participation in family and community life. The report makes clear the importance of understanding what independent living actually means, following concerns raised by disabled people on this issue. Therefore, independent living is having access to the resources and assistance required to go about daily lives, not, as some assume, simply doing everything for yourself (see Chapter One). In terms of housing, the report's stated intentions involve improving disabled people's opportunities and choices in several ways. These include: increasing the availability of information and advice; ensuring adherence to LTH standards for all public sector housing by 2011, and setting a target for new housing to adhere to these standards by 2013; promoting the use of Accessible Housing Registers (see Chapter Four); setting up and investing in a rapid repairs and adaptations service; ensuring early identification of people at risk of health and care crises; improving the DFG system; and continuous investment in the Supporting People programme. In terms of DFGs, intentions include increasing the maximum grant limit, removing working tax credit and child tax credit from the means test, improving the system to aid local authorities in providing small-scale adaptations and generating a more flexible system to allow the applicant to move to a new dwelling if suitable (see ODI, 2008, p 46). Time will tell if the work (and funding) required to implement the report's recommendations is carried out in practice.

At the end of New Labour's period of government, therefore, a range of grants and services was available to disabled people in relation to housing, offered by state, private and voluntary organisations. Some of these were set up before New Labour came to power, but remained in place in 2010. For people wishing to stay in their own home, for instance, there were support services for domestic help, and financial or other assistance for equipment and adaptations (such as Supporting People and HIAs). Financial assistance was available in the form of direct payments (offering control over services required), through the ILF (to employ someone for personal and domestic support) and via DFGs. For social tenants, there were different options available, depending on whether additional support was required. These included housing association properties specifically designed for people with particular impairments, care homes and sheltered housing. Furthermore, the range of Home Buy and low-cost home-ownership options allowed disabled people to take part in schemes where they could purchase their social rented accommodation if desired, albeit with some exceptions (see Chapter Five).

Despite some positive developments under the New Labour government, there is still a range of areas that needs tackling. Some examples include the continued provision of 'special needs' housing, which separates disabled people from the rest of the community and from friends and families, and still reflects, to some extent at least, the practices set in place during the 19th century. Such housing caters for some needs, but the provision of this type of accommodation remains small and should not detract from the aim to increase the availability of accessible, flexible properties within the general stock of housing across all tenures (see Chapter Four). We have seen a general shift towards better use of language that seems to draw on the social model of disability, and greater user involvement, but in practice we are yet to see a full acknowledgement of the principles of this model. In fact, Clapham (2005) argues that the discourse of community care that has dominated housing provision to date – and that views disabled people's needs as homogeneous and 'special' – largely remains in place. In addition, while choice and control have been the aim of many policies introduced during the period, choice is still lacking for many disabled people (see Williams et al, 2008), and residential care accommodation remains the only option for many. Finally, some of the programmes and support in place are also in need of development. One example is the Supporting People programme, which has been met with criticism in terms of issues of 'cost shunting' from social services. As Lund (2006) states, this stems from the difficulties associated with making '... distinctions between "treatment" (provided by the National Health Service), "care" (provided by social services departments) and "support" (supplied by social landlords)' (p 213). It seems unlikely that these issues will be addressed by the coalition government in the current economic climate, but we take a look later at what the government has proposed in relation to housing for disabled people.

Chronology of relevant UK housing policy and key events for disabled people: an overview

1834	Poor Law Act
1845	Lunacy Act
1862	Lunacy Amendment Act
1886	Idiots Act
1890	Lunacy Act
1908	Report of Royal Commission on Care and Control of the Feeble-Minded
1913	Mental Deficiency Act
1918	Tudor Walters Report
1919	Ministry of Health Act
1927	Mental Deficiency (Amendment) Act
1930	Mental Treatment Act
1942	Beveridge Report
1944	Dudley Report
1944	Disabled Persons (Employment) Act
1944	Education Act
1946	National Health Service Act
1948	National Assistance Act
1959	Mental Health Act (1960 Scotland)
1961	Parker Morris standards
1968	Social Work (Scotland) Act
	Health Service and Public Health Act
	Seebohm Report
1970	Chronically Sick and Disabled Persons Act
	Local Authority Social Services Act
1972	Chronically Sick and Disabled Persons (Scotland) Act
1974	Housing Act

Department of the Environment (DoE) and Welsh Office Circular *Housing for People who are Physically Handicapped* 'Mobility Housing' and 'Wheelchair Housing'

Cullingworth Report

1977 National Health Service Act

Housing (Homeless Persons) Act

1978 DoE *Housing Services for Disabled People* and *Handicapped Children:Their Homes and Lifestyles*

1978 British Standard 5619

1980 Housing Act

Tenants' Rights (Scotland) Act

1981 International Year of Disabled Persons

1983 Mental Health Act

1986 Disabled Persons (Services, Consultation and Representation) Act

1988 Housing Act

Independent Living Fund

Office of Population, Censuses and Surveys (OPCS) *Surveys of Disability in Great Britain*

Griffiths Report, *Community Care:An Agenda for Action*

Wagner Report, *Residential Care:A Positive Choice*

Social Security Advisory Committee *Benefits and Disabled People:A Strategy for Change*

1989 Children Act

Local Government and Housing Act

Lifetime Homes standard launched by the Helen Hamlyn Trust

Caring for People White Paper

1990 Disabled Facilities Grants

National Health Service and Community Care Act

1993 Independent Living Fund 1993

1995 Disability Discrimination Act

Carers (Recognition and Services) Act

Mental Health (Patients in the Community) Act

1996 Community Care (Direct Payments) Act

Housing Act

Housing Grants, Construction and Regeneration Act

1999 Part M (Access to and Use of Buildings) of the English Building Regulations

Access Committee for England & Centre for Accessible Environments standards

2001 Health and Social Care Act

Social Care Institute for Excellence established

Valuing People White Paper (DH, 2001a)

2002 Homelessness Act

2003	Disability Discrimination Act (1995) (Amendment) Regulations
	Homelessness etc (Scotland) Act
	Supporting People programme
2005	Disability Discrimination Act
	Mental Capacity Act
	PMSU report *Improving the Life Chances of Disabled People*
2006	Disability Equality Duty
2007	Mental Health Act
	Equality and Human Rights Commission established
2008	ODI independent living strategy
2010	Equality Act

The Conservative-Liberal Democrat coalition: new possibilities?

In May 2010, the Conservative-Liberal Democrat coalition government came to power. Since then, we have heard repeated claims for the urgent need to implement public expenditure cuts, and we are currently in a period where such cuts are swiftly taking place. The key areas for cuts were announced on 22 June in the emergency Budget, with further cuts announced in October's comprehensive spending review. Despite government claims that the most 'vulnerable' would be protected from these cuts, it would seem that disabled people could potentially lose out (*The Guardian*, 2010a). We look now at some of the key proposals made in the coalition government programme and emergency Budget, and the likely impact on disabled people's housing opportunities. Although it is difficult to predict exactly what will be put in place, we can make some observations relating to what the coalition government has been saying.

Certain proposals from the government programme would appear to be beneficial for many disabled people and lower-income groups, such as the continued support for low-cost home-ownership initiatives. There are claims, for instance, that the government will '... promote shared ownership schemes and help social tenants and others to own or part-own their home' (HM Government, 2010, p 12). The coalition government also proposes to '... extend the greater roll-out of personal budgets to give people and their carers more control and purchasing power' and to use '... direct payments to carers and better community-based provision to improve access to respite care' (HM Government, 2010, p 30). Nonetheless, many of the proposals are likely to have a less positive impact on disabled people. There are plans, for example, for fixed tenancy terms on social rented housing, which some argue could see disabled people losing specifically adapted homes and moving into inaccessible private rented housing because of income assessments (Muscular Dystrophy Campaign, 2010). This is problematic, for, as we will see in Chapter Four, there are very few accessible properties in private renting. In relation to employment, the government plans to encourage 'responsibility' and 'fairness' through '... providing help for those who cannot work, training and targeted support for those looking for work, but sanctions for those who turn down reasonable offers of work and training' (HM Government, 2010, p 23). Its plans under this section are to '... create a single welfare to work programme to help all unemployed people get back into work' and to '... re-assess all current claimants of Incapacity Benefit for their readiness to work' (HM Government, 2010, p 23). This suggests a strengthening of the work imperative promoted by the New Labour government, but it seems at present that targeting the barriers that disabled people encounter in the workplace are as yet overlooked (Disability Alliance, 2010a).

In relation to public spending cuts, the emergency Budget in June reported on several key proposals that will affect disabled people's income and housing opportunities. First, DLA and benefits for families are being targeted. DLA costs around £11 billion a year, and government plans to reduce this figure involve the introduction of a tougher medical assessment (using a similar approach to the Work Capability Assessment for Employment and Support Allowance [ESA]), aimed to determine those who 'really need' the benefit (Ramesh and Butler, 2010). Such a measure, aside from being a costly exercise in itself (Disability Alliance, 2010b), arguably '... confuses the care and support needs of disabled and older people with being in work. DLA simply recognises that there are extra costs associated with day-to-day living if you are a disabled person and indeed many of those who receive DLA do work' (Essex Coalition of Disabled People, 2010, p 1). There are also fears that people labelled with learning difficulties will particularly lose out through the medical assessment (*The Guardian*, 2010b), and that there may be a reverse in the trend for growing numbers of people being able to live independently as a result of loss of the benefit (Essex Coalition of Disabled People, 2010). Following further public spending cuts announced in the comprehensive spending review, there is some suggestion that disabled people may face greater disadvantage in relation to income and employment, which will affect funds available for housing. There are plans, for instance, to reduce the numbers of people in receipt of ESA, and the length of time that it can be claimed (see Chapter Five). Similarly, measures relating to VAT, which are argued to have a greater impact on disabled people

(Disability Alliance, 2010b), and cuts to housing benefits (*The Guardian*, 2010c) may see some disabled people's incomes reduced further. In addition, the ILF closed to new applicants '... less than three months into the financial year' (*The Guardian*, 2010d, p 1) due to lack of funds and despite government claims that its budget had not been cut. More recently, it has been announced that the ILF is set to close (Peck, 2010).

Another public spending cut proposed by the coalition government is the reduction in Support for Mortgage Interest, which could potentially lead to an increase in the numbers of disabled people falling into arrears. It has been argued in one press commentary, for instance, that:

> Around 59,000 disabled people use the benefit to help them pay mortgages on homes they have bought. A further 5,000 people with profound physical disabilities and mental health problems have used the state payments to secure niche mortgages to pay for shared ownership.... Most of those who take up the benefit are first-time buyers with a total household income of less than £60,000. A sizeable minority are home owners who can show that their houses are no longer suitable for their needs. They may have long-term support needs, have a full-time carer, or need to live close to a medical facility. (*The Guardian*, 2010a)

Furthermore, as we shall see later, some mortgage lenders' failure to accept benefits as income can relate to distrust of government commitment to maintain benefits payments. In the current era of credit constraint and public spending cuts, this may become even more common among lenders and have further impact on access to the owner-occupied sector for disabled people. There are, then, some important proposals from the coalition government that could potentially affect disabled people's housing opportunities. Some of these have been welcomed, but it would seem that many are likely to negatively affect disabled people. Unfortunately, in a period of cuts we are likely to see a decline in the provision of services, but it remains to be seen how great the impact of that may be on disabled people.

International insights: housing and disabled people outside the UK

The housing rights of disabled people are recognised in the United Nations Convention on the Rights of Persons with Disabilities, which states that disabled people should have the right to live in the community and have equal choices to others. Article 19 of the Convention asserts that disabled people must '... have the opportunity to choose their place of residence and where and with whom they live on an equal basis with others and are not obliged to live in a particular living arrangement' (in addition to having access to residential and community support services) (UN, 2008). Article 28 states that disabled people and their families have a right to an adequate standard of living, which includes housing. A full review of international policy is not the intention here, nor is there scope to provide it. Rather, the aim is to draw the reader's attention to selected examples that have come to light from the literature and from which useful insights or good practice can be drawn. As Lund (2006) argues, among other benefits, comparing housing policies across different countries can '... supply ideas from programme development in the UK by identifying what policies are in operation elsewhere and, perhaps, assessing their effectiveness in relationship to UK policies' (p 74). He states, for example, that the choice-based letting scheme in the UK (see Chapter Six) was actually based on the Delft lettings model that emerged in the 1980s in the Netherlands. Furthermore, there have been important developments, such as CILs, that have their counterparts in the US following the emergence of the first CIL in Berkeley, California in 1972. The American ILM was also a considerable inspiration in the development of 'Project 81' described earlier (Oliver and Barnes, 1998). Thus, international comparisons enable the selection of features of successful developments and the avoidance of those that are less effective. Nonetheless, comparisons can be complex and affected by a lack of comparable data. Indeed, comparative work on housing and 'difference' in western countries is limited, let alone in those countries with different cultural contexts (Harrison and Hemingway, 2011), and issues of policy transfer are restricted by the different welfare systems in place (Brown and Yates, 2005). Thus, we draw here on some useful case examples in relation to disability and housing, bearing in mind the complexities of comparisons, and policy transfer, in different contexts.

Deinstitutionalisation has been under way in many countries, but is apparently particularly advanced in the US, Canada, Scandinavia, Australasia and the UK (Mansell and Beadle-Brown, 2009). The UK has made good progress towards community living options for disabled people, shifting away from institutional provision. Nonetheless, this form of accommodation still exists for disabled people, especially for particular groups, and some community-based housing resembles more institutional provision (Townsley et al, 2010). In addition, as we will see in later chapters, housing conditions and options available to disabled people within the community or within mainstream housing are far from unproblematic. There may therefore be a lot to learn from countries where institutional provision has been diminishing. For example, large-scale institutional accommodation for disabled people does not exist in Denmark, Norway or Sweden. In Sweden, '... community-based residences are designed to accommodate a maximum of six individual units, or apartments, and are situated in ordinary buildings' (Townsley et al, 2010, p 19). There may also be lessons to learn from Australia, where various approaches to providing 24-hour support, as an alternative to institutional care, have been introduced, each guided by the concept of independent living. See Fisher and colleagues (2009) for an evaluation of these approaches.

Outside of the UK, one of the strongest areas in other countries, as evidenced in the literature, relates to the physical element of housing. Housing design can be important for addressing physical barriers for disabled people, and solutions to inaccessible environments tend to rest on the dominant understanding of disability in a country (as well as broader principles underpinning welfare provision). Sweden is a useful example here. With earlier acceptance of the social creation of disability than in Britain, as well as greater involvement of disabled people in policymaking processes, Sweden has adopted an approach to housing design that aims to address diverse needs, rather than developing segregated 'special needs' housing. Thus, in the 1980s and 1990s, Sweden introduced a range of legislation '... to regulate the internal design requirements of all new dwellings' (Allen, 1999, p 60). In addition, the approach taken to the existing housing stock was to introduce programmes to adapt all dwellings to '... consider the complexities of functional competence' (Allen, 1999, p 60), facilitating a collective approach to inclusion. There was also apparently a strong connection between physical access in design solutions and social planning to enable greater social inclusion of disabled people. Furthermore, in Sweden, '... it is a condition of wholesale transfers of housing stock and major redevelopment/regeneration programmes that the accessibility of dwellings is improved' (Goodridge, 2004, p 21). The Lifetime Homes approach (see Chapter Four) that is currently being adopted to some degree in the UK shows some recognition of these issues, but there may be much to learn from the Swedish approach to collective design solutions.

On the other hand, more individualised housing solutions, such as adaptations and assistive technology, can be important for some households. As we will see in Chapter Four, in the UK, access to equipment and adaptations within the home can be subject to a lengthy process of application and assessment. It may be that a scheme currently being piloted in Norway could provide some guidance to avoid some of the '... bureaucracy involved in applying for equipment or aids'. This involves a '..."user pass" (brukerpass), in which a person who already has access to the type of equipment in question can use the brukerpass to gain access to replacement, repairs, etc.... This system has been shown to reduce the cost of administration, and also to reduce time lags in supply' (Townsley et al, 2010, p 38). Additional individualised solutions to physically inaccessible environments include developments in 'smart home' technology (see also Chapter Four). One example cited by Chan and colleagues (2009) provides an indication of the range of devices that can be integrated into the dwelling. They discuss the Gator Tech Smart House developed by the University of Florida for older and disabled people:

> It is based on environmental sensors for comfort and energy efficiency, safety and security, activity/mobility monitoring, reminder/prompting technologies, fall detection systems, smart devices and appliances (smart phone, smart mail box, etc.), social distant dining with family members, and biometric technologies for physiological monitoring (weight, temperature). (Chan et al, 2009, p 91)

In Northern Ireland, too, 'smart' technology has been applied to accommodation for older people with dementia to improve the safety of the residents. In the scheme run by the Clanmil Housing Association, 'Sensors watch the 24 flats for fires, floods and falls and monitor the night-time movement of residents' (Randall, 2003, p 22), although this seems to reflect more of a 'top-down' approach.

In the UK, as we will see in Chapter Four, the building regulations – while a step towards improved access standards – have been of limited success in creating fully accessible environments for disabled people. In Australia, however, Prideaux (2006) found that the Disability Standards for Access to Premises had proved a particularly important development. Here, the Australian government has '... effectively amended the DDAA [Disability Discrimination Act of Australia] to allow for the development of prescribed national minimum standards ... contained within the Premises Standard itself' (p 50), which means that there is consistency between the anti-discrimination legislation and building regulations. As such, '... anti-discrimination legislation relating to access can be enforced through the daily activities of building surveyors' (Prideaux, 2006, p 52). Furthermore, he argues that

'... the introduction of a Premises Standard has introduced mandatory Performance Requirements. As a consequence, Australia is now on the verge of creating a national code of practice that can be adopted and enforced by regional policies, practices and agencies' (Prideaux, 2006, pp 59-60). In contrast, in the UK and Northern Ireland, lack of consistency in the application of access standards results from the responsibility for enforcement and compliance of access standards in building regulations resting on building inspectors (Prideaux, 2006).

Looking at trends in housing tenure, it is useful to examine examples across the European Union (EU). While similar tenures exist across the EU member states, differences in social housing exist in terms of size of the sector and allocation criteria. As Czischke (2007) explains, allocation criteria include approaches based on 'universalistic' or 'targeted' provision. Universalistic provision is based on the principle of decent quality, affordable housing for general needs (as seen in Sweden), whereas targeted approaches provide housing to either employees, or the most 'vulnerable' (including disabled people) (as increasingly has been the trend in the UK). The sale of much of the higher-quality or better-located social housing stock in the UK has caused a decline in available accommodation, and has arguably contributed to the residualisation of the tenure (Murie, 2007; Malpass, 2010). There are concerns that disabled people are more commonly housed in stigmatised, segregated social rented dwellings, and in response there is some argument for a '... broad-based social rental sector with a diverse dwelling stock and a differentiated resident profile ... an approach which is now reflected in the "universalistic" model' (Czischke, 2007, p 12). Although this does not '... necessarily guarantee the absence of segregated communities' (Czischke, 2007, p 12), such an approach would contribute to the reduction of stigma associated with the tenure, and might have positive outcomes for disabled people. Access to owner-occupation would also be improved through schemes that recognise the additional outgoings that many disabled people have. In Western Australia, for example, the statutory authority Homewest is responsible for assisting those who cannot afford their own home to buy or rent. As DTZ Pieda (2003, pp 48-9) explains, Homewest uses an allocation policy for housing that considers disabled people's additional costs; calculates rent at 25 per cent of household income (which is reduced if the disabled person is employed, as an incentive to work); provides purpose-built housing with consultation at design stage; and offers an Access Home Loan that pays for 50 per cent of the property for an individual.

Finally, various schemes have been introduced to address homelessness in different countries, especially for mental health service users. One notable example has been applied in the US, and is a scheme that differs from the commonly used 'treatment-first' approach to tackling homelessness (whereby the provision of housing is conditional on receiving treatment beforehand). Research showed that those who received housing through the 'Pathways' approach (immediate housing provision that was not contingent on treatment, plus choices with regard to support and integrated management services) demonstrated greater signs of housing stability than those offered housing through the 'treatment-first' approach (Padgett, 2007). While this is a small selection of some of the policies, programmes and schemes relating to housing for disabled people currently under way in different countries, it would seem that lessons can be learned from several of these approaches that may be beneficial in the UK. As can be determined from these examples, approaches that address wider social and environmental barriers and tackle general rather than specific needs provide greater opportunities for improving the housing options and opportunities for disabled people.

Conclusion

Various regulations and policies have been introduced that address disabled people's housing needs, and disabled people have played a crucial role in influencing many of these developments. These include more generic anti-discrimination legislation such as the DDA, specific Acts that have given local authorities greater responsibilities to provide for disabled people's housing needs, and improved access rights for disabled people via building regulations and LTH standards. National strategies such as the ODI's independent living strategy have also been important, and specific initiatives have introduced greater support for particular groups (especially people labelled with learning difficulties). Furthermore, there are general expectations for more user involvement in services and planning and these have begun to affect disabled people along with other people (although there are claims that policy has not gone far enough). Finally, there is evidence of successful approaches to housing in countries outside the UK that suggest that there may be much to learn from international strategies for tackling housing problems for disabled people. Nonetheless, housing provision for disabled people has largely been predicated on an individual understanding of disability and discourse of community care. This has meant that disabled people's actual needs within housing have either been neglected or have been addressed by specific, specialised provision; useful in some cases, but often exclusionary. There are arguments, too, that some disabled people – such as disabled people from minority ethnic groups – have been neglected in the creation of housing policies (Drake, 1999) and that limited resources have restricted the provisions made.

We are currently in a period of transition involving major public cuts, and while it remains to be seen whether services for disabled people will suffer as a result, initial impressions are that disabled people may lose out in the coming years. In particular, the lack of resources available for positive initiatives is likely to have a negative impact on future developments and improvements. Nonetheless, continued support for, and monitoring of, existing legislation are needed. Furthermore, in line with the current public spending cuts, researchers need to monitor the differential impact of benefit cuts and changing levels of participation. Any decline in housing investment, such as adaptations, will have a direct impact on disabled people. Overall, it would appear that progress has been patchy, and initiatives that apparently enable choice, control and greater independence have not always been achieved in reality. Poor understanding of what the social model means in practice may have played a role here. Thus, the next chapter provides an overview of approaches to disability for policymakers, housing practitioners and researchers, with a view to clarifying ways of thinking about disability and impairment.

Summary of key issues

- There have been some important developments within housing for disabled people, including generic anti-discrimination legislation and specific housing policies. The move away from more institutional settings has also been an important step towards independent living for many.
- Despite policy developments, housing provision has tended to separate disabled people's needs from those of the non-disabled population; to exclude or neglect certain groups; and to rely on individual or 'medical' ideas about disability. Provision has largely been professionally defined and resource-led, which has failed to appropriately address the housing needs of many.
- The public spending cuts in place under the coalition government will affect everyone, but seem likely to substantially affect the income and housing opportunities of disabled people.
- International examples of good practice in relation to housing for disabled people can offer important insights, albeit different contexts and welfare systems require consideration.

Recommended further reading

Milner, J. (2005) 'Disability and inclusive housing design: towards a life-course perspective', in P. Somerville and N. Sprigings (eds) *Housing and Social Policy: Contemporary Themes and Critical Perspectives*, London and New York, NY: Routledge.

ODI (Office for Disability Issues) (2008) *Independent Living: A Cross-government Strategy about Independent Living for Disabled People*, www.odi.gov.uk/docs/wor/ind/ilr-executive-report.pdf.

Oliver, M. and Barnes, C. (1998) *Disabled People and Social Policy: From Exclusion to Inclusion*, London: Longman. (Useful for a general history of disability policy.)

Prideaux, S. (2006) *Good Practice for Providing Reasonable Access to the Physical Built Environment for Disabled People*, Leeds: The Disability Press. (Useful for international examples of good practice in the built environment that may provide useful starting points for informing UK housing development, policy and provision for disabled people.)

PMSU (Prime Minister's Strategy Unit) (2005) *Improving the Life Chances of Disabled People: Final Report*, London: Cabinet Office, www.strategy.gov.uk/downloads/work_areas/disability/disability_report/index.htm.

THREE

Understanding disability: from 'personal tragedy' to social disadvantage

There has been a shift in thinking about what constitutes 'disability' in recent years, from restriction arising through individual functioning and based on medical interpretations, to that which is caused by social, environmental and cultural barriers. This transition from an individual or 'medical model' interpretation of disability to a socio-political approach has been crucial for highlighting the constraints that disabled people encounter every day of their lives, and is hugely significant for housing policy and provision. It has been argued that housing providers and policymakers, as well as those involved in the 'disability business' (Albrecht, 1992), have largely been influenced by the former, to the detriment of disabled people. There are, then, two key models of disability: the individualistic 'medical' model and the social model (there are also several variations of these; see Priestley, 1998 and later in this chapter). This chapter offers an overview of these models, and highlights how the approach taken by a person or institution can affect the treatment of disabled people and the services that they receive. With this in mind, it is essential that housing practitioners and policymakers question their understanding of disability and the impact it has on their work with disabled people, and – following a social approach to disability – need to engage in initiatives for more inclusive practices that challenge disabling social processes.

Individual understandings of disability: personal disadvantage?

The more individualistic understanding of disability and impairment, often referred to as the 'medical model' or 'personal tragedy' approach, began to emerge in the 19th century, alongside the rise of institutionalised forms of housing and the increasing influence of medical professionals. As mentioned in Chapter One, the model is based on the premise that an individual has an impairment or 'functional limitation' that prevents them from doing something (Oliver, 1990a, 1996a). It is the presence of a real or perceived impairment (Barnes,

2005) that becomes a defining characteristic of the individual and is presumed to prevent them from doing things for themselves or fully participating in society. Thus, it is the impairment that is ultimately regarded as the *cause* of disability. Accordingly, disabled people are deemed dependent on others for support, such as their families and the state. The assumption made is that the 'functional limitation' can be remedied in some cases through the use of medical or rehabilitative intervention (often by the non-disabled 'expert' or 'professional'), and this is believed necessary for the transition of the individual to a more socially acceptable condition (Oliver, 1992). In this way, the model is based on notions of supposed 'normality', where disabled people are marked out as different from the 'norm' (see Davis, 1995). Within such an approach, then, notions of 'care', 'cure' and 'normality', as well as assumptions about 'vulnerability', 'personal tragedy' and disabled people as 'victims', are vital to understandings of disability.

This model has been central to official definitions of disability, often produced by non-disabled professionals that have overlooked disabled people's own views and accounts. These definitions have, for instance, been used in surveys on disability in the UK (OPCS, 1988; now the Office for National Statistics) and within important UK legislation such as the 1995 Disability Discrimination Act. The approach is often associated with the World Health Organization International Classification of Impairment, Disability and Handicap (ICIDH), which was introduced to provide a common language on disability and impairment. The definitions within the ICIDH have now been superseded by the International Classification of Functioning, Disability and Health, which has attempted to draw together elements of the individual and social models (sometimes referred to as the biopsychosocial approach), although its success in this regard has been questioned (see Hurst, 2000; Pfeiffer, 2000; Baylies, 2002; WHO, 2002).

It can be argued that the individual or 'medical' model of disability constitutes a deficient basis for understanding disability and impairment, as a result of two key factors. First, it creates the image of disability as one of 'personal tragedy' (Oliver, 1990b; Barnes et al, 1999) that leads to dependency on others and the state or notions that disabled people should be 'cared' for. Consequently, policies tend to concentrate on either rehabilitating or 'curing' '... the medical problem' (Imrie, 2006a, p 31), or providing 'separate' or 'specialised' provision as a form of 'containment' (Drake, 1999) or 'compensation' for people with impairments (Hyde, 2000). This is evident in the education system, where segregated schooling exists for disabled people (Barton, 1997; Whitaker, 2001; Ainscow, 2007), and in 'special needs' housing (Stewart et al, 1999; French and Swain, 2006). Here, medical and social care professionals' opinions and perspectives take priority over disabled people's own voices and the focus is almost entirely on the impairment, instead of acknowledging disabling forces inherent in the cultural and physical environment (Swain et al, 2003). Second, research that is based on this model is criticised for oppressive practices (Oliver, 1992; 1996a) and for utilising methods and terminology that fail to accurately represent disabled peoples' experiences, as demonstrated in the 1988 OPCS surveys of disability (see Abberley, 1990, 1992). The language used in 'medical' model accounts promotes the presumption that impairment is the primary cause of disabled people's disadvantage, which is believed by critics to reinforce the prejudice and discrimination that many disabled people experience.

The social approach: broadening our perceptions?

The individual model of disability began to be challenged in the 1960s and 1970s, when disabled activists drew attention to the failure of society to cater for diversity in the human body. Looking briefly at the trajectory of disability politics and understandings of disability, we see that during the 1970s the Independent Living Movement (ILM) emerged in America. This was inspirational for the disabled people's movement in the UK, offering a philosophy and notions of choice, control and autonomy (see Zarb, 2006) that influenced the development of social model definitions and accounts (Finkelstein, 1980; Oliver, 1983, 1990b) and later the operationalisation of the social model approach through the seven needs for independent living (see especially Davis, 1990). Other disabled activists were also influential here, including Paul Hunt in 'A critical condition' (in the edited collection *Stigma*) in 1966 and more formally the Union of the Physically Impaired Against Segregation (UPIAS) (1976).

With the introduction of the social model of disability, we have seen a shift in thinking about disability, from an approach that focuses on the individual impairment as the 'cause' of disadvantage to one that focuses on social and environmental barriers, and human rights. In a report entitled *Fundamental Principles of Disability*, UPIAS (1976) began by redefining disability, moving away from the prior focus on an individual functioning interpretation to a more social understanding, and rejecting discriminatory terminology such as 'handicap' (Barnes et al, 1999). Here, two distinct terms emerged. While impairment remained the functional attribute or condition of the individual, disability became known as that which is socially created – a result of social, environmental and attitudinal barriers experienced by the individual. Importantly, it was disabled people themselves who developed these definitions, rather than the non-disabled 'professionals' who were responsible for earlier attempts (Abberley, 1999). Accordingly, the definitions are informed by the actual experience of disability. These were later extended by Disabled People's International and the British Council of Disabled People (now the United Kingdom Disabled People's Council) to incorporate all forms of impairment, such as cognitive or intellectual impairments and 'mental illness'. The principal strategy adopted by advocates of the social model is, therefore, to remove social barriers and prejudice, in acknowledgement that people '... are disabled by society's reaction to impairment' (Morris, 1993b, p x). It is important to note that challenging these barriers has an impact not only on disabled people, but also on '... those with whom they share their lives, including partners, children, carers, household, friends, colleagues and neighbours' (Crowther, 2000, p 17). So, for instance, a lack of accessible properties will mean that the whole family may not be able to move to certain houses or locations; poor consultation during the adaptations process could mean that the entire family is affected by lack of (or poor use of) space; or inaccessible housing may make it difficult for disabled people to visit the homes of family, friends and neighbours.

The social model was developed further during the 1980s and 1990s through the work of key writers such as Vic Finkelstein (1980) and Mike Oliver (1983, 1990b). Finkelstein (1980) suggested that disability resulted from the rise of capitalist society, especially the changing forms of labour during industrialisation that saw disabled people excluded from participation in paid employment and, instead, moved to residential institutions. Finkelstein's work, although not without criticism, has been especially influential in the development of the social model approach. In particular, the work of Oliver follows a similar idea, and it was through Oliver's work that the phrase the 'social model of disability' originated in the early 1980s. While his earlier work outlines the social model approach, it is his 1990 publication *The Politics of Disablement* that is considered a key writing on the social model. Like Finkelstein, Oliver situates disability in the rise of capitalism, as well as the growth of the institution, which led to the segregation of disabled people from society. This gave way to a growing need for medical 'professionals' and changing ideas about what constituted 'normal'. In addition, there was a rise in negative stereotypes and the notion of disability as 'personal tragedy'. Oliver argued that it is not the individual who should be changed to fit the environment, but rather it is the environment that should be made more accessible for the individual.

Finkelstein and Oliver's materialist perspectives are among some of the most influential accounts of the rise of disability in contemporary society. We have also seen social model ideas that are idealist in emphasis (rooted in cultural attitudes and beliefs), as well as feminist and post-modernist approaches. (For more information on different perspectives within social model accounts, see Morris, 1996; Oliver, 1996a; Gleeson, 1997; Priestley, 1998; Barnes et al, 1999.)

The social model of disability therefore looks at collective disadvantage experienced by people with impairments within a socially, physically and economically unaccommodating environment. The focus is on society's role in 'disabling' people with impairments, as it fails to cater for diversity in the human body. As such, 'Disability ceases to be something that a person *has*, and becomes instead something that is done to a person' (Swain et al, 2003, p 23, emphasis in original). In this way, a person with an impairment does not necessarily experience disability. Disability is thus regarded as socially constructed and solutions are sought in structural changes, with policy and legislation targeting social and environmental barriers. In relation to the built environment, for instance:

> By focusing on structure, one can move from asking what *bodies* can function in a particular context (or looking at 'needs' in the abstract) to asking what types of structures can accommodate the widest range of bodies. From individual bodies, we need to move to the 'social body' and its materiality. (Freund, 2001, p 691)

At the same time, it should be acknowledged that disabled people are a diverse group and that different people will experience different barriers in different ways. As Crowther (2000) puts it, 'What unifies disabled people ... is the experience of barriers and discrimination' (p 16). It is the focus on barriers that has proved central to the social model, and is therefore addressed in detail in the following chapters of this book (in addition to looking at institutional practices and the impact of the differential treatment of individuals).

Questioning the effectiveness of the social model

There has been a vast amount written on the social model since its introduction, including that which raises criticisms of the approach. This critique has emerged both from within and outside the disabled people's movement. We look now at some of the most common claims made against the model, but for more detailed reviews, there are several useful summaries available (see Tregaskis, 2002; Barnes, 2003; Oliver, 2004). Most of the criticisms of the social model refer to its apparent failure to address the experience of impairment or other social divisions (such as age, ethnicity, gender and sexuality). It is often argued that the personal experience of impairment and disability is neglected, as it focuses on collective disadvantage and structural factors. It therefore overlooks the very real experience of individual impairment, and pain, which can be a daily issue for some (Morris, 1991; Crow, 1992, 1996). Hyde (2000) states, for instance, that, 'It is possible to imagine circumstances in which impairment is a considerable influence on a person's inability to perform social activities ...' (p 187). Others have argued for the need to incorporate the psycho-emotional dimensions of disability into social model accounts (Thomas, 1999; Reeve, 2004). It is claimed that these apparent omissions prevent disabled people from being able to fully identify with the model. It is also proposed that the focus on commonality of experience disregards the importance of differences between disabled people and that these differences can be significant in experiences of disability. It is suggested, for instance, that the social model has neglected to explore difference in relation to gender (Morris, 1991), sexuality (Corbett, 1994; Shakespeare, 1997), impairment (French, 1993; Crow, 1996) and the lives of people from various minority ethnic groups (Begum et al, 1994; Vernon, 1996, 1997).

In response to such claims, it has been argued that the social model does not deny the importance of impairment (or its effects), but rather advocates a focus on collective experiences of barriers (environmental, cultural and economic) as a more appropriate tool for removing these obstacles (Oliver, 1996b). The social model was developed as just that, a model or practical 'tool' for action (Oliver, 2004) to improve insights into disability through an alternative approach (Finkelstein, 2001). Moreover, it is argued that a focus on impairment over social explanations of disability can, in fact, blur the necessary distinction between disability and impairment (Finkelstein, 1996), and further that, even when people have a similar impairment, experiences can vary considerably (Rae, 1996). Medical and rehabilitative interventions are not considered unnecessary by the social model; rather, it is claimed that they should not be the sole interventions in disabled people's lives. Furthermore, it has been suggested that:

> Accepting that pain and illness are involved can ...be very
> well accommodated in the model, and this is particularly

true for the housing factors. Housing can be disabling, and quite clearly can harm health. It is important to bring these links to the attention of housing professionals. (Oldman, 2002, p 799)

While the claims around the apparent neglect of such experiences have been important for highlighting difference and perhaps demonstrate the need for an awareness of this in social policy and service provision, it might be argued that these criticisms do not detract from the social model's central focus on strategies that tackle collective disadvantage.

In terms of the supposed failure of the social model to deal with other social divisions, it is suggested by some that too much focus on difference can be at the expense of examining what these groups have in common (Freund, 2001). In addition, Oliver (2004) argues that while the social model has not yet addressed these, it should not be assumed that it could not do so. In fact, the structural emphasis may imply potential links to other kinds of divisions, as this book will indicate regarding risk. If the social model is understood as having an emphasis on the material and structural, it fits with other material and structural approaches that deal with alternative forms of divisions. It could also be argued that these debates have contributed significant insights into difference and that this only enriches our understanding of structural processes through listening to a range of different accounts and experiences. It does not seem to devalue the social model or, indeed, remove the need to focus political attention and action around collective disadvantage.

Other criticisms we have seen include the supposed outdated nature of the model in relation to impairment and identity. Some post-modernist writers have also expressed concerns in relation to the separation of impairment and disability as advocated within the social model. As they see matters, disability and impairment are essentially the same, being influenced by socially constructed discourses (Shakespeare and Watson, 2001; Tremain, 2002; Shakespeare, 2006). Furthermore, it has been argued that while the medical model portrays disabled people as 'victims' of their impairment, the social model also runs the risk of presenting disabled people as passive victims, but this time of an exclusive society (Shakespeare, 2000). In relation to the supposed inaccurate distinction between impairment and disability (Shakespeare and Watson, 2001; Shakespeare, 2006), it has been suggested that such critics are denying the materiality of disabled people's impairments (Rapley, 2004; Hughes, 2005). While there are issues around the social construction of *perceptions* of impairment, it may be that impairment is a practical issue for many disabled people and it is important to acknowledge that within the social model impairments must be considered in order to understand and remove barriers (Barnes, 1999). In addition, while post-modernist and post-structuralist writers have presented useful insights into the ways in which impairment and disability are '... socio-culturally and historically situated', their accounts can also be considered problematic as '... given the almost exclusive emphasis on language and discourse, there is a tendency in these approaches to de-emphasise sociomaterial contexts' (Freund, 2001, p 702). Moreover, the claim that the model is 'outdated' in terms of impairment and identity has overlooked developments evidenced through the affirmation model (Swain and French, 2000) or the 'social relational' model and introduction of 'impairment effects' (Thomas, 1999).

The affirmation approach is an extension of the social model in the sense that barriers are viewed as social and environmental, and in offering a critique of the personal tragedy notion of disability (Swain and French, 2000). According to this approach, while disabled people may experience disadvantage linked to their impairment, many people with appropriate support (such as contact with other disabled people or disability culture) reinforce a positive, affirmative identity (Swain and French, 2000). This, Swain and French (2000) suggest, is most apparent in the Disability Arts Movement, and is a '... non-tragic view of disability and impairment which encompasses positive social identities, both individual and collective, for disabled people grounded in the benefits of life style and life experience of being impaired and disabled' (p 569). As such, it is a direct challenge to the ideas of personal tragedy and dependency that often surround disabled people's lives and '... is born of disabled people's experiences as valid individuals, as determining their own lifestyles, culture and identity' (Swain and French, 2008b, p 75). For Swain and French (2000), it is important not to entirely disregard impairment, as this leaves it open to be viewed as personal tragedy. They suggest that asserting the negative implications of having an impairment should be avoided, for impairment may be valuable for the individual.

The social relational model is also an extension of the social model of disability and shares many of its principles, including the notion that disability is socially caused. It is an attempt to draw elements of the social and medical models together, providing a biopsychosocial model of disability, and is largely advocated by Thomas (1999, 2002, 2004). Within this approach, disability is shown through unequal relationships, or through '... the relationship of ascendancy of the non-impaired over the impaired' (Thomas, 1999, p 40). In addition, Thomas suggests that a distinction should be made between restrictions of activity that are social (which is 'disability') and those whereby impairment may be the cause, which she calls 'impairment effects'. These are '... shaped by the interaction of biological and social factors, and are bound up with processes of socio-cultural naming' (Thomas, 1999, p 43). Within this book, while the importance of the experiences and histories of individual impairment is recognised, it is the external issues that may affect disabled people that are emphasised more strongly. So its focus is not *impairment experiences* or *trajectories* as such, but rather an interest in *housing experiences*. As mentioned earlier, other attempts to bring together the medical and social models have resulted in claims to have provided a biopsychosocial model of disability (WHO, 2002). The concern with these approaches relates to the links between impairment and disability, for as Oliver (1996b) points out, it is important to assert no causal relationship between impairment and disability.

We can see, then, that there have been many criticisms of the social model. One way in which we can distinguish between these is to see them as attacks on, first, the action purposes of the model and second, the explanatory strength of the model (see forthcoming paper by the current author, Harrison and Hemingway, 'In defence of the social model of disability: further developments in understanding structural factors'). It would seem that the majority of critics focus on the latter of the two – its explanatory powers. Such conceptual debates are ongoing and are likely to continue, but what interests the current author is the practical merits of the model. Considering that criticisms of the social model focus less on its practical, or action purposes, we can perhaps assume that this remains a key strength of the model. While experiences relating to impairment and other dimensions of difference can provide important insights into the processes at work in disablement, it is the focus on the structural, and on collective disadvantage, that provides a valuable tool for action.

Barriers and opportunities: the social model in practice

In focusing on the action purposes of the social model, this book aims to show how a social understanding of disability can be employed to highlight the importance of structural factors, institutional discrimination and 'barriers'. It is also possible to see, however, that the social model can be extended through exploring specific actions and processes. These issues are explained below, with reference to the research carried out by the current author. The social model usefully highlights the holistic nature of disability experiences, identifying oppressive practices that are linked to a range of structural factors. This book does not attempt to explain these forces in depth, although some observations are made that point to influential factors (such as market processes and risk). Rather, the focus is on how these forces affect disabled people's choices and experiences within housing, in order to highlight potential factors that need tackling. Such structural factors or institutional forces influence people's behaviours, decisions and assumptions and shape disabled people's pathways. Choice, for instance, can be affected by financial systems and administrative processes in both public and private sectors of housing provision, and while ideas about diversity are increasingly catered for within both sectors, there are ingrained assumptions and ideologies that can constrain and condition opportunities for disabled people or lead to discriminatory practices. Structural influences can also be positive, however, providing options, support and 'enabling' environments.

It has been argued that structure should not be viewed in too deterministic a way, for structural factors simply '... set the stage and scenery, provide a range of possible texts and performance traditions, and lay out suits and props for the actors' (Harrison, 2004b, p 59). It is therefore difficult to ascertain the impact that structure will have on individuals, as people have the capacity and resources to act in various ways within structural contexts (and have the potential to resist structure, as in the case of the disabled people's movement). Attention should therefore also be paid to the role of human agency – the part played by individuals as opposed to organisational behaviours. Individuals are not passive recipients of environmental influences, as a reciprocal relationship exists in which structure affects agency and agency affects structure (Harrison, 2007). Furthermore, there are '... identifiable human contributions in processes that are oppressive' (Harrison, 2004b, p 59). These may relate, for instance, to employees of housing providers implementing practices that have a damaging or discriminatory effect on disabled people (perhaps unknowingly). In this way, human agents are manifesting the power and forces that are part of the wider picture. The relationship between structure and agency is thus more complex than suggested at present in many studies and as such, the effects of structural factors and the roles of 'agents' need exploring in specific settings. Within the research that informed this book, the role of agency was investigated through the voices and experiences of the human 'agents' themselves, both the 'service providers' (housing and mortgage representatives) and the 'users' (disabled people). The experiences and voices of disabled people helped to highlight exclusions and barriers in housing; while through listening to the experiences and opinions of housing industry informants it was possible to document how these barriers work.

People are affected by structural factors in different ways, depending on their circumstances and lifestyles, and so it is significant to bear individual differences in mind in relation to both structure and agency. Here we can emphasise the importance of the interactions between human agency and structural forces. It is important, for example, to look at institutional practices that can have more of a discriminatory effect for some than for others. This might be evidenced in relation to impairment group. So, for example, the housing industry may discriminate in an institutional way through the practices, relationships and assumptions that are embedded in its operation. An argument for the recognition of the diversity of experience is not new, but what this book emphasises is how *perceptions* and *classifications* of specific impairments may affect opportunities, rather than how *impairments* may affect opportunities. Accordingly, impairment may be incorporated into the social model, via the external reactions to a person's impairment rather than restrictions associated with the impairment itself. One example is the way in which individuals are assessed for risk when applying for a mortgage, as this can have more of a disabling effect for some disabled people than for others. So, experiences can be diverse and structural factors should be examined not only in relation to commonalities (as in the social model), but also for variations such as those relating to impairment (see also below in relation to risk).

The social model implies that there are important institutional effects of a discriminatory character. Some writers (such as Barnes, 1991) have gone so far as to refer to institutional discrimination in a broad way in relation to disability, which is fostered in the structure of society itself and is reflected in the inequalities of outcome for disabled people. The research informing this book looked beyond examining outcomes or unequal patterns, however, asserting the necessity of exploring specific actions and processes. Drawing on the concept of institutional discrimination used in ethnic relations (MacPherson, 1999), which relates to the practices, understandings and sensitivity of organisations towards diversity, we can certainly see that there are possibilities that institutions may have practices that result in discriminatory effects, even if these are not direct. So, for instance, it is the idea that the social rented sector or the 'owner-occupation industry' may discriminate in an institutional way, through the practices, relationships and assumptions that are embedded in its operation. Furthermore, if the social model is alerting us to institutionalised barriers and, in a way, structural obstacles, it is also necessary to explore whether those are found in relation to having an adequate home and being able to choose tenures (see Chapter Seven).

The social approach to disability is a useful tool for identifying 'barriers' to participation, of which there are several overlapping or mutually reinforcing types and some of which can be impairment-specific (Oliver, 2004). These include physical, attitudinal and financial barriers, and those that relate to communication. Physical (or access) barriers within this book represent those aspects of the environment that do not cater for a variety of bodily forms, largely relating to inaccessible environments (both within the dwelling and outside it). Communication (or information) barriers relate to the limited availability of information, the provision of inaccessible information or the failure to provide equipment or support for communication. Attitudinal barriers are evident in many areas of society, but in terms of this book refer to the attitudes of housing providers and financial industry representatives. While attitudes relate to 'agency', they are likely to be institutionalised and thus also represent a 'structural' constraint. Finally, financial barriers range from those arising from wider social disadvantage (such as income and employment) to lender perceptions of benefits in mortgage applications. Issues relating to life insurance and mortgage payment protection insurance have also been included in this category. Financial barriers can mostly be regarded as structural (institutional and economic), but are also affected by agency (for example, in terms of personal contacts). These barriers come together and affect not only the ability to acquire or secure housing, but also *experiences* of the dwelling. So, for instance, the social model allows us to see how personal relationships can be affected by unsuitable or inaccessible housing. It should be noted, as also mentioned earlier, that while this book predominantly draws attention to barriers, there may be circumstances in which disabled people are given priority in the allocation of housing on health grounds (particularly within social renting). In this sense, there may be certain situations in which disabled people may experience opportunities through welfare provision via systems based on 'priority needs', thus demonstrating the caution that must be exercised during an investigation into barriers. As has already been highlighted, while the barriers approach is important, examination needs to move beyond barriers and more collective disadvantage in order to more fully understand the role of structural factors in the disabling process.

The concept of risk can be useful when looking at how barriers work within housing. Disabled people have, throughout history, been considered a risk to both themselves (hence the practice of incarceration) and to the economy. This may be because disabled people have been defined as a risk and this risk is evident in society's attitudes to economic agents. If we apply or extend social model thinking to risk, we can say that where risk is likely to be crucial is for understanding institutional behaviours. We need to look at barriers and outcomes to investigate and highlight discrimination against disabled people, but it is also important to look at the processes that affect or lead to these and it is here that notions of risk can be utilised. In this way, we see how risk is manifest in institutional responses to disability, demonstrating the ways in which it can inform the perspectives and practices of institutions and the implications of these for particular groups of people. Risk can affect housing provision within the rented sector, with assessments of housing need focusing on 'risk of harm' (as conceived by both family and housing practitioners), or exclusion from eligibility for housing on the grounds of risk to housing providers (such as meeting rent payments) or the community (especially for mental health service users) (see Chapter Six). People with different impairments can also be perceived as more vulnerable or 'risky' by the owner-occupation industry, or classified and measured according to risk. It may be, for instance, that some disabled people are perceived or labelled as higher risk to finance or housing providers, or to other consumers (see also Harrison and Hemingway, forthcoming). As such, risks might represent barriers and constraints, relating to issues of risk assessment that lead to labelling, stereotyping and measuring. It is these institutional practices that may have a negative impact on disabled people's opportunities to access particular housing options. Thus, the social understanding of disability and risk come together to demonstrate how barriers work, by illuminating the mechanisms and practices of institutions, and highlighting how the institutional measuring of risk is a potentially crucial contributing element within structural factors. Such a model, it is hoped, could be applied to other potentially excluded or disadvantaged groups.

Conclusion

It is hoped that this chapter has demonstrated the importance of understanding different approaches to disability and the effects that these can have on housing opportunities and barriers for disabled people. Limited understandings based on more individualised, 'medical' interpretations have tended to dominate housing provision for disabled people, and, as we saw in Chapter Two, this has often resulted in housing and related services that fail to meet many disabled people's needs appropriately. The social model of disability emerged in the 1970s, but it is only in the past decade that it has begun at least to be acknowledged within housing policy and provision. While the social model has been subject to some criticism among disability writers for its explanatory potential, its strength lies in its practical use in identifying barriers, discrimination and oppressive practices. As we have seen in relation to investigations of barriers, there are several overlapping variables that need to be considered, which can be categorised as physical, attitudinal, financial and related to communication. We can also go further than this to look at how some processes can have more of a disabling effect for some disabled people than for others. This highlights the potential of considering impairment-specific issues within a social model approach, by focusing on the external reactions to a person's impairment rather than those restrictions associated with the impairment itself.

Overall, the essential claim here is that while debates are ongoing about the social model – and some broadening of approach is necessary in terms of both agency and structure – the core elements of the model remain central to looking at housing for disabled people. Thus within housing, for example, by identifying the barriers, constraints and opportunities that may result from the assumptions and practices of housing and related service providers, practitioners and policymakers can begin to question their own assumptions, judgements and practices and make adjustments to the ways in which they work. The social model therefore remains a valuable tool and inspiration for action within housing policy and practice (with its emphasis on structural constraints), albeit in a modified form that considers aspects of 'difference'.

Summary of key issues

- The individual model of disability has dominated disabled people's lives for many years, and regards disability or disadvantage as being caused by a person's impairment, which leads to individual difficulties and 'personal tragedy'. Housing policies influenced by this model have therefore focused on 'curing' or 'caring for' individuals, or providing separate, specialised provision for individual needs.

- The social model of disability is increasingly recognised as a more accurate understanding of disability and sees disability as socially caused. The disadvantage that disabled people experience is therefore a result of social, physical and economic environments that rarely cater for people with impairments. Thus, it is physically inaccessible houses, disadvantage in the labour markets, and the attitudes and practices of housing providers that 'disable' people with impairments. Solutions are sought in identifying and removing barriers, and creating environments that cater for diversity, difference and more 'general needs'.

- There has been some criticism of the social model, including its apparent failure to address experiences of pain, impairment or difference among disabled people, as well as questions around the distinctions made between disability and impairment. These criticisms have contributed important insights into differential experiences, but arguably do not detract from the practical use of the model.
- The strength of the social model lies in its practical application, its focus on structural factors and collective disadvantage, and its identification of barriers. It can also be taken further to show how barriers work, by looking at difference in relation to perceptions of impairment and risk.

Recommended further reading

Barnes, C., Mercer, G. and Shakespeare, T. (1999) *Exploring Disability: A Sociological Introduction*, Cambridge: Polity Press.

Oliver, M. (1990) *The Politics of Disablement*, Basingstoke: Palgrave Macmillan.

Priestley, M. (1998) 'Constructions and creations: idealism, materialism and disability theory', *Disability and Society*, vol 13, no 1, pp 75-95.

Swain, J. And French, S. (2008) 'Affirming identity' in J. Swain and S. French (eds) *Disability on Equal Terms*, London: Sage Publications.

Thomas, C. (1999) *Female Forms: Experiencing and Understanding Disability*, Buckingham and Philadelphia, PA: Open University Press.

FOUR

Physical and communication barriers: the built environment and access to information

The built environment plays a key role in '... shaping the ways in which people lead their lives' (Imrie and Hall, 2001, p 333), yet it poses a challenge for many disabled and older people in both public and private spheres, segregating, excluding and restricting movement. The design of buildings, public amenities and streets; the presentation and positioning of signs; and the inaccessible transport system neglect to cater for diversity in the human body, creating an environment that excludes almost everyone at some point in their lives (a process some have referred to as 'architectural disablement'; see Goldsmith, 1997). While everyone can potentially be affected by building design, disabled and older people are disproportionately 'designed out' of the physical environment, which restricts their opportunities to participate in the everyday life of society (Imrie, 1996; Burns, 2004). Much like the architecture of the public sphere, the design of housing rarely considers diversity in the human form and as such, the general stock of housing in the UK has been designed primarily for the non-disabled population. It is not just the experience within the home that is important, for there are various components of housing as a physical dwelling that need to be considered. So while access into the home, movement around the inside of the dwelling and general usability of facilities within it are all important, the accessibility of the immediate environment outside the dwelling (for example, the garden and communal areas) and the surrounding neighbourhood also require consideration. Furthermore, albeit that barriers created by physical design are experienced more commonly by people with mobility impairments (Imrie, 2006a), people with a range of impairments encounter these types of barriers, such as people with visual or hearing impairments or mental health service users. It is these issues that form the focus of this chapter. In addition, access to appropriate information, communicated in an accessible and effective format, is essential to disabled people making informed choices about housing and allied services. This chapter therefore also explores information and communication issues within the housing and mortgage industries.

Accessible housing: from 'special needs' to 'universal design'

The term 'accessible housing' can be applied to various forms of accommodation, including so-called 'special needs' housing, or wheelchair and mobility housing that has been designed for people with specific access requirements. It also applies, however, to housing designed to be flexible enough to meet the general needs of the majority of the population, whether a disabled person or not, such as Lifetime Homes (LTH) or those that adhere to 'universal design' principles (see later). Despite these differences, numbers of accessible dwellings tend to be limited across all tenures, and so for the majority of the population, housing fails to adequately address diverse and changing needs. The following oft-cited statement highlights the issues here:

> Are you male, fit and aged between 18 and 40, not very tall nor very short? Do you have good sight, good hearing and are you right handed? If you are, you need read no further. You are part of the 18% of the population for whom British houses are designed. If you are not, stay with me; this report concerns you and the rest of the 82% of the population who tolerate what is forced upon us by the 'average' housebuyer. (Smart, cited in Rowe, 1990, p 3)

This quotation, which was part of a report on Lifetime Homes, demonstrates the limiting and exclusionary approach taken to housing design. Aspects of housing design that are often taken for granted but can present numerous difficulties for disabled people include access to the property and use of outside space; access into the building, which may be restricted by steps, narrow doorways or raised thresholds; movement around the inside of the dwelling, which can be constrained by narrow doorways and hallways, space and layout; the facilities such as kitchens, which may have high counters and cupboards, or small bathrooms, which may restrict manoeuvrability for wheelchair users; and fixtures and fittings, such as inadequate lighting, high shelves and cupboards, and shiny tiles (the glare from which may cause difficulties for people with visual impairments). Such exclusionary design features can lead to disabled people being dependent on others (including the informal care of family and friends) to carry out everyday activities, which can have a negative impact on household relationships and sense of 'home' (see Chapter Seven).

Specially designed and 'visitable' housing: meeting specific needs

Early interventions by various governments relating to inaccessible housing have resulted in the construction of specifically designed properties for disabled people ('special needs', mobility and wheelchair housing). Such interventions gained specific emphasis during the 1960s, but the discourse of 'special needs', Clapham (2005) argues, was also '... associated with the growing targeting of housing policy in the 1980s with the increasing political pressure to reduce public expenditure' (p 217), and so state support was limited to those labelled as having 'special needs'. Groups categorised in this way were subject to stereotyped assumptions about their requirements and were subsequently provided with specialised accommodation to meet those needs. Although this special needs discourse proved advantageous for many, in the sense that it '... unlocked resources at a time when state support for housing was being reduced' (Clapham, 2005, p 218), it has also been stigmatising, reinforcing assumptions of disabled people that are based on an individual understanding of disability, and overlooking socially caused disadvantage.

Special needs housing is built to a different standard to – and separated off from – mainstream housing, and tends to be mainly available through the social rented sector (CLG, 2009a). Social rented properties have, in the past, most commonly been provided by local authorities, but more recently have come to include provision by charitable and non-charitable housing associations, some of which may specialise in housing for disabled or older people. The availability of accessible accommodation clearly provides a partial explanation for the predominance of disabled people residing in the social rented sector (alongside greater affordability and support), and has contributed to its reputation as the 'special needs' provider (Stewart et al, 1999). Three of the informants in the current author's research reported being very satisfied with their social rented accommodation (all from local authorities), citing the ease with which repairs and maintenance are carried out, and the support provided by their landlord as advantageous. One informant, Nancy, also described how effective her landlords had been at adapting her property. Despite such benefits, the stock of accessible housing within the sector is still limited (see later), some dwellings may not be suitable, and it seems that very few disabled people have access to housing adequately adapted to their needs (DRC, 2007a), particularly disabled children (Beresford and Rhodes, 2008).

With small numbers of accessible properties, it might be assumed that all are being utilised by those who need them, but as Stewart

(2004) asserts, much of the wheelchair housing available is occupied by people who do not use a wheelchair (although it must not be assumed that all wheelchair users require specialised housing; see Harris et al, 1997). There may be many reasons for this occurrence (including reasonable explanations such as low take-up or rejection of these properties by disabled people), but these are under-researched. Nonetheless, Stewart (2004) offers some possible explanations. These include the high numbers of wheelchair-accessible properties with only one bedroom, which are unsuitable for many disabled people (presumably resting on the assumption that disabled people are single and do not have families); properties being declined on the basis of the '... concentration of specialist facilities on one site' (Stewart, 2004, p 153); and the impact of the poor or slow process of communication between housing agencies and social services.

There may be some cases, however, where wheelchair-accessible properties prove more suitable for people with different types of impairments than general housing. The current author's research showed that such dwellings could be important for people with visual impairments, especially in relation to level thresholds: Jenny, for instance, has found her options very limited and moved into social rented housing as a last resort. She was offered no choice over where she was to live, and claimed to be very unhappy with the location of the property, which she believes to be in a 'horrible' neighbourhood:

> 'I have been on the transfer list since I moved in initially, but the council have made it quite clear that it's unlikely I will be re-housed in suitable accommodation, as this is kept for elderly people and wheelchair users. Where I live impacts on many aspects of my life: I dread coming home, I have little to no motivation for making the flat my own because I hate living there so much, I don't like people visiting because I am embarrassed and I have concussed myself twice on the concrete steps outside my door....'

Jenny's situation appears to highlight the problems that can arise around distinctions made by the local authority between impairments and the consequent services that are provided to the tenants. It is understandable, for instance, that wheelchair-accessible properties should be reserved for wheelchair users, especially when much wheelchair-accessible housing is occupied by people who do not use a wheelchair, but it is not clear why Jenny's safety has not been taken into account, especially if her example of being concussed twice has been noted by the housing providers. So perhaps in such a case as this, moving Jenny to a more 'accessible' property should be a priority. This case also highlights one of the criticisms that is often made of 'special needs' housing: that it tends to focus on people with physical impairments (French and Swain, 2006).

Even when accessible properties are provided within the social rented sector, they may still not meet the access needs of the individuals living there. The current author interviewed Holly, a wheelchair user, who has always lived in council accommodation, and tended to be quite critical of social renting. She described her and her husband's experiences over the last few years. After they had temporarily moved into a 'prefab' that leaked and had no heating (while a new property was built by the local authority), the council took out the old kitchen and put a brand-new, inaccessible kitchen into the property, resulting from a failure to consult her about her access requirements. Holly was forced to live with the inaccessible kitchen and poor conditions in the property for a year, until the council moved her and her husband into more temporary accommodation (also inaccessible) while building the bungalow that they now live in. When asked if their current property was accessible, she stated:

> 'It was completely accessible when it was done, but subsequently my husband has started to need to use a wheelchair. He has always been disabled, but he now needs to also use a wheelchair and it is not really big enough for two people who are wheelchair users. But we would never be re-housed because we would always be regarded as being adequately housed.'

Holly's story therefore also seems to highlight one of the key failures of local authorities in the provision of housing for disabled people: the lack of communication, or consultation. So while social renting provides more accessible properties than alternative tenure types, it would appear that these are still limited, and can sometimes fall short of meeting the needs of inhabitants. Furthermore, 'special needs' housing is not ideal, with segregated, and often stigmatised, accommodation resting on assumptions that disabled people are different and thus require separate provision. As we will see later, a more appropriate solution lies in building accessible housing for all.

While accessible housing is limited in the social rented sector, there are even fewer accessible properties in the private sector – both within private renting and owner-occupation – which has a considerable impact on choice within housing. The lack of accessible properties within private renting has been especially noted (see PMSU, 2005; Imrie, 2006a). This can be particularly problematic for young disabled people, whose non-disabled peers predominantly rely on private renting for independent housing when leaving the family home (Morris, 2002). For disabled students, the lack of suitable privately rented accommodation may force a reliance on university-provided housing, which can also be limited in terms of accessibility (see Shevlin et al, 2004; Harrison et al, 2009). Homeless disabled people can also be affected by physical access issues, with many homeless shelters failing to cater for disabled people (Goodridge, 2004) and other forms of accessible temporary accommodation lacking. Doherty (2006) found, too, that available temporary accommodation in Scotland for homeless disabled people is often located in high-rise flats in low-demand areas, which can cause additional concerns for mental health service users who may be '... affected by stress and the environment around them' (p 4).

Attempts have been made to improve the accessibility of the general stock of housing via the introduction of Part M of the building regulations in England and Wales (and the equivalent regulations in Northern Ireland and Scotland) (see Chapter Two). These have meant that new-build properties are required to meet certain standards of accessibility, and such properties have enhanced 'visitability' to other people's homes. While these are undoubtedly a step in the right direction, some have argued that such guidelines are not sufficient to constitute 'accessible' housing (Imrie, 2003; Milner, 2005; Thomas and Ormerod, 2005). The requirement that the property should be 'visitable', allowing access for a wheelchair user into the dwelling but not necessarily around it, is still limiting, and does not appear to greatly improve the stock of accessible properties for people to actually *live* in. As Imrie (2006a, p 4) states, the regulations do not question '... the basic layout and design of the dwellings', instead simply 'adding on'... design features in order to facilitate some flexibility of use'. He also points out that builders tend to display little regard for the regulations, often failing to see disabled people as part of their target market (perhaps because of perceived additional costs for building accessible properties). Concerns have also been raised in relation to the consistency of the application of the standards – with compliance being the responsibility of building inspectors (as raised in Chapter Two) – as well as the conceptual implications of marking disabled people out as a separate group to be catered for through the regulations (Imrie, 2003). Such a limited approach to accessibility can be regarded as ineffective, exclusionary and damaging for people with impairments, as well as their families.

For more information, see Imrie's (2006a) *Accessible Housing: Quality, Disability and Design*, which offers a detailed appraisal of Part M of the English building regulations.

Accessible housing for all: focusing on general needs

LTH standards go much further than the building regulations in attempting to provide housing that is flexible, adaptable and liveable (rather than simply visitable) and address the needs of a diverse population. The LTH concept gained formal expression in a seminar held by the Helen Hamlyn Trust, and has been enhanced and promoted by the Joseph Rowntree Foundation (JRF) (Milner and Madigan, 2004). It refers to flexible, accessible housing that incorporates 16 design criteria. These include the fitting of sockets and switches at appropriate heights for the majority of users; the installation of an accessible toilet; the provision of adequate space standards; the inclusion of walls that are capable of taking hand rails; and the ability to incorporate facilities for future needs through fixtures such as a floor lift or a hoist to be used from the bedroom to the bathroom, among others (see the JRF website for more details). Thus, the LTH dwelling caters for changing needs throughout the life course, which is important, for as Barlow and Venables (2004, p 797) state, '... the intensity with which the home is used varies with the stage in the lifecycle', so, for instance, '... older people tend to use the home for longer periods'. This can also be the case for some disabled people.

The individual benefits of Lifetime Homes are clear: increasing inhabitants' independence in the dwelling and providing greater control over one's environment. LTH standards enable people to remain in their own home for longer, enhancing feelings of security and allowing people to retain their local social commitments, relationships and community links. It is also less stigmatising to live in dwellings of this type. Supporters of LTH standards have also drawn attention to the more collective advantages of Lifetime Homes, such as the creation of mixed communities and the potential cost savings to be made from reducing the need for home support, alternative accommodation (such as residential care homes) or the implementation and removal of adaptations (Cooper and Walton, 1995; PMSU, 2005; ODPM, 2006). It has been argued, for example, that it is more economical to build accessible houses than adapt inaccessible ones at a later date (Rowe, 1990; French and Swain, 2006). LTH standards are not without their drawbacks, however, with questions arising around their ability to meet a variety of needs within one design and the suggestion that they neglect the needs of people with visual impairments and children (see Milner and Madigan, 2004). Concerns have also been raised (mainly by builders) about the impact of practical design on aesthetic appeal and sense of 'home' within the dwelling (Cooper and Walton, 1995). The latter critique, however, as Imrie (2006a) argues, is actually '... more revealing about ... [builders'] ... lack of creative (design) imagination than ... about the alleged lack of design options in relation to designing for accessibility' (p 66). Finally, numbers of dwellings that meet LTH standards remain small.

The 2007 English House Condition Survey provides figures on the availability of housing considered 'visitable' and that which is defined as 'accessible and adaptable' (incorporating 11 features of the LTH standards). In terms of 'visitable' homes:

> About 740,000 (3.4%) of homes across the whole stock had all four features that enable a person with mobility problems to readily visit (level access to main entrance, flush threshold to main entrance, WC at entry level and circulation space). Only minor work would be necessary to provide these in an additional 2.6 million (12% of) homes. It was not feasible to provide all four features in 28% (6.2 million) of homes. (CLG, 2009a, p 189)

It was also shown that over a quarter of the dwellings had none of the four features, meaning that simply entering these buildings would be either difficult or impossible for some disabled people. For those dwellings labelled 'accessible and adaptable', 11 features derived from LTH standards had to be evident, although a wheelchair-accessible lift and changes to the floor level, which are considered necessary to constitute accessible housing, were not included (due to insufficient information). It was found that 'Around half (51%) of all homes had six or more of these features ... only around 110,000 homes or 0.5% of the existing stock had all eleven features' (CLG, 2009a, p 205). Despite limited numbers of properties meeting the standards to date, support for Lifetime Homes has been strong and there is some indication that the situation will improve in the coming years. The Joseph Rowntree Housing Trust, for instance, has been building all new homes to LTH standards since the late 1980s (JRHT, 2008), and, reporting in 2004, Stirling with Lloyd discussed how LTH standards have been introduced in Wales for all new-build housing association properties. Furthermore, the Homes and Communities Agency (HCA, 2010) state that the standards are '... currently included as an optional element within the Code for Sustainable Homes' (p 1). A commitment to improving adherence to the Lifetime Homes standards has been documented in the 2008 government report *Lifetime Homes, Lifetime Neighbourhoods: A National Strategy for Housing in an Ageing Society* (HCA, 2010) and the ODI (2008) independent living strategy. These state that adherence to the standard will be mandatory for all public sector housing by 2011, and plans are under way for new housing in the private sector to follow suit by 2013.

Going further than LTH standards, the concept of 'universal design' in the US is based on the idea of creating environments that are accessible for the majority from the outset (rather than having to add or adapt features at a later date). From this perspective, and reflecting a social model approach to disability, the '... emphasis ... is not on the different and special needs of particular mind-bodies, but on flexible spaces for *all* bodies' (Freund, 2001, p 702). The Center for Universal Design (1997) offers seven principles of universal design, including: equitable use (practical and saleable to people of various abilities); flexibility in use (caters for different preferences and abilities); simple and intuitive to use (easy to understand); perceptible information (information effectively communicated to user); tolerance for error (minimises hazards from accidental misuse); low physical effort (can be used with little energy); and size and space for approach and use (appropriate for users of all body shapes, sizes and capabilities). Examples of the application of the latter principle, in relation to housing, would mean the positioning of plug sockets, light switches, shelves, cupboards and so forth at levels to be reached by people of different sizes, whether sitting or standing. It might also mean the provision of enough space to cater for the use of assistive devices or personal assistance (Center for Universal Design, 1997). Thus, in addition to catering for parents with children, older people and people with impairments, universal design would account for variations in bodies that might not be considered impairments, for as Freund (2001) comments, being '... "very" tall, or short, small or large can be disabling in a "one size fits all" socio-material environment' (p 692). The idea of 'inclusive design' is similar in approach to universal design, but there is a preference in the UK for this term (see CEBE, no date). The principles of universal design are clearly desirable, but some have questioned whether they are actually *achievable*. People's needs and requirements differ, and environments are not used or experienced in the same ways. The differences between disabled people demonstrate the complexities here, for as Barnes and Mercer (2003) assert, 'Mobile disabled people may require a narrow toilet compartment with rails securely fixed at either side with walls to lean against for support, whereas wheelchair users typically need more space to manoeuvre' (p 52). In this way, '... some people will always be excluded' (Hanson, 2004, p 14). Nonetheless, such difficulties must not detract from *aiming* for a more universally accessible environment that caters for the majority.

Making housing more accessible: adaptations and assistive technology

With limited numbers of accessible properties, it may be necessary when looking for a suitable dwelling to find one that is 'adaptable'. Thus, it may be that adaptations or assistive technology (or both) are necessary to make the dwelling accessible for the inhabitant. Adaptations might involve small-scale adjustments, such as, for example, adjusting lighting, installing handrails, hoists or ramps, widening doorways, installing adapted smoke alarms or flashing lights for the front door (see Heywood with Smart, 1996), or larger structural modifications such as building extensions or altering access into, or around, the dwelling. While adaptations are not in themselves the solution to inaccessible environments, they play an important role in improving the lives of disabled people and their families (including informal carers), facilitating greater independence, confidence and control, and improving health and feelings of safety. As Heywood with Smart (1996) assert:

> Housing adaptations allow people to come and go from their own homes, to move around within them, turn on lights, open windows, cook for a friend or put a child to bed. They allow an older person to have a bath if they so choose and not only when someone else decides. They allow children to play safely within their own home. All these things are perfectly ordinary activities and it is the purpose of adaptations to make them possible for disabled people. (pp viii–ix)

Adaptations can also greatly reduce the need for home care or support, or for people to live in more institutionalised forms of accommodation, which can improve the lives of inhabitants and save on long-term costs (ODI, 2007) (although, of course, these benefits would also be achieved from more accessible environments generally).

Despite the recognised advantages of adaptations, many people who need them do not have them (Williams et al, 2008). For some, this can result from lack of information or knowledge about the support available (see Hanson et al, 2002), or about how to start the adaptations process (Williams et al, 2008). The process of arranging, funding and using adaptations is also far from straightforward. As shown in Chapter Two, disabled people can apply for financial assistance to help with the costs of aids and adaptations through Disabled Facilities Grants (DFGs), Home Improvement Agencies or the Supporting People programme. There are also various charities that can provide help with both equipment and housing adaptations (see Woodin et al, 2009). Most grants tend to involve some form of assessment – often by an occupational therapist or social worker – as resources tend to be small and waiting lists long (Foundations, 2007). Although these other funding options are available in some cases, DFGs tend to be the main form of funding for adaptations, and while these have been helpful for many, such grants also have limitations. Crawford and Foord (1997, p 99) point out that although DFGs are 'mandatory', this is only the case, '... as long as the authority has got the money, the applicant qualifies under the test of resources, and is classed as not just a "priority", but a top priority'. Some home owners and private tenants may be discouraged from applying for the grants on this basis.

Exclusions can also apply that make some disabled people ineligible for assistance. Thomas and Ormerod (2005) discuss the example of 'Eve', who was buying a home with her partner and applied for the DFG to help with adaptation costs. Her claim was apparently rejected on the basis that she was living in an accessible property already and was choosing to leave it. This would appear to demonstrate some restriction of choice for disabled people. If they inhabit an accessible property, it seems they may be expected to remain there indefinitely, whether or not circumstances or aspirations change. It has also been shown that if adaptations are required by a social tenant, these can sometimes be avoided in favour of moving the tenant to another property; that if a tenant is on a transfer list, the social landlord may be unwilling to adapt their current property, despite the likelihood of them remaining on the list for several years; and that within some local authorities, adaptations may be refused for people who do not have mobility impairments (Goodridge, 2004). This partly relates to the pressures on local authorities to meet as many needs as possible within limited levels of expenditure, and therefore to target resources (Heywood, 2001). Thus, as Oliver and Barnes (1998) argue, the actual numbers of adaptations tend to be small, leading to some disabled people having to rely on their own limited resources. This can mean only partial improvements taking place, and in some cases, they state, '... mobility may be limited to only one room' (p 46).

Difficulties relating to DFGs may arise, too, if adaptations are required before moving into a property, and for some people, having a multitude of requirements can make the process particularly lengthy. The experience of one informant from the current author's research highlights the issues here. Phillip, who is a wheelchair user, moved to his current house out of the need for a more accessible property. He discussed the many features that he and his wife were looking for (or hoping to be able to add) when viewing properties. These included ramps to exterior doors, a through-floor lift, a large, open shower and spacious rooms for manoeuvring a wheelchair. They also had to consider the neighbourhood, in terms of its physical accessibility, within their search. Their situation was distinctive in that when they found a property, they had to pay for two mortgages on separate dwellings for eight months because they were unable to apply for a DFG until they owned the property and could not move in until the adaptations were carried out. They believed that this had been their only option, and stated that they were lucky enough to be financially able to do this (although with some difficulty). Presumably, few people would have had the financial capacity to do this in a similar situation. Tenants can encounter similar issues, with some having to pay two rent bills when waiting for adaptations to be put in place, or they may find that their rent or service charge is increased following adaptations (Goodridge, 2004). As mentioned in Chapter Two, however, DFGs have been recognised as important to independent living for disabled people within the more recent ODI (2008) independent living strategy, with plans to both improve the system and increase funding in the grants. The coalition government has shown continuing support for DFGs, although it is uncertain whether the plans set in motion by New Labour will be carried through.

For disabled people living in private rented accommodation, arranging adaptations may be difficult for a variety of reasons. Not only do dwellings tend to be small and located in higher-density areas, which can make adaptations problematic (CLG, 2009a), but research by Goodridge (2004) for the Disability Rights Commission (DRC) also found that tenants can be '... reluctant to request adaptations for fear of jeopardising their tenancies' (p 9), and that even if a tenant did request an adaptation (either to be carried out by the landlord or themselves), landlords may refuse on the presumed basis that their property will be devalued or that the 'disruption' would lead to complaints from neighbours. Furthermore, people living in private rented housing can be placed under pressure to move to a new property rather than waiting for adaptations to take place (Crawford and Foord, 1997). As of December 2006, however, a duty has been placed on all landlords '... to make reasonable adjustments' and they '... cannot unreasonably withhold consent for disability-related improvement' (Cook, 2005, p 2).

Where people have managed to arrange for adaptations to take place within their home, some have found that the adaptations have been ineffective for their needs (and their family), have remained unused or have negatively affected the dwelling and relationships within it (Oldman and Beresford, 2000; Heywood, 2004). This has resulted from either cost constraints for providers (JRF, 2001), lack of choice in the adaptations provided for the disabled person (Williams et al, 2008) or lack of consultation with users about their needs. It has been suggested, for instance, that particular groups can be disadvantaged in the adaptations process, including families with disabled children and mental health service users (Beresford and Rhodes, 2008; Williams et al, 2008). Finally, there may be concerns over selling adapted properties later on (DTZ Pieda, 2003) (see also Chapter Five).

Like adaptations, assistive technology has the potential to improve independence in the home and lead to financial savings in terms of the hours of care or support required (Allen et al, 2006). Various types of technology can be employed within the home environment, from assistive technologies to wearable, implantable and microcapsule devices (see Chan et al, 2009). Assistive technology includes small items or devices designed to help with individual day-to-day activities like cooking or bathing (Barlow and Venables, 2004), and devices that are used by the individual to move around, such as electronic wheelchairs and through-floor lifts (Chan et al, 2009). Wearable, implantable and microcapsule devices, on the other hand, can be:

> ... worn by the user or embedded in the house, and connected through wired or wireless networks to a service centre with environmental and diagnostic facilities. These devices can assess sounds, images, body motion, and ambient parameters (light, temperature, humidity, etc.), vital signs (blood pressure, respiration, body temperature, heart/pulse rate, body/weight/fat, blood oxygenation, ECG, etc.), sleep patterns and other health parameters, daily activities, and social interactions. (Chan et al, 2009, p 92)

Electronically enhanced assistive technology can enable the user to control '... visitor access, door opening and closing ... furniture and beds ... the ambient environment and operation of home entertainment and communications equipment' (Barlow and Venables, 2004, p 801).

It may be that even if more accessible properties, such as Lifetime Homes, become available within the mainstream housing stock, assistive technology might still be required for meeting certain needs, such as the safety and support needs of older people, especially as such standards only apply to new dwellings (Barlow and Venables, 2004). Despite this, the costs of equipment (often being specifically designed for a particular individual), and its installation and maintenance, can be high. It can also become 'redundant' if users are not made central to the process of designing and installing the assistive technology in the home (Dewsbury et al, 2004).

Taking the use of assistive technology even further, we have seen the emergence of 'smart homes'. These are flexibly designed dwellings with integrated electronic assistive technology '... so that an entire home can be controlled centrally or remotely as a single machine' (JRF, 2000, p 2). They are tailored to the individual needs of the inhabitant, can provide greater safety and security, and can monitor health in an 'unobtrusive' way (JRF, 2000; Chan et al, 2009). Such dwellings, it has been argued, offer a cost-effective solution to meeting the needs of older and disabled people, and can provide a '... sustainable and viable alternative to institutional living' (Martin et al, 2005, p 33). Various types of smart home have been developed in different countries (see Chapter Two and Chan et al, 2009) and some of these make use of 'telecare' for risk management and the delivery of health and social care. Telecare exists in a range of forms, including systems that provide information or support and those that increase safety within the home (Barlow and Venables, 2004). They have the potential to save time and money for the inhabitants (although less so for healthcare staff) by preventing the need to travel to appointments, and '... can provide the infrastructure for coordinating multidisciplinary care outside the hospital (scheduling visits with health staff and community health workers, automating collection of clinical findings and test results)' (Chan et al, 2009, p 93).

Several writers have drawn attention to the practical, social, legal and ethical limitations of telecare and smart home technology (JRF, 2000; Barlow and Venables, 2004; Dewsbury et al, 2004; Chan et al, 2009). Concerns have been raised, for instance, about confidentiality, privacy and data protection; associated costs and limited affordability; difficulties with inhabitants learning how to use systems and devices; people not using the technology as intended; the failure of systems to meet the users' needs appropriately due to poor design; the reduction of user control; the replacement of more personal, human-provided care with technology; and the lack of a legal framework for telemedicine in the European Union. Nonetheless, these approaches offer additional support options for disabled people, which have the potential to increase independence within the home environment.

Finding suitable housing in inaccessible surroundings

The inaccessibility of the general stock of housing has obvious implications for disabled people when viewing potential properties to rent or purchase. Whilst it is unlikely that a disabled person would be interested in buying or renting a dwelling that is clearly inaccessible, they may want to view properties with potential for adaptation. Previous research has highlighted the obstacles that some disabled people face when viewing properties due to estate agents' failure to inform the customer about their inaccessibility (Hemingway, 2004a; Thomas, P., 2004; Hamer, 2005a). As Paul and Carol from the current author's research explained, the estate agents appeared to ignore their requests for particular features or types of property:

> 'I asked the estate agent, I said, right I only want properties that are either ground floor or bungalows and they just sent you everything. I mean, I think that's true of everyone from what I understand but there was no thought about what I actually want, so you'd get upstairs flats sent to you and stuff like that, it was just a waste of time.' (Paul)

> '... estate agents messed me about, and that's from somebody in spite of having many impairments, they're all invisible, so I can only imagine what estate agents give to people who are very visibly disabled people.... Estate agents need to wise up about access issues. My experience about estate agents is that they just don't know the first thing about access ... I want them to actually start noticing things like whether they are level entry, or they have a threshold, and actually measuring door widths. That's not a lot to ask them to think about and do.' (Carol)

Several informants who encountered difficulties here explained how they often took friends or family along to viewings to check properties over first. As Paul recalled:

> 'The biggest problem was actually going round the houses because you just couldn't do it on your own, like with an estate agent you had to have somebody to go with you. I

remember my friend went lugging me up these steps to see these inaccessible houses to see whether you could possibly do anything.... He actually got me in but it was that difficult to get out I had to actually get out of my chair and crawl down the steps and then get back into my chair, so it was a very dignified exit!'

Some disabled people, however, may not have people to accompany them, or the desire to do so. Perhaps a more suitable arrangement would be for estate agents to give prior warning of inaccessible features so that the client could decide whether or not the property was worth viewing. Disabled people may also have to contend with poor physical access in the premises of housing providers, estate agents, building societies and banks (although some companies may overcome difficulties here by travelling to people's homes).

Not only is the accessibility of the dwelling significant, but for some, the residential environment in which the property is located may also be an important concern (although choice for social tenants can be limited in this respect; see Fitzpatrick, 2002). For example, it might be necessary to investigate the accessibility of shared areas when considering buying or renting a flat, apartment or house in a communal building or development. As the current author's research showed, the inaccessibility of communal areas can restrict housing options for disabled people within an already limited stock of accessible housing, and make the search process even more difficult. The accessibility of the neighbourhood is also an important concern for many disabled people, especially as a '... barrier free house can become a prison for disabled people if the surrounding built environment is not barrier free or if transport is inaccessible or unaffordable' (Herd, 1999, p 65). Despite the need for an accessible neighbourhood environment, finding one can also prove difficult for some disabled people. Adam, who has a visual impairment, highlighted the difficulties he encountered, especially as he was not familiar with the different parts of the city to which he was moving:

'I guess we were looking for six months or so. It was quite difficult. A, it was sort of getting to know different parts of [the area], and B, it was getting to know about properties in the different parts of it. Then once you had found out about them, it was going to see them, which are all quite visual things so we basically sought advice from friends who knew [the area] better than us and we used quite a lot of taxis. Taxi drivers tend to know different parts of town pretty well, so we would sometimes get advice from [them].'

The location may even be considered more important in a person's criteria than the accessibility of the dwelling itself. There is some overlap here with social needs. While the accessibility of the neighbourhood, for instance, may be important, the desire to achieve a feeling of safety within the local environment may also be significant (see also Chapter Seven). So while, strictly speaking, this is not an entirely physical issue, it does demonstrate related considerations. Jessie discussed her concerns in relation to local reactions to both her impairment and her ethnic background. For her, local attitudes to her ethnicity were important in her search for a dwelling, supporting research reviewed by Harrison (2003) that showed that the fear of potential racial harassment may affect the residential area selected. Also significant for Jessie, however, were the anticipated reactions to her impairment. This was evident in her claims that:

> 'I am registered blind, but ... I insist on not using a white stick around, because I don't feel safe if people in my neighbourhood know that I am visually impaired because I would feel more vulnerability. I have heard a lot of visually impaired women talking about being attacked, so I am aware that when people notice you can't see them, then you are more likely to be attacked, so for that reason I don't use my white stick around where I live if I can avoid it.'

It therefore appears that while this need for secure personal movement is a concern potentially experienced by everyone, it may be a particular consideration for some people with visual impairments. Derbyshire (1998) also found, for instance, that people with visual impairments tend to highlight concerns with safety and possible harassment, and 'In particular, they often cite estate properties that are accessed by poorly lit walkways and passages as a cause for concern' (p 71). Unfortunately, much 'special needs' housing is located on less desirable council estates, which is perhaps part and parcel of the gradual adjustment of social renting to cater for lower-income groups or more 'vulnerable' people through the residualisation of the tenure discussed earlier. For mental health service users, too, this may cause particular unease. As a study into neighbourhood conditions found, '... the rate of neighbourhood disorder (e.g, abandoned housing, high amount of vandalism, problematic public behavior) and perceptions of neighborhood problems (problems with transportation, crime activity, problems with street lighting) are associated with greater fear of crime, depression, anxiety, and somatic symptoms' (Kloos and Shah, 2009, p 317). Central to the requirement for an accessible area might also be the need for good transport links, services and facilities. It has been shown, however, that disabled people encounter a range of difficulties associated with inaccessible public transport systems and inadequate private transport options, with disabled people living in rural areas at a particular disadvantage (see Finkelstein, 1994, Matthews, 2002, and Chapter Seven for further information on transport issues).

Thus, inaccessible properties can pose difficulties for disabled people, and these may be further compounded by difficulties with viewing potential properties and finding suitable communal and neighbourhood areas. Together, such barriers can have a huge impact on disabled people's ability to find a home. The experience of one disabled informant from the current author's research is helpful here. Katie, a wheelchair user, was moving to London for a new job, but after finding her options for private renting limited by few accessible properties, she decided to look at owner-occupation. She came up against further difficulties when attempting to find an accessible property to buy (or at least one that could be adapted). Furthermore, when a suitable flat had eventually been located, the inaccessible communal step and the refusal of the management committee to agree to erecting a ramp (despite her offer to pay for it) meant that she once again had to continue her lengthy search for a home.

Addressing physical barriers in housing

Strategies for addressing the inaccessibility of the built environment, and of housing and residential environments in particular, have, to date, been very different in approach. Whereas adaptations and assistive technology offer individual solutions for tackling the inaccessible built environment, the construction of accessible dwellings (in terms of LTH or universal design standards) constitutes a more collective solution. In the short term it may be that specifically designed housing retains its value, perhaps being considered '... superior to more fully institutionalised paternalistically controlled accommodation' (Harrison with Davis, 2001, p 125). A balance may therefore be required between housing interventions that focus on specific impairments on the one hand and those that address general living environments on the other. It is important, however, that practices that concentrate on responding to individual impairments do not hinder or prevent efforts to improve practices and housing environments in general. The move towards more accessible housing in general terms, or environments as a whole, is a clear objective and one that has been advocated by many (Burns, 2002, 2004; Imrie, 2006a, 2006b).

Improving the stock of accessible properties available appears to involve two key measures: encouraging more universal and inclusive building standards, and challenging building industry attitudes. The building industry is currently required to comply with access guidelines within building regulations, so minimal access standards are now (or should be) being incorporated into new-build properties, but as we have seen, these tend to result in properties that are 'visitable' rather than 'liveable'. The development of access standards, such as LTH standards, that go further than those currently in place would therefore be beneficial, but there needs to be more formal enforcement of these if we are to see improvements. The move to accessible housing has previously been encouraged but voluntary, resulting in slow progress, and so the willingness to implement LTH standards has largely been restrained by a building industry motivated by profit and competition. Lifetime Homes are a step in the right direction, and may mean accessible dwellings in the future, but getting at least these standards accepted will take time. Therefore, '... embedding a requirement in the planning system and in the building regulations' (ODPM, 2006, p 361) for these standards should be a priority. Concepts such as 'inclusive' or 'universal design' also demonstrate how the design of the physical environment can offer the opportunity for independent living, greater choice, control and equality within housing environments designed for the majority of the population. With the number of people aged over 75 expected to rise by 60 per cent over the next 15 years (Marshall, 2009), and with an increasing prevalence of impairment in the older population (Barlow and Venables, 2004), the case for providing a more accessible environment becomes even more urgent. For guidance on implementing universal design principles in practice within housing, see Steven Winter Associates (1997) and the Center for Universal Design (2006). Different organisations have also been established to provide information and support on universal design in different countries (see, for instance, the Australian Network for Universal Design).

The move towards more universal standards would need to work alongside the pursuit of a change in building industry attitudes so that, rather than perceiving the construction of more accessible properties as a hindrance (and added cost), the building industry would recognise the desirability of catering for a larger customer base. The perception of accessible accommodation as costly should also be challenged, for as we saw in Chapter Four, there are significant long-term savings to be made from building to Lifetime Homes standards (although these savings are not necessarily made at the building stages). The building industry should, however, see the development of more accessible housing as an opportunity to produce products that address a growing market of consumers (particularly in an ageing population). Greater involvement of disabled people is also needed in dwelling design and in the training of building and construction industry employees, if changes are to occur here. As Hanson (2004, p 21) argues, inclusive design '... demands a user-centred approach' that involves '... working with people, not for them'. Furthermore, the design of inclusive environments goes beyond creating physically accessible spaces and incorporates aspects of maintenance and management into the process (Hanson, 2004).

It may also be possible to implement initiatives to promote more suitable accommodation in the private rental sector. Landlords could be offered grants, for example, to make their existing properties more accessible to a wider range of people and to improve general accessibility along the lines of LTH standards. In relation to the adaptations process, the need for increasing funding and for improvements to the application of DFGs has been recognised in the ODI's (2008) independent living strategy, and it is hoped that proposed plans will be supported by the coalition government. It is also important during the adaptations process that professionals and builders understand both the needs of the individual and their family (Heywood, 2004). This can be especially so when considering cultural differences, and assessments of need should take into account the use of space within the home as it relates to different generations living together, religious obligations and domestic equipment (JRF, 2002). Effective consultation with users can be enhanced by increased staff knowledge of adaptations and their uses (see Derbyshire, 1998, and for further information on the adaptations process, see Bradford, 1998).

There are therefore various strategies in place for tackling inaccessible environments. We should not forget, too, that people may also have individual strategies for dealing with the physical barriers encountered. As Imrie (2006a) points out, disabled people '... are not passive victims of insensitive design' and there have been many examples where disabled people have demonstrated '... the capacity to generate usable spaces out of the social and physical impediments that are placed in their way' (p 104). The work of Allen and colleagues (2002) also suggests that the design of the environment is not always experienced as oppressive. It was shown, for instance, that children with visual impairments developed 'memory maps' to work out – and navigate their way around – the environment:

> They did this by using their cognition (for example, counting steps), sense (for example, listening for sounds) and by establishing routines (for example, habitual ways of walking 'particular routes'). The fourth strategy involved transposing their cognitive, sense and habitual orientations towards environments they had become familiar with, onto unfamiliar environments (for example, by using the memory map of home to make sense of a friend's house). (Allen et al, 2002, p 10)

The study also found that while the built environment was not necessarily problematic, '... mobile objects, unpredictable movement and an intensity of movement' (p 16) were aspects of the urban environment that could be. Again, however, strategies were developed here to cope with perceived problems (albeit parents' strategies differed to those of the children, with the former preferring to remove children from potential risks by keeping them at home). Nonetheless, this does not diminish the need to address wider social and environmental barriers, for as Thomas, P. (2004) points out, even when disabled people are proactive in challenging barriers, they may still encounter exclusion.

Communication constraints in housing provision

Access to information is essential for making informed choices about housing and allied services. Indeed, as Brown and King (2005) state, '... one of the essential prerequisites for rational choice is information. One needs to access accurate and correct information before one can come to a considered decision' (p 66). Despite this, information and advice on housing tends to be lacking for disabled people. Communication, or information, barriers are therefore extremely significant in disabled people's housing choices and opportunities. This lack of access to information has long been recognised, and disabled people have been active in addressing the problem in different ways. The setting up of Centres for 'Independent', 'Integrated' or 'Inclusive' Living and the Disablement Information and Advice Line in 1976 are important examples. Nonetheless, gaps remain in the availability of accessible information from housing and allied service providers, and these can affect disabled people's knowledge of their housing rights. There are four key issues relating to the availability of information and the ways in which it is communicated. First, there is limited general information available on housing options for disabled people; second, the language used tends not to be straightforward or presented in plain English; third, information is not always available in different formats, whether written or verbal; and fourth, service providers may fail to make equipment or support available to ensure information is communicated effectively.

The lack of general information and advice on housing options, entitlements and support for disabled people, their families and 'carers' has been highlighted in various studies (Hudson et al, 1996; Derbyshire, 1998; Stirling with Lloyd, 2004; Gilbert et al, 2008). Problems relate to generic and impairment-specific disability services tending not to offer housing advice, and those agencies that offer housing and disability advice specialising by either '... dealing with adaptations or equipment, home care or personal assistance, finance or specialist schemes' (Goodridge, 2004, p 16). Research has also shown that some groups may experience particular difficulties in obtaining advice and information on housing options and rights, such as families with a disabled child (Oldman and Beresford, 1998; Bevan, 2002), people labelled with learning difficulties (Fitzpatrick, 2002), people with sensory impairments (Goodridge, 2004) and people living in residential care homes or with their parents (Hudson et al, 1996).

Not only has information not been *available* for many disabled people, it has also largely failed to be *accessible*. Information about services that uses 'technical jargon' has been found to be too complex for different audiences, especially people labelled with learning difficulties or people whose first language is not English (such as disabled people from minority ethnic groups) (Molloy et al, 2003). In addition, it is a legal requirement under the 1995 DDA that all information on offer from housing organisations and providers, be it general information, applications for tenancies, property particulars, rent or mortgage statements, tenancy agreements or information on repairs and maintenance, should be made available in a range of different formats. This may include different-sized fonts on various coloured backgrounds, Braille, audio tape, signs and symbols for people labelled with learning difficulties, or electronic information via email. Disabled people should therefore have access to the full range of information available relating to their housing situations, options and responsibilities, just as non-disabled people already do.

A report for the Department for Work and Pensions (DWP) by Aston and colleagues (2007) looked at how landlords had been responding to the requirements laid out by the DDA and the more recent duties of 2006. They found that 'Changes to methods of communication were some of the most commonly cited adjustments by landlords of all types' (p 97), with examples cited of materials being provided in different formats, tenants being met in person (rather than being sent a letter), and more time being allowed for meetings with tenants. There was some distinction between social and private landlords, however, with social landlords being more likely to have already made adjustments and to mention the changes they had made than private landlords. It seems from the current author's research that other private sector housing and finance providers (including estate agents and mortgage lenders) have also been less effective at making adjustments than organisations in the social sector. The experiences of the disabled people interviewed provide some useful illustrations here and relate mainly to problems encountered in acquiring materials, including general company information, statements and mortgage contracts. Such experiences were mainly applicable to people with visual impairments (although this may reflect the research sample). Carol discussed her experiences of dealing with a mortgage lender as follows:

> 'I was very clear from my very first interview that I had a visual impairment so any information would be needed in 14 point font. And he said that shouldn't be a problem because he'd be printing quotes off the computer. Of course, he'd forgotten about the brochures. But actually, when he tried to print things off the computer, it wouldn't do it. So I didn't get anything accessible. Even when I was dealing with head office, I kept reminding them and saying could you please write to me in an accessible way, and they'd say, "Oh yes." But I never got a single thing from them that actually followed my requests.'

Similarly for Robert, none of the information supplied by the lender was provided in an accessible format, so his broker approached the lender on his behalf to request that all forms and correspondence be produced in Braille:

> '... so eventually they did it and believe it or not we got this absolutely massive box with about 30 different tapes in. They must have gone through every single leaflet they had in the place and Brailled it, whether it was relevant or not! And *then*, believe it or not, the mortgage consultant got a bill from them for doing the Braille. She told them where to stick it. So it really was an experience to say the least.'

It would seem that in this particular case, while the lender eventually provided the information in Braille, it failed to grant the disabled client equal access to its services, as it required payment for generating the information in an accessible format. Nonetheless, Robert was optimistic that his experience reflected the fact that it had taken place seven years previously, and he believed that the situation might now have changed for other people with visual impairments. For Jessie, however, whose mortgage was arranged more recently, such barriers were still evident. She appeared to be understandably quite angry about the lack of accessible information made available to her and stated that:

> '... people have an understanding about how to put a ramp up to a building, or a rail or something like that, but they haven't grasped the need for accessible information, they haven't grasped that if they make even information generally in a larger print, even 14 [font size], then a lot more people will be able to read it, and elderly people.'

Gaining access to personal information such as rent and mortgage statements in an accessible format can be especially important, as clients' privacy can be compromised in these circumstances (Derbyshire, 1998), but the current author's research indicated that such provisions were not always made for disabled people (including one social tenant, Simon).

In addition, important contracts are not always provided in accessible formats. Robert described how the solicitors for his mortgage lender had been unwilling to sign the mortgage contract because Robert and his partner could not 'read' it. Consequently, he had to arrange for his own solicitors to oversee the signing of the contract. Had the contract been produced in an accessible format, the situation may have been more straightforward. A similar situation arose for Adam and his wife, although rather than the solicitors refusing to sign the contract, they read it out to Adam and his wife, before asking them to sign it. Adam stated that, "It did feel like we were being placed in a position where we were having to trust the people we were dealing with to a much greater degree than anybody else would have to and that is quite a common situation for a blind person to be in." Attitudes here appear to be a little naïve and lack understanding. It would be interesting to find out if the solicitors would have been confident about signing such important documents that they had not been allowed to read for themselves. Some of the lenders interviewed did appear to be making an effort to reduce the barriers within their institutions, as highlighted by one informant who stated that, "For deaf customers we will book and pay for sign language interpreters, speech or text transcribers, whatever it is to make the interview accessible to the deaf person. For blind people we will get all the paperwork in an accessible format for them." It was apparently not quite so easy for another lender to achieve this, though, as seen in the following admission:

> 'It may be more difficult communicating if their disability is related to speech or hearing. We would also have difficulties in providing literature specifically for the blind. For those suffering from mental difficulties we would need to ensure through their solicitors or a representative that they have some awareness as to the contract they are entering.'

The inconsistency among lenders in terms of their willingness and ability to provide accessible services to disabled people is certainly a concern. The experiences of disabled informants would suggest that this is an area where lenders need to make vast improvements, for as Jessie pointed out, "… in terms of the DDA and accessible information, I can see that is one of the areas that organisations are not taking very seriously".

Estate agents also reportedly often fail to provide information in accessible formats (Hamer, 2005a), and this was reflected in the statements of many of the disabled people interviewed for the current author's research. Adam stated, for instance, that:

> 'Even though stuff was on their website, the people I was speaking to didn't know how to, or didn't want to, email stuff to me. Getting emails of specs would have been the preferred option for us, because you don't have to ferret around on inaccessible websites and you don't have to spend lots of time on the phone, but we didn't get any stuff emailed to us…. What we were told was that the system was not like a Microsoft Word document or a WordPerfect or whatever, it wasn't a standard package and therefore it was impossible or more likely it was difficult to convert this file into something that could be emailed and read over the email. There's a lot of compatibility, I mean computers aren't perfect, but there's a lot of ways of converting one file type to another, but I think if you ask for something and you are not exactly sure whether they can do it, and they tell you that you can't, you don't really know where to go after

that. I think maybe next time round if we did, we would push things harder again, but sometimes you get tired of it!'

Further interviews with six estate agents provided additional insights. Given the responses of disabled people, of particular interest here was whether companies would provide information on properties in accessible formats, whether a sign language interpreter could be arranged for clients, and whether these would be at the clients' or the estate agents' cost. Four informants claimed that such services were rarely requested, which seemed to influence their opinion on the topic: if the demand is not there, there is no reason to provide them. This may appear to be a reasonable response, but one could argue that not providing information in a format available to everyone means certain groups are being excluded or even discriminated against. Taking discussions further, three informants stated that providing large print would be possible, as it would involve relatively little effort, and one informant stated that she would do her best to get a document converted into Braille at request (although she may charge the client for the service, depending on how 'genuine' a customer she perceived them to be). Three informants claimed that providing Braille or sign language interpreters would not be possible. After prompting further, one informant stated, "That's not my opinion of what I would do, unfortunately that is the company opinion. It's disgusting, really." When asked why these services would not be provided, she stated that the cost was the main issue:

> '... especially if it is just once in a blue moon ... then again, if it was someone who needed a sign language interpreter, then we would just write everything down ... there would be ways and means of getting around it, but they just wouldn't be the most politically correct or convenient method. If we needed to get somebody up a flight of stairs then we would get them up a flight of stairs, but its not the most convenient way or the "correct" way of doing it.'

Half of the respondents claimed that the cost of providing these services would be charged to the client (despite the fact that it is unlawful to charge disabled people for such services, see Mind, 2006). Nonetheless, not all responses were so negative, with one informant stating that the estate agents that they worked for would take on the cost themselves, and another claiming that it did not seem fair to charge disabled people. This respondent also stated, however, that neither did it seem fair on the estate agent. It is difficult to see how this issue would be resolved. Finally, one informant claimed that their company were starting a marketing scheme for people with visual impairments and would ensure that they "… have the correct communication tools".

Disabled people may face barriers when attempting to access housing information and advice via the internet. A report by the DRC, for instance, found that among '1,000 UK websites covering Government, business, entertainment and e-commerce … 81 per cent failed prevailing web access guidelines' (Lobel, 2004, p 45). It is a requirement under the DDA, however, for websites to be accessible for people with different impairments. This came into force in 1999, with additional changes in 2005 to include small employers in the duty. The Royal National Institute for the Blind (RNIB) (2009) provides details of inaccessible aspects of websites that may contravene the DDA. These include the provision of links and PDF documents that are inaccessible to a screen reader, or web pages that make use of text size, colour and formatting in such a way as to make them inaccessible for some people with visual impairments . The current author's research found that the estate agents interviewed had done very little to make their websites accessible, with many failing to offer even basic features such as options for larger font sizes or audio players (although one informant claimed that the website for his firm was in the process of being developed and that the inclusion of possible features would be discussed with his colleagues). Two companies did provide virtual viewing, however, which they believed to be particularly useful for some disabled people.

Finally, in terms of housing provision, particular groups can face different types of communication barriers relating to the limited availability of equipment or support. For people with hearing impairments, for instance, British Sign Language interpreters, loop systems or '… provisions for people who lip-read' (Crowther, 2000, p 30) may be lacking. Disabled people from black and minority ethnic groups can also encounter difficulties resulting from insensitivity to cultural and linguistic issues (Begum, 1992). Some people face communication barriers due to housing providers' unwillingness (or lack of knowledge of how) to communicate. In the current author's research, for instance, Chris describes himself as having dyslexia, dyspraxia and a speech impairment, and there was some suggestion from his experiences (see Chapter Six) that people with speech impairments may encounter problems here. In addition, one of the informants working for a disabled people's organisation stated:

'I had somebody from a council housing department on the phone telling me that they had someone in their office that couldn't speak, but he had one of our cards explaining what aphasia was and she asked if she put him on the phone, maybe I could understand what he wanted. When I pointed out that that was probably very difficult from a distance because I wouldn't get the clues either, but that this chap might be able to write, she then asked how they would know that, so I suggested a pen and paper where he proceeded to write his name and address and I then explained what aphasia was and that it doesn't affect intelligence. She then shouted across the office, "Oh, he's understood everything we've said!" I guess from that experience there is a huge training need.'

The following account of one of the financial services representatives in the current author's research seemed to suggest that some employees may have personal difficulties with talking to some disabled people:

'From a personal point of view I find dealing with mental disabilities or speech impediments difficult to cope with and as a manager would tend to delegate these applicants to a more sympathetic member of staff. I appreciate this is a personal "cop-out", but I hope by recognising it and delegating I avoid any prejudice.'

While this informant felt that his honesty made up for his unwillingness to deal with people with certain impairments (and he may have genuine difficulties here), this kind of reluctance or insecurity about mental health service users and people with speech impairments, and the resulting behaviour, may perpetuate misguided assumptions and reinforce the barriers and prejudice that some people endure. This seems to support the claims made by Harrison with Davis (2001, p 129) that there are '... possibilities of hierarchy among disabled people in regard to consultation, with those most able to articulate their needs, and who present the "socially acceptable face of disability" (without speech problems or visible disfigurement) being responded to more fully'.

Addressing communication barriers in housing

It has been shown that inaccessible information may present a key barrier to housing for disabled people, affecting choice and the ability to make informed decisions. The DDA has, however, encouraged positive changes in the field of information provision in many ways, and there is some evidence that housing providers are addressing the problems encountered here, although there is much scope for improvement. Developments appear to have been slower in the private than in the public or voluntary sectors, for example, which would suggest that further enforcement or monitoring of duties under the DDA may be necessary. Service providers need to recognise the importance of providing accessible information for different groups as a right, rather than regarding it as an added cost or burden. Understanding that different groups may require different styles and formats is also important. For example, alternative forms of communication to speech and written language (such as the use of pictures, photos or symbols) may need to be employed for some people labelled with learning difficulties (see Mencap, 2010, for further information). There are various guidance documents available offering advice on meeting information needs; see, for example, the RNIB and Housing Corporation good practice guide for housing workers and policymakers on housing management and service provision for people with visual impairments (Derbyshire, 1998).

We have seen how simply finding information on available properties can be difficult for some people. There have been some small-scale, yet important, attempts to address these difficulties, including the emergence of the Accessible Property Register, a website set up and run by disabled people for disabled people that advertises accessible and adapted properties for sale and rent. The use of accessibility symbols on documentation concerning properties in both the rental and owner-occupation markets has also been introduced in some areas to improve the process of finding a suitable property (Hamer, 2005a; DRC, 2007a). Some local authorities, for example, use a symbol to indicate accessibility when advertising rental properties. Within the choice-based letting scheme for social renting in Leeds, wheelchair symbols are placed next to particular properties to indicate the inclusion of accessibility features (see *Leeds Homes* magazines). Similar schemes have been established in some cities in relation to owner-occupation to improve information on accessible homes for disabled people within estate agencies (for details, see Hamer, 2005a). Such schemes could prove useful for many disabled people, but would require national expansion if the benefits were to be fully witnessed. Finally, efforts need to be made to address the communication barriers that different groups can encounter, and as with access to information, these need to be recognised as a right. People with hearing or speech impairments, or people labelled with learning difficulties, seem to experience particular disadvantage here. As mentioned earlier, while some equipment (such as hearing loops) is being more widely used by service providers, it is important that staff are trained in how to use this equipment. Communication barriers can also be exposed and tackled via the use of Person Centred Planning, particularly for people labelled with learning difficulties. As Morris (2004) states '... it was only after Person Centred Planning was introduced for one man that staff realised how he communicated that he needed to go to the toilet. Prior to this he had been "incontinent"' (pp 435-6; see DH, 2001b for further information on Person Centred Planning).

Conclusion

The 'disabling' physical environment presents serious challenges for many disabled people in terms of housing. There are few accessible properties available, with additional difficulties posed by inaccessible communal areas and neighbourhoods (and inaccessible local transport systems), even accounting for differences in tenure. Such barriers contribute to homelessness among disabled people. The general trend in addressing such physical barriers, framed by an individual understanding of disability, has been to provide specifically designed housing for disabled people, in recognition of a need to cater for bodies that fit outside of the apparent majority. Although this approach has been considered necessary and practical for addressing the needs of disabled people – designing properties specifically tailored to individuals would seem an appropriate solution – the outcome has been less than ideal. Low take-up of these properties, and the stigmatised, separated and 'ghettoised' housing that has emerged, has made this form of housing the subject of much criticism. While voluntary segregation is not always negative, this enforced segregation, operated behind a discourse of professionally defined housing need, arguably is. Separate provision also takes the focus away from providing accessible housing in general, and prevents disabled people from accessing the housing available to everyone else. Thus, while so-called 'special needs' housing caters for many people, the provision of this type of housing should not detract from the aim of increasing the availability of accessible, flexible properties within the general stock of housing across all tenure types. Physical constraints can also be encountered during the viewing process, making the search even more complex, or when visiting the premises of housing and mortgage providers. Various strategies have been employed to tackle these physical barriers, including adapting existing housing and building new properties to more accessible standards. Whereas adaptations offer opportunities for greater independence, building more accessible properties is a more suitable solution and demonstrates greater recognition of the role the residential environment plays in 'disabling' processes.

As mentioned previously, the physical environment alone cannot be held responsible for disability; it is more complex than that. Not only are there different factors to consider – earlier categorised as attitudinal, financial and relating to communication – but the physical environment does not affect everyone in the same way (see Chapter Seven) and we cannot always guarantee that it is the physical environment that has had a direct causative effect (see Harrison, 2004b). This chapter has also looked at difficulties that disabled people encounter in relation to information provision and communication (including a lack of information and advice, and support for communication). These are important barriers to address, for access to information communicated appropriately is crucial to the ability to exercise choice within housing. Such barriers tend to be more often experienced by people who have sensory impairments (both visual and hearing), as well as people with speech and cognitive impairments, and so before we have even explored the barriers relating to financial and attitudinal factors, we see that many disabled people face considerable constraints within housing. We look now at financial factors that can affect disabled people's housing opportunities and pathways.

Summary of key issues

- The physical environment is an extremely significant component in the creation of barriers for people with impairments (and their families), and can be 'disabling' in a variety of ways. These include the general inaccessibility of properties, communal areas and neighbourhoods, and the premises of housing and allied service providers.
- Different strategies have been used to address physical access issues, including the use of adaptations and assistive technology for existing housing and the construction of housing tailored to individuals, but these have largely focused on addressing 'specific' rather than 'general' needs. Access standards in building regulations have partly improved accessibility for some, but LTH standards and 'inclusive' or 'universal' design address a more diverse range of access needs within mainstream housing designed for the majority of the population.
- Communication, or information, barriers are crucial to disabled people exercising choice within housing and refer to the limited availability of general information on housing options, the inaccessible presentation

of material and the lack of available equipment or support for ensuring that information is communicated effectively.

• There have been some significant attempts to improve the accessibility of information for disabled people in relation to housing, particularly via the DDA, but further work is needed to improve the situation more generally.

Recommended further reading

Aston, J., Hill, D. and Williams, C. (2007) *Landlords' responses to the Disability Discrimination Act*, Leeds: Department for Work and Pensions.

Derbyshire, F. (1998) *Better Housing Management for Blind and Partially Sighted People: A Good Practice Guide*, London: RNIB.

Hamer, R. (2005) *House Hunting for All: Opening up Property Search Systems to Disabled People*, Edinburgh: Ownership Options in Scotland.

Heywood, F. (2005) 'Adaptation: altering the house to restore the home', *Housing Studies*, vol 20, no 4, pp 531-47.

Imrie, R. (2006) *Accessible Housing: Quality, Disability and Design*, London and New York, NY: Routledge.

Rowe, A. (ed) (1990) *Lifetime Homes: Flexible Housing for Successive Generations*, London: Helen Hamlyn Foundation.

FIVE

Financial considerations: income, affordability and risk assessment

The role that financial factors play in the housing and disability relationship is extremely significant, and yet it has been relatively overlooked in UK research. Financial issues affecting housing access and experiences can be broadly defined as including employment security and history; income (including benefits); additional costs relating to impairment, the physical dwelling and life insurance; and issues associated with risk assessment (including credit rating) in the mortgage application process. Whereas some of these factors (such as income and employment) affect access to all housing tenure, others (such as life insurance and risk assessment for housing finance) are more specific to owner-occupation. This chapter shows how a social approach to disability can be used to emphasise these structural constraints, but also stresses the importance of exploring structural factors in further detail, and of recognising the ways impairment is treated by institutions and individual actors. This is shown through the concept of risk, which is significant in terms of understanding how different groups are perceived as more vulnerable or 'risky' by the owner-occupation industry and examining how certain groups are classified and measured. Thus, the institutional measuring of risk can be seen as a potentially crucial contributing element within structural factors, generating barriers identified by a social model approach. This chapter is presented in four parts, and several sections are informed from the author's own work in particular. The first examines financial situations common to disabled people in terms of employment, income and living costs, and the implications of affordability for housing options. The second part focuses on access to owner-occupation, looking specifically at risk assessment procedures within lending institutions and the effect that these have had on disabled people. We then take a look at the situation following the recent economic crisis and the potential implications for disabled people in relation to housing. The final part examines potential strategies for addressing some of the barriers identified throughout the chapter.

Money matters: income and employment for disabled people

The changing role of the labour market, namely the increase in part-time, less secure employment, has had consequences for everyone in society. Such a transition has affected housing (and particularly the ability to meet mortgage payments) considerably (Ford, 1998). It is well known, however, that disabled people experience particular disadvantage in the labour market, in some cases leading to a reliance on benefits. Recent figures from the ODI (2010) show that while the employment gap has reduced, and disabled people's employment rates have improved, disabled people are still less likely to be in employment than non-disabled people. The employment rate for disabled people is currently 47 per cent, compared with 77 per cent for non-disabled people. It has also been shown that the employment level for disabled people is lower than any other disadvantaged groups such as minority ethnic groups (PMSU, 2005). Within these figures there are further variations in employment *between* disabled people (Beresford, 2000; PMSU, 2005; Evans, 2007). Mental health service users '... have the lowest employment rates of all impairment categories, at only 21 per cent' (DRC, 2007b: 5), and only one in 10 people labelled with 'severe' learning difficulties are in employment (Evans, 2007). For mental health service users and survivors, the difficulties related to employment often lie in the disincentives of returning to or finding work, such as loss of support (Turner and Beresford, 2005). Thus, it may be difficult for a mental health service user to look for employment, particularly when they may lose out, both emotionally and financially, if employment does not continue. Other variables may also be significant in employment opportunities. Barriers to the labour market could be greater, for instance, if a disabled person is a member of a black or minority ethnic group (Sefton et al, 2005). In addition, disabled women are less likely to be employed than their male counterparts (Roulstone and Barnes, 2005a).

Various sources address the employment situations of disabled people (see Arthur and Zarb, 1995; Barnes 1999; Burchardt, 2000; Roulstone and Barnes, 2005b; DRC, 2007b; Evans, 2007; ODI, 2010). These point to how employment is often low status and low paid, in conditions that are less than adequate. Disabled people are more likely than non-disabled people to spend longer periods out of employment and seeking and remaining in jobs is often more difficult for disabled people than non-disabled people. It has also been shown that direct discrimination against disabled people may exist during recruitment (including through medical questionnaires used during the job application process). This more direct form of discrimination has been challenged by the 1995 Disability Discrimination Act (DDA) and, more recently, by the 2010 Equality Act (Wollenberg, 2010). Different impairment groups may, however, encounter different types of barriers. For people with visual impairments, for instance, it has been argued that employer discrimination can work at every stage of the process of recruitment. As Simkiss (2005) states, 'Job advertisements that are too small or indistinct to read, application forms and information packs that are inaccessible, and which arrive late, and interview practice that fails to provide reasonable adjustments for candidates are common' (p 255). It seems, too, that the negative attitudes of employers may affect employment opportunities for disabled people (and sometimes for specific impairment groups) and that disabled people are more likely to experience unfair treatment at work than non-disabled people.

Low morale among disabled people and concerns about perceived discrimination or low skills might also affect employment opportunities. Moreover, as Abberley (2002, p 130) argues, jobs are '... designed around the capacity, stamina and resources of the average worker, nine-to-five, five day a week employment ... which are incompatible with the needs of a wide variety of citizens'. In addition, it has been shown that inadequate support services may prevent some disabled people from being able to enter the labour market, as reflected in the following account by Steven, one of the informants from the current author's research:

> '... to get employment right, you have got to be in a situation where you have got space in your day to go out there, and normally it is between nine and five pm. If you are having any kind of district nurses coming, or injections or whatever, or carers, hospital appointments, it gets to a point where you are unemployable because you are fitting into those services which are only available at certain times of the day. What I am trying to say is you have got to provide those services at different times and in different ways, so it frees a person up to make employment a possibility. I think that is one of the stumbling blocks. We have a lady who comes in every day, she helps me, I struggle getting dressed now so she helps me. I have to wait for her, she can't get here before eight, so it's a bit frustrating because I want to get down to work, but I get round that. When I do have to

> be here early, I don't wear a shirt and tie, just a polo neck
> or something, I can manage that.'

Such constraints clearly affect opportunities for employment. Add to these the sometimes inaccessible work environments, transport issues and difficulties of moving to areas where jobs are available (due to a reliance on social renting), and it becomes clear that while many disabled people want to work, barriers within employment can prevent this, or restrain an individual's employment position.

Income is obviously a significant factor in the path to housing choice. Disabled people, however, generally have lower incomes than the rest of the population, as shown by the PMSU (2005, p 46) report, which states that the '... income of disabled people is, on average, less than half of that of non-disabled people. Even after direct taxes and benefit payments have been accounted for – disabled people still earn 30% less than non-disabled people.' A report by Woolley (2004, p 12), based on the questionnaire responses of 98 families from the Family Fund databases, found that for families with a disabled child/children, the mean income was £293.67 per week, 23.5 per cent below the UK mean income of £384 before housing costs. At the time of writing, there were several benefits available to disabled people. Disability Living Allowance (DLA), which includes both mobility and care elements, is neither means-tested nor reliant on employment, and is regarded as a benefit for addressing extra costs. There are also no restrictions on how this money is used (Simons, 1998; Hamer, 2005c). In addition to DLA, various premiums exist that provide extra income (but are means-tested): the 'disability premium', the 'severe disability premium' and the 'enhanced disability premium'. For people who acquire an impairment during military service or employment, the War Disablement Pension and Industrial Injuries Disability benefit may be available (PMSU, 2005). The Armed Forces Compensation Scheme also provides funds for those injured during service from 2005 onwards, and the Industrial Injuries Disablement Benefit may be available to those who have acquired an impairment as a result of an accident or conditions at work (Directgov, 2010a). In addition, Attendance Allowance is available to disabled people over the age of 65 who require assistance with everyday activities. Finally, Housing Benefit is available to those disabled people paying rent and on low incomes. As mentioned in Chapter Two, however, levels of financial support available from Housing Benefit are currently subject to cuts, so the financial assistance offered here is likely to be reduced.

Those who are not in employment are eligible for Employment and Support Allowance (ESA). This replaced Incapacity Benefit (IB) and

Income Support in 2008 as the main form of income replacement benefit available to people with impairments, conditions or short-term sickness. Following a Work Capability Assessment (WCA), which is a medical assessment, claimants are categorised into one of three groups: first, those who can start work immediately; second, those able to start work with further support (the Work Related Activity Group), and third, those not expected to look for work because of the 'severity of their impairment' (the Support Group) (Directgov, 2010a). The significance of categorising people into these groups goes beyond mere economics. As Piggott and Grover (2009) argue, '... distinguishing between the work-related activity and support groups ... is a strategy for weakening the opposition to the ESA by dividing it and concentrating resources on those held to be more deserving' (p 166). The conditionality inherent in the provision of ESA has caused concern among organisations of disabled people, especially with the failure to address disabling barriers in the labour market (as mentioned earlier). Concerns have also been raised about continued support for the WCA despite claims that it is 'seriously flawed' and thus ineffective (Disability Alliance, 2010a). Furthermore, recent announcements in the comprehensive spending review suggest that claimants of ESA will be restricted to one year of payments before being moved to the considerably lower income provided by Jobseeker's Allowance. This will further decrease some disabled people's incomes.

Despite the range of benefits available, it has been argued that for those solely reliant on benefits for their income, the level is '... approximately £200 less than the weekly amount required for them to ensure a minimum standard of living' (JRF, 2004, p 3). As we shall see later, reliance on benefits for income can have a negative effect on access to the owner-occupied sector, but it can also affect access to private renting. Research by Shelter (2010, p 1) showed that '... one third of advertisements for private rented properties barred housing benefit claimants outright. Phone calls to landlords that did not specify such a bar found as few as one in six landlords willing to accept a housing benefit claimant as a tenant'. As well as poor employment opportunities and low incomes derived from a reliance on benefits, there may be extra costs and financial considerations relating to disabling barriers or to impairments that further reduce income available for housing. The added costs of assistance, aids and adaptations (in cases where financial support via provisions such as the Disabled Facilities Grant is not available, is less than needed or requires substantial personal contributions) can considerably reduce resources. The Joseph Rowntree Foundation (JRF, 2004) states that additional costs arise in almost all areas of everyday life, including for equipment or personal assistance and '... ongoing higher expenses for ... food, clothing, utilities and recreation' (p 1). There may also be additional costs for heating for people with mobility impairments who are in the dwelling for long periods of time (Goodridge, 2004), and for repairs and maintenance for some owner-occupiers (although Home Improvement Agencies may offer support here). Young disabled people often become adults with few financial resources, both because living with an impairment in an inaccessible environment can be costly, and because their families are less likely to be able to help them financially, having themselves had the additional expense of bringing up a disabled child in a disabling society (Oldman and Beresford, 2000; Woolley, 2004).

For those entering the owner-occupied sector, additional financial resources may be necessary for paying life insurance premiums or mortgage payment protection insurance (MPPI). These may be required when taking out a mortgage and for some people can result in high premiums as a consequence of industry perceptions and classifications of impairments. Life insurance (which involves the underwriter assessing risk in terms of mortality or premature death) could, in the past, prevent disabled people from securing a mortgage if life insurance was rejected due to perceived high risk of claimants (Burns, 2002; Hemingway, 2004a). It is now more likely to cause difficulties in terms of affordability. One informant from the current author's research, for instance, found that her premiums rose by 50 per cent on her second mortgage, following the requirement to assign life insurance to the mortgage. An underwriter from a large building society also pointed out the effect that life insurance could have on the amount possible to borrow for a property:

> 'I suspect that some health conditions would result in
> very high premiums being applied to the life policy. For
> a customer on a tight budget, this could have a knock-on
> effect on the amount they have each month to fund the
> mortgage payment which could in turn reduce the amount
> they are comfortable borrowing.'

The introduction of MPPI, which is a common recommendation of lenders, may present similar difficulties. MPPI is a form of insurance that protects the mortgagor in times of unemployment, illness or accident through payments made while they are not working. The current author's research found that some companies now insist on MPPI with all mortgage applications, and (as with life insurance) disabled clients may find that they are paying higher premiums than their non-disabled counterparts.

The socio-economic environment therefore plays a significant role in people's realisation of the home. Everybody's opportunities and choices are affected by employment situation, income and available resources. As we have seen, however, disabled people encounter greater disadvantage in the labour markets than non-disabled people, which results in limited resources for participating in the private sector and weaker positions in the housing market. The recent public sector cuts are likely to further exacerbate the situation here. For some disabled people, for instance, the combined effects of cuts to Housing Benefit, DLA and ESA are likely to have a huge impact on income. Furthermore, additional costs reduce available resources. As shown in Chapter Four, this can mean that disabled people are more likely to reside in social rented housing. Thus, the notion of social renting for the 'vulnerable' may be affected by the socio-economic status of those commonly housed in the sector. A Communities and Local Government report (CLG, 2009a) demonstrates a clear relationship between income and tenure, with over half (53 per cent) of those living in social rented accommodation having a total joint income of less than £10,000 a year, compared with with 11 per cent of owner-occupiers and 25 per cent of people living in the private rented sector. This can limit opportunities to progress to owner-occupation (if the individual so desires) (Morris, 2002). Extra expenses may also arise through the need for larger houses that may facilitate wheelchair users, such as bungalows (which are generally higher priced). For Holly and her husband, difficulties accessing home ownership partly related to buying their first property. As she stated, it was not possible for them to begin as first-time buyers usually do; starting small, maybe with a terraced house, and working their way upwards. She explained:

> 'I think the whole area of owner-occupation is something that we haven't been able to access, because normally your first home may well be, assuming that you haven't been left any money by your family or something like that, may well be a small terraced house, or small semi or whatever. But as a disabled person we have certain requirements that we have to have, so it has to be a fairly large property because there are two wheelchairs, so the cost of that sort of accommodation we couldn't afford. Do you see what I mean? We can't work our way up the property ladder in the same way.'

It may be that certain schemes provide opportunities for people on low incomes to access the owner-occupied sector. The Right to Buy, for instance, has given many council tenants the chance to buy their homes, although as Chapter Two showed, disabled people were excluded from being able to buy their own homes via the initiative until 1988. It also appears from the responses of some of the informants within the current author's research that some exclusion persists, particularly for wheelchair users. Holly and Rebecca, for example, found that their wheelchair-accessible properties were exempt. Holly explained her thoughts on this:

> 'I have very mixed feelings about it, to be honest, because my personal politics really is that I don't agree with the Right to Buy legislation anyway, as a general principle. I think the net result of it has been that the council accommodation that has been left is the council accommodation that people don't want, and now we are in a position that if you live in council accommodation you are seen as being lower than the low in some respects, whereas previously that wasn't the case, it was seen as being okay to have a council house.... So as a political thing I don't agree with it. But personally, it seems sort of wrong that everybody else has the Right to Buy but as a disabled person you don't.'

As this exclusion was unexpected in the findings, the researcher contacted a Yorkshire local authority to enquire further about claims that some disabled people are exempt from the Right to Buy. The authority confirmed this to be the case in certain situations. Further examination of the Right to Buy does reveal that exclusions for certain properties are allowed if the properties are part of a group specifically used for disabled people (CLG, 2007). The same applies to the Right to Acquire, which enables people to buy their rented property at a discounted price if they have lived in properties rented from Registered Social Landlords for five years, but some disabled people are not entitled to exercise this right. Exclusions apply, for example, to '... housing provided to people who have special needs or who are physically disabled' (Directgov, 2010b, p 1). Most disabled people, however, should be able to exercise the Right to Buy (although there are some restrictions on bungalows and ground-floor flats), if they entered the tenancy before the age of 60. Holly lives in a bungalow, and, albeit not to condone such policies, the housing association may therefore be within its rights in relation to the Housing Act to refuse the Right to Buy, but Rebecca, who lives in a house with a through-floor lift, should be eligible for the Right to Buy, so to deny her may be regarded as discrimination.

With low incomes, and extra costs incurred by disabled people, there may be increased susceptibility to poverty (Oliver and Barnes, 1998), and as Beresford (2000) asserts, this can particularly be the case for mental health service users. Prideaux and colleagues (2008) state that '... a third of disabled adults of working age are living in poverty (this is double the rate for non-disabled people, and the gap has widened in the last decade)' (p 6). These figures are likely to underestimate the extent of poverty for disabled people, as the additional costs associated with impairments mentioned earlier are rarely considered (JRF, 2004). Furthermore, the link with low-income ownership means that disabled people are more likely to live in poor housing conditions (Morris, 1993c). Limited income can also have a negative impact on suitability of housing and location of rented accommodation as rents tend to be higher in urban areas (where most services and accessible facilities are located) as do rents for ' ... ground floor, larger and therefore more flexible accommodation' (Goodridge, 2004, p 14). In addition, limited financial resources may lead to homelessness. As Mojtabai (2005) has shown, the reasons for loss of housing and continued homelessness among mental health service users are the same as for those without 'mental illness', relating to insufficient income and unemployment (as well as lack of suitable housing), thus demonstrating structural rather than individual 'inadequacy' as the cause of homelessness. It is important to bear in mind that low income may also provide opportunities to access housing in the social rented sector, with circumstances placing disabled people in positions of priority need. Nonetheless, the disadvantaged socio-economic position of many disabled people has a significant impact on housing options and choices.

Assessing individuals: owner-occupation and risk evaluation

This section looks closer at financial considerations that have not been examined in detail in previous research by exploring the mortgage application process for disabled people in relation to risk assessment (although, for some important contributions, see Burns, 2002; Hagner and Klein, 2005; Hamer, 2005c). Here, we look at how the mortgage industry may play a role in creating and reinforcing the barriers encountered by disabled people. The evaluation of attributes of potential applicants during the mortgage decision process, for instance – which can be inconsistent and may put undue emphasis on impairment – may prevent access to the owner-occupied sector. Thus, when risk is assessed, disabled people's circumstances (in relation to employment and income) may be viewed in a negative light. The next chapter takes this further by looking at the way in which distinctions between impairments can be made by institutions or intermediaries, suggesting that people with particular impairments may be classified as 'higher risk' and hence experience further disadvantage.

It is worth clarifying a few terms here. There are, for example, many different 'intermediaries' involved in the home purchase process. When a person begins their search for a property to purchase, they may employ the services of an estate agent, who provides property particulars on numerous dwellings, and arranges viewings of these properties. Once a suitable property has been located, arranging the funds for buying the property (through a mortgage) may require the services of a mortgage broker or independent financial adviser (IFA), or direct contact with the mortgage lender or lending institution. These are presently regulated by the Financial Services Authority (FSA) (although the coalition government plans to replace this single body with three separate regulators) and are thus required to hold specific qualifications, as well as adhere to certain rules when arranging a mortgage. For many people, a mortgage loan from a lending institution will be required to assist in the purchase of a property. This consists of two key elements, the debt or loan, and the interest payable on that loan, but the treatment of these elements depends on the type of mortgage applied for (see Garnett and Perry, 2005, p 135). The amount that a person borrows may be decided by the lending institution using *loan-to-value income bands/ratios* or *income-multipliers*, which look at the amount a potential mortgagor wishes to borrow (according to property price minus the deposit) against their earnings. Earnings are often multiplied by between two and six times (depending on the lender) and if the resulting figure covers the mortgage applied for, the loan may be agreed. As will become apparent, however, underwriters increasingly rely on *affordability models*, which assess available income slightly differently, being based on individual budgets. A mortgage can be secured through several different institutions, known as 'lenders', which lend money to a client for a particular property in return for mortgage payments plus interest over an agreed term. Banks, building societies, insurance companies and specialist lending companies (including sub-prime lenders that lend to clients considered 'high risk') can be classified under this label. Finally, in distinguishing between building societies and banks, a traditional building society would be classed as both prudential and mutual (owned by and for the benefit of borrowers and lenders rather than for separate profit-driven shareholders, as is the case with banks).

Assessing risk in the mortgage industry

Risk assessment or evaluation within lending institutions is used to determine the probability of a client failing to make repayments, hence helping to decide the client base, and is an inherently exclusionary approach that relies on some form of 'discrimination' (see also Burns, 2002). In recent years, there has been a shift from a more traditional, qualitative calculation of risk to an increasingly complex system of quantification that is now widespread (Leyshon et al, 1998). These two forms of risk assessment both involve assessing the 'riskiness' of the client in relation to repayment of the loan, and within each approach the lender may examine similar factors. Actions often include assessing the credit history of the client, carrying out some form of assessment for affordability, and checking for fraudulent applications. The methods used for such assessments differ, however. In more traditional approaches to underwriting, manual processes are more commonly used, with affordability calculations based on income multiples and greater flexibility (albeit also subjectivity) (Leyshon and Thrift, 1999; Aalbers, 2005). In contrast, credit scoring is a more automated underwriting process focusing on assessment by generalisations and involving increasingly sophisticated databases to construct the profile of the client, and hence their label as high or low risk.

Looking a little closer at credit scoring, we see that lenders use 'scorecards' – where client details are examined to determine a score that informs the decision to lend – and often automated affordability models. Scorecards vary between institutions, and sometimes between products *within* institutions, but several standard variables are used within this information-gathering stage, including age, gender, residential status, occupation, time in employment and income, as well as marital status (Bridges, 2005). Sometimes additional factors such as nationality and number of children will also be considered, as well as the client's health if linked to life insurance (Aalbers, 2005). Although there are commonalities to a degree, there are some subtle differences. In the current author's research, for example, one lending institution claimed to look at the number of children an applicant has, which may not be the case with other lenders. As the informant from this building society explained, even here there may be different perspectives to consider, as having several children can be perceived in both a positive and negative light. It may be viewed as positive because the customer's responsibility to their children would presumably mean that they would aim to keep up their payments. It may also be perceived as negative, however, in that the client would presumably have fewer financial resources available. This variation in the perception of an attribute (whether deemed positive or negative) was evident in relation to a range of variables within and across different institutions.

Once a score has been obtained, it is compared with the current thresholds used by the lender on accepting or rejecting the client (Leyshon and Thrift, 1999). If the score is above a certain level, the lender may be willing to take the risk on that customer. So the higher the score, the less risk the client is perceived to represent. As one informant explained:

> 'You get certain points for certain things; let's take a figure of 250 which is fairly common. 250 means accept, 230-250 means refer to a human being to make the decision, 270 and above means extremely good … or less, the interest rate is higher. So credit scoring is literally adding up points for each factor, for example, have a telephone, yes, five points. Credit scoring is based on your history, your employment and income.'

Scorecards may be designed by a credit reference agency or by the lending institutions themselves, in which case they tend to be drawn using details of the lender's current client base. One informant, who was an underwriter, explained that scorecards were developed on the basis of the performance of the company's own customers. They build on and maintain their own scorecards for the type of customers they want to attract and their cards are reviewed twice every year, with the cut-off point being reviewed according to the movements of the market. It was explained that if more customers are desired, they might relax the scorecard. It was also described as standard practice within lending institutions to use different cards for different types of application, including 'prime', adverse credit, 'sub-prime', and buy-to-let applications, as well as those from self-employed clients.

Many lenders, whether using traditional or credit-scoring approaches, also use behavioural scoring techniques, which involve investigating the previous purchasing activities of the customers to assess the likelihood of them meeting mortgage repayments (Leyshon and Thrift, 1999). Authorised intermediaries and financial institutions, for instance, have access to databases such as Equifax and Experian that provide credit reports on anyone in the UK, relating to, for example, the number of county court judgements a person has against them (if any), their worst status on default, any outstanding loans or credit cards, payment records, details of addresses held and total number of defaults. Some lending institutions have additional tools in place to further assess potential clients' characters. As one lender (an advocate of more traditional methods) explained, it may conduct detailed checks for deception, whereby it looks for:

> '… coincidences and contradictions within the application. This might be … differing signatures on the application and direct debit (contradiction), which should be signed by the same person. These can sometimes be small and apparently meaningless but often evidence of an attempt to deceive.'

Following such checks, some lenders may look at the property itself, as some lending policies do not lend on a property that has certain restrictions, for example "if only particular people can live in it, such as those above a certain age". In terms of valuation, this perceived restriction is seen as too high risk, as it affects the future sale of the property. This could perhaps raise concerns for disabled people who wish to adapt their properties or buy adapted properties. When questioned on the implications of this for disabled people, one informant stated that lending on 'specially adapted houses' could cause some difficulties, as the lender has to consider the future saleability of the property in its assessment. What lenders are concerned with is the ability to sell properties in the event of default or continued non-payment. If properties are sold at an auction, they rarely attain market value and so the lender will primarily be concerned with recovering its debt. Some lenders, however, charge a 'higher lending fee' when the mortgage is taken out. This is a single premium that insures the lender in the event of repossession.

Once the character of the client has been checked or the credit score obtained, which tends to determine *whether* the institution will lend, the use of affordability models determines *how much* it will be willing to lend. As one informant explained, affordability can be assessed using traditional income multiples (for instance, three times annual gross income) or using an analysis of debt-to-income ratio. The latter, according to this informant, represents a 'true' affordability calculation that "… takes account of the applicant's income and cost of servicing their existing debt (plus the new mortgage loan) as per the information received from the credit search". The score obtained for affordability differs from the credit score in that the lower the score the better, as this is perceived to be a lower risk. Van Dijk and Garga (2006) point out that the larger institutions are more likely to use affordability models, suggesting that size of institution may inform the practices used. This was supported in the current author's research, whereby all of the institutions using credit scoring used affordability models, and all of the institutions using traditional underwriting methods (which tended to be smaller) used income multipliers to assess affordability.

While the move towards quantification is problematic in many ways, the alternative, more qualitative, methods of risk management are not without their limitations. While the more subjective nature of this type of underwriting can be positive for clients (by not reducing them to statistics), it is also potentially problematic in terms of the personal prejudices and judgements of the underwriter that may influence the decision to lend. Furthermore, many institutions champion the alternative – credit scoring – (Association for Payment Clearing Services et al, 2000; Van Dijk and Garga, 2006), with claims that it represents a fairer, more precise, unbiased approach to lending as practitioners purport to use objective, mathematical methods in risk assessment and thus remove human error. Credit scoring has also speeded up many of the processes of mortgage application, providing both the lender and the client with faster decisions, enabling more efficient and consistent business practices and opening up the market to more borrowers. One informant also claimed that the use of credit scoring made it easier to "… comply with FSA mortgage regulations". Additionally, the increased use of affordability models rather than income multiples may be an improvement for some disabled people if different forms of income are accepted, and may be more suitable for responding to the individual needs of each case (Hagner and Klein, 2005).

It is also possible that credit-scoring practices may exclude some people while improving access for others (Aalbers, 2005), as well as being more beneficial to the company than the client. The use of credit-scoring techniques, databases and information systems allows the industry to pursue segmentation (the process of dividing customers into particular groups) (Leyson and Thrift, 1999). Thus, customers are transformed into calculable units to be used for profit, or rejected as high risk on the basis of their categorisation. It has been argued, too, that risk assessment should not be based on such technical principles, whereby the 'expert', who has little knowledge of the person they are assessing, calculates the level of risk (Beck, 1992; Jaegar et al, 2001). The use of information supplied by credit reference agencies in the decision-making process can also negatively affect certain groups of people through the use of models that assess risk using data on people with similar lifestyle circumstances (Moneyfacts, 2005).These customers may experience either total rejection of their mortgage application, higher interest rates (to reflect the higher perceived risk of the potential borrower) or higher premiums on their life insurance if such a policy is a condition of the mortgage. Furthermore, Aalbers (2005) highlights the potential problems arising from the use of personal information on the customer that has been acquired for other means, as a consequence of the linking of databases across institutions. This has implications for disabled people, as, depending on the type of data accessed, it may be possible to identify someone as being a disabled person even if this has not been declared on their mortgage application form. While it may appear therefore that being a disabled person will have no influence on a lending decision, this may not actually be the case.

Disabled people and risk evaluation

The different forms of risk assessment used within mortgage lending can, then, be loosely classed as two key types: 'traditional' underwriting techniques and those that implement credit-scoring systems. While many of the characteristics of the client examined in traditional methods and credit scoring are similar, there is some indication that they tend to vary according to institutions' own practices and as such, it is difficult to generalise about lending practices at the very detailed level. Nonetheless, there are potential implications of underwriting for disabled people in general terms. Disabled people may be disadvantaged as a consequence of the underlying principles of risk assessment, the particular assumptions that may inform these and the variables on which the assessment is based. These factors relate to three key issues within the scope of industry perspectives and consequent practices: first, perceptions of disabled people; second, perceptions of income situations to which disabled people might be more commonly associated; and finally, perceptions of impairment in relation to risk. As mentioned earlier, there is an overlap in the following discussion with issues addressed under the broad label of attitudinal barriers, in terms of the assessment of individuals by institutions. While risk assessment is introduced here in relation to income issues, the next chapter examines how people with different impairments may be evaluated when accessing a mortgage. We draw now on interviews held with 52 financial services representatives (including intermediaries, lending institution employees and underwriters).

The language used by industry informants and their descriptions of disabled people within the current author's research appeared to imply an individual or 'medical' model understanding of disability (see Hemingway, 2008). This could potentially affect industry practices and behaviours, which may disadvantage disabled people both in their encounters with industry staff and their application for a mortgage. Within the underwriting process, for instance, such an understanding has the potential to influence decision makers' perceptions, which may consequently affect disabled people. One way in which this may occur is if particular impairments are made known to the lender. Assumptions about these impairments may then affect the application if, perhaps, a particular impairment is regarded as restricting a person's ability to earn or shortening their life expectancy, assumptions that may be generalisations. While this may be so, however, it is important to acknowledge that behaviour is not simply shaped by attitudes. The lending institutions' employees are likely also to be influenced in their practices and decisions by the rules and regulations of their organisation or their job (particularly with the DDA legislation in place). Furthermore, the primary motivation for the lenders is the desire for profit, so while it is important to highlight the industry's understanding of disability and disabled people, its perspective on income and employment situations common to disabled people may prove to be more significant here.

Financial circumstances are of obvious importance in accessing the owner-occupied sector and are evidenced through both economic and institutional arrangements. In exploring these issues, Burns (2002) notes a distinction between two main groups of disabled people. Her research indicated that disabled people who had developed an impairment while in the owner-occupied sector had the least difficulties in obtaining a mortgage. For this group, the barriers were reduced because they were '... more established in their housing careers, which often meant they had some collateral behind them, being in some cases "asset" rich' (p 224). The second group, those who had an impairment prior to purchasing their first home, met with considerably more constraints. For these people, employment issues and the failure of institutions to accept benefits as income slowed their progress. An important issue therefore arises in relation to the extent to which the variables examined in credit scoring and other underwriting practices influence the final decision to lend and what effect this might have on disabled people. The work of Andreeva et al (2004) is relevant here, and suggests that more indirect forms of discrimination may occur in credit scoring (through economic disadvantage) even if more directly significant variables (that can lead to direct discrimination) are not included. In a similar way, within the current author's research, when asked if 'disability' or impairment is a factor considered within the scorecard, several underwriters claimed that there is nothing within their scorecards that distinguishes a disabled person from a non-disabled person, with suggestions that it would not be permissible under the DDA to do so. As another informant pointed out:

> '... not building anything into our scorecards regarding a person's disability ... demonstrates that we do not see (and experience bears witness) that the disabled are any greater credit risk than those not suffering from a disability.'

This was a common response to this question and seemed to indicate that impairment is not directly assessed in relation to risk. It may be possible, however, to identify a disabled person from the other variables used in the scorecard, perhaps on account of their income, such as being in receipt of DLA (Hemingway, 2004a). Thus, the potential for this to affect the assessment cannot be entirely ruled out. In addition, a reliance on computer software may mean that certain negatively perceived attributes are disproportionately associated with disabled people, causing them to be effectively 'screened out'. These may include, for instance, low income, employment circumstances or, as Burns (2002) suggests, lack of *credit history*. Burns (2004, p 174) states, for instance, that if disabled people '... are in receipt of housing benefit there will be no record of their rent payments from which forecasts of prompt payment of mortgages are made'. So within credit scoring, even if impairment is not a factor considered in the scorecard, other variables that are (and that may be more common to disabled people) may lead to disadvantage.

Employment is clearly influential with regard to mortgage application. Lenders often require borrowers to be in full-time, permanent employment and to have remained in that employment six months prior to application. Many lenders also examine clients' employment histories in risk assessment. It may be that the typical employment situations of disabled people are therefore viewed in a negative light in relation to this. The type of employment that disabled people most commonly have may not, for example, be rated highly on a scorecard. This is demonstrated through the claims of one informant, an IFA (previously an underwriter), who explained how classifications of employment could work within credit scoring:

'Some lenders have special mortgages for special people, including doctors, dentists, optometrists and teachers. Then you have graduate mortgages, for graduates under the age of say thirty-five. Generally lenders will consider someone in a professional occupation, so they would be white-collar or blue-collar management. Really, the classification of A, B, C1, C2, D and E is used, A being professional, B semi-professionals like managers, civil service and so forth, C1 manual, C2 semi-manual and so on, so that classification is taken into account.'

As he stated, the lower the classification (with E being the lowest), the higher the perceived risk. Within this classification system in particular, disabled people may therefore experience indirect exclusion if employed in low-paid, low-status occupations, as is often the case (see earlier in this chapter). Those not in employment may score low or even 'zero' on a scorecard that makes use of such classification systems. Similarly, a focus on income variables may have a detrimental effect on some disabled people because, as shown at the beginning of the chapter, income may be low as a result of general disadvantage in the labour market or due to reliance on benefits. It may also be that the length of time that some disabled people spend in employment is reduced, or at least disrupted, as a consequence of health. As one disabled informant, Holly, stated, one of the biggest barriers to home ownership for her was the fact that "... no one knows how long they are going to be able to work for, but for a disabled person that is even more of an issue. I do know that I am not going to be able to work until I am sixty, I know that for a fact."

It has been shown in the existing literature that some disabled people experience discrimination from lenders merely because they receive state benefits, even though such support is disability-related (Burns, 2002; Goodridge, 2004). This is something that was also raised by some of the disabled informants within the current author's research. Being denied a mortgage as a consequence of benefits constituting part or all of income was an issue for at least two of the informants within the study. Joyce, who was trying to arrange a remortgage with her husband on their property, discussed being turned down by a large, high-street lender:

'He gets the carer's allowance and that's not counted; my attendance mobility is not counted. I get a pension from work, thank God, and they can only take half of that. I get industrial injury benefit and they can only take ten per cent of that, so according to them I was on about, sort of £15 a week.'

The whole process left her feeling exhausted and deflated, and she equated the lender's refusal to take her benefits into account to the fact that she was a disabled person. She said: "I never had this problem and then suddenly because you're in a wheelchair, you're not wanted. And yet, all of the benefits I've got are for life." She also described being turned down by two other high-street lenders. In the end, she managed to secure a remortgage through a sub-prime lender that charged a much higher rate, apparently three times what she would have paid with a regular lender, but accepted all of her benefits as income.

When Robert and his partner decided to apply for a mortgage, they approached the same lender that Joyce had initially applied to. They had established a relationship with the bank, with a total of four accounts already open there. The lender, however, refused to take into account either of their DLAs or Robert's partner's Severe Disablement Allowance, only accepting Robert's earned income. Robert therefore enlisted the assistance of a mortgage broker, who managed to find a lender on the couple's behalf. What is interesting about these cases is that the informants circumstances are very different. Joyce is nearly twice as old as Robert, is not in paid employment and was applying to remortgage, so one might deduce that the difficulties she faced were a combination of age, employment situation and mortgage type. Robert, on the other hand, is a lot younger and is employed in a steady job, and he and his partner both have long-term benefits that increase their joint income. What is more interesting here, however, is that the particular lender that rejected both applications was described by the financial services representatives interviewed as being one of the most likely lenders to accept benefits. Clearly, actual practice suggests that the organisation does not.

Nearly half of the financial services informants interviewed highlighted the problems that disabled people might encounter in relation to benefits. While some asserted that there definitely would be difficulties, others suggested that there 'may' be difficulties in certain circumstances. These circumstances included clients being in receipt of income comprising 'pure' benefits (so in other words, they had no other form of income, particularly earned income). Several lenders stated that the decision whether or not to regard benefits as adequate income would depend on the size of the loan required. So, for example, if the applicant had a small deposit, the lender might be less inclined to accept benefits than if a large portion of the value of the mortgage had been paid off. It was also stated that the acceptance of benefits could depend on whether or not the benefit was payable for life, or could simply depend on the particular lender's rules and criteria. The issue therefore appears to be lending institutions' failure either to accept benefits or assess them in the same way as earned income. The matter of the acceptance of benefits as income was therefore investigated further within the underwriting informants' responses. Four stated that benefits were generally not accepted within their institution, with two of these informants justifying this rejection on the presumed insecurity of benefits. Five informants, however, claimed that benefits were fully accepted as income, including DLA and IB, with one informant stating that they would also be accepted as sole income (as in her mind some benefits could be more secure than earned income). This acceptance of benefits as sole income appears to be quite a rare occurrence within lending institutions, and, as one informant asserted, a lot of lenders would be willing to take a range of benefits into account, but only alongside an earned income (so some form of employment income would be necessary to satisfy most lending institutions). The other four informants claimed that only a certain percentage of benefits would be accepted as income, with 50 or 75 per cent being the usual figures accepted. One of these informants stated that their lending institution would accept a percentage of benefits, but that the application would actually be treated 'more cautiously', and other factors taken into consideration, if the payments constituted sole income. Such factors may include, for example, whether the client has a current account with the lender, as the branch manager will know the client's circumstances in more detail, and this could be judged in the assessment.

Discussions with IFAs and mortgage brokers suggested that banks and building societies differed in their acceptance of benefits, with building societies apparently being more likely to accept benefits as income. Some brokers suggested that the larger institutions would be more likely to accept benefits than smaller institutions. Thus, institutional context may be important here. Investigating this further through the underwriter findings, it is interesting to note that the larger institutions were actually less likely to fully accept DLA as income and that both banks interviewed only accepted a certain percentage of DLA. As numbers were small, however, it was difficult to draw any further conclusions in relation to this. Informants' responses, therefore, seemed to illustrate the level of inconsistency within the industry. This was reflected both in the opinions informants had of benefits (whether they believed that benefits would represent a difficulty or not) and in terms of different lenders' willingness to accept them. For one IFA, however, this inconsistency should not present a significant obstacle, given the number of products and lending institutions available to choose from (albeit there may be a small price to pay, quite literally). As he stated: "Okay, you are not getting the keenest rates, perhaps a little more expensive than you might get under a prime case, but there is no reason why you couldn't just get a self-cert mortgage and bypass the problem completely." Perhaps in the current economic climate, however, there is likely to be less choice available, especially as, according to the Council of Mortgage Lenders, there has apparently been '... a further concentration of lending activity among the seven largest lenders, who can access funding' (CML, 2009, p 2). There has also been a total withdrawal of the self-certification of income facility previously available to both employed and self-employed applicants.

The current author's research suggests that lender antipathy towards benefits mainly relates to the belief not only that the received income is low, but also that it is insecure. One underwriter stated, for example, that the lending institution he worked for:

> '... would treat a disabled person in work in the same way as any other person in work but would be inclined to be far more cautious if the sole form of income was from state benefit (irrespective of disability). This is simply because successive governments can tend to "muck about" with benefit in a way that an employer may not within the contract of employment. We obviously have to try to peer into the future when lending over 25 years and a person on benefit is less likely to see as substantial an improvement in financial circumstances as an employed individual (although this may not always be the case it is a useful rule of thumb).'

Such distrust of the government in relation to the security of benefits is likely to heighten as public expenditure is cut, particularly in relation to DLA. Research by Hamer (2005c, 2005d) found further reasoning behind lenders' rejection of benefits, noting five key lender responses. First, it was asserted that lenders exclude all benefits from loan applications, and are therefore not discriminating solely against disabled people; second, it was argued that benefits are provided for particular purposes (such as additional living costs) and are not designed to be used as collateral against a mortgage; third, it was claimed that benefits are insecure; fourth, that if a disabled person began paying a mortgage on IS but then became unemployed, they may not be able to meet mortgage payments; and finally, it was argued that benefits are not accepted as the disabled person's circumstances may change. All of these perspectives have been criticised by Hamer (2005c) as inherently discriminatory. He begins by pointing out that most lenders accept some form of benefits, using the example of Working Tax Credits. Lenders are therefore being selective about the benefits that they will accept. In order for the claim that benefits are for a set purpose to be fair, lenders would therefore have to ask non-disabled, employed people whether they were carers and deduct accordingly. This is unlikely to happen, so, Hamer argues, why ask disabled people? The government is also unlikely to remove benefits if they would result in homelessness, which would suggest that benefits are secure, at least to some degree. Even if this were not the case, many forms of employment are insecure, but do not receive such attention. Finally, the claim that circumstances may change suggests that they do not for non-disabled people. Hence, refusing benefits on these grounds appears somewhat discriminatory.

It seems, then, that there is some inconsistency inherent within industry perceptions and treatment of benefits. It is also evident that there may be a range of income or employment variables through which disabled people score low in comparison with non-disabled people (on account of general disadvantage). These may either contribute to excluding them from obtaining a mortgage or result in higher interest and therefore higher repayments.

The 'credit crunch' and its aftermath

The recent economic crisis, sometimes referred to as the 'credit crunch', has had implications for everyone, but we look here at the impact that it may have had on disabled people's opportunities within housing. The credit crunch, at its simplest, '... means that lenders won't lend, borrowers can't borrow, builders can't build and buyers can't buy' (Parkinson et al, 2009, p 4). While the processes involved have been complex, a brief note on its causes is made here, drawing on several sources to provide an overview of key issues (Birch, 2008; BBC, 2009; CLG Committee, 2009; Parkinson et al, 2009). The economic crisis witnessed in the UK and internationally has its roots in the US sub-prime market collapse, the decline in inter-bank and general lending, and the house price rise and fall (resulting in negative equity, default and repossessions). While many relate the cause of the credit crunch simply to the sub-prime market collapse, it is unlikely that this was the sole cause of the financial problems that led to the crisis.

By the end of 2000, the UK was experiencing a thriving economy and house prices were on the rise. Around this time, the international financial sector saw the introduction of the credit default swap (CDS), an insurance contract that paid out if an investment failed, giving banks greater confidence to pass their risks to one another. In 2001, following the collapse of the World Trade Center, the global markets froze, and, with the economy in need of help, the Central Bank cut interest rates from 2001 to 2004, making it cheaper for banks to borrow money. Following this, investors' returns in financial markets were reduced, and so banks took bigger risks to generate higher profit margins. During this period, then, there was an increase in the availability of 'cheap money', but also significant at the time was the rise in the number of new financial products on offer and the presence of a 'light touch' regulatory system. Then property played its part in the crisis. US sub-prime mortgages had become increasingly popular (as they had in the UK), supporting lower-income groups to become home owners. As Parkinson and colleagues (2009) state, for instance, in 2006, '... around 20% of all new mortgages in the US were rated sub-prime' (p 5). 'Stated income' mortgages had also risen in the US (similar to self-certification mortgages in the UK), and so it had become much easier to secure loans at this time than in previous years. Interest rates then began to rise, and meeting mortgage repayments became increasingly difficult for many owner-occupiers.

American lenders were financed by banks around the world, including British banks. Through a process known as securitisation, where mortgages are packaged up and sold on, UK banks bought the mortgages from the lenders for the gradual income they would yield (assuming that the borrowers could afford to continue with payments). These residential mortgage-backed securities were repackaged and resold by banks, many of which were insured by CDSs that were not being regulated. In the UK, there was an assumption that risk had disappeared because it was being spread around, but with regulation being the responsibility of three different bodies (the Bank of England, the Treasury and the FSA), it would seem that some level of uncertainty surrounded the role of each. So at the time, risks attached to the financial products were undervalued. UK average house prices had previously been on the rise, but at the height of the boom in the summer of 2007, repossessions in the US increased rapidly within the sub-prime mortgage market and house prices began to decline (due to a combination of rising interest rates and falling house prices). It has been suggested that this was more to do with the packages that had been sold than with the sub-prime mortgages themselves, as banks were unaware of what products they had within their packages that were still profitable. Confidence therefore declined and banks stopped lending to one another or to customers (or charged higher interest rates). So the origins of the crisis predominantly lay in the 'age of risk' (BBC, 2009), and the trigger was securitised sub-prime mortgages, which then resulted in wider financial problems.

The credit crunch led to a property crisis all over the world, causing the number of house sales and new constructions to drop dramatically. This has had an effect on both the public and private sectors. With new housing being built at a slower rate, some commentators have highlighted the potential design implications of those properties that gain planning permission, especially in terms of reduced space standards (Finch, 2010). In terms of future housing stock, this is bad news for some disabled people, particularly wheelchair users. In addition, in 2006, Doherty stated that:

> Recent new build programs have only been averaging 30 new wheelchair accessible and barrier free properties a year. If new builds continue to increase at the current rate it will take approximately 133 years to make up the *current* estimated shortfall of barrier free and wheelchair accessible properties within Glasgow. (p 3, emphasis in original).

With the credit crunch affecting the rate at which new-builds have been constructed, and with the recent public spending cuts, the effect is likely to be even more negative. It has also been suggested that '... the condition of the housing stock' may be '... worsening due to owners and landlords being unwilling or unable to spend on repair and maintenance' (CML, 2010, p 1). There may be implications here for adaptations in the private rented sector too. Furthermore, older disabled people may have fewer choices available to them as privately run sheltered housing companies affected by the recession begin to withdraw development plans and lose staff (Marshall, 2009).

Despite lower house prices, which should make owner-occupation more attainable, the fact that lenders are more risk averse means that it is more difficult for potential buyers to purchase properties. Many lenders have withdrawn mortgage products, reduced loan amounts, tightened lending criteria and now offer lower loan-to-value ratios (Birch, 2010). As Parkinson and colleagues (2009) state, 'Mortgage loans for house purchase were down 43% in the first six months of 2008 compared to the first half of 2007' (p 14). Furthermore, with the recent 'funding crisis', we have seen the withdrawal of a vast number of mortgage products from the sub-prime industry. The schemes that are left are less generous with their loan-to-value income multiples and affordability calculations. It may be that the withdrawal of more flexible loans once offered by sub-prime lenders will result in less choice for people solely in receipt of benefits. Both prime and sub-prime lenders have been affected by the decline in the availability of mortgage funds, and the tendency for lenders to sideline those perceived as higher risk has made it difficult for many people, but potentially more so for disabled clients, to access the owner-occupied sector.

Those already in the owner-occupied sector, particularly those who bought their properties when the market was at its peak and those with high loan-to-value mortgages, have seen a sudden decline in the value of their homes, and many people have been left with mortgages for more than the house is worth (negative equity). People with low or insecure incomes may be unable to keep up repayments, thus increasing the likelihood of default or repossessions. This is often because home owners from low-income groups tend to commit above-average amounts of income to housing costs and are therefore less able to accommodate difficult times (Stephens et al, 2008). As we saw earlier, disabled people are more likely than non-disabled people to be on low or insecure incomes, which may increase their susceptibility to repossession. A Communities and Local Government report (2009b, p 16) on repossessions in 2008 found that:

> For England as a whole, 13 per cent of households buying with a mortgage reported either some difficulty in paying the mortgage or that they were in arrears. Over 30 per cent of unemployed households, those with at least one sick or disabled member, and those who had previously been repossessed reported some difficulties or being in arrears.

One of the wider consequences of more repossessions and evictions is that they push the price of housing down, causing more borrowers to default, which further depresses the market.

Since the 1990s, there has been a decline in state financial support for home owners and individuals have been encouraged to make their own provision through insurance such as MPPI. Governments have, however, shown an interest in intervening during the recent period of 'market collapse', and there have been some (albeit limited) efforts to stabilise the situation in the UK, including help for both current and potential home owners. In terms of broadening access to owner-occupation, we have seen a rise in the stamp duty threshold and the availability of more low-cost home ownership initiatives such as shared ownership and Homebuy. Although there are several different types of Homebuy schemes, they generally entail the arrangement of an equity loan from a housing association for part of the purchase, with a mortgage for the remainder of the purchase cost. The housing association may then enforce a charge or gain equity from the sale of the property at the current market price (Mullins and Murie, 2006).

Shared ownership has been around for some time and involves part-purchase, part-renting from a housing association. Most lenders require the scheme to allow 'staircasing' (the ability to purchase further shares from the housing association and eventually acquire full ownership) before they will lend to the customer (MacErlean, 2003). Shared ownership schemes provide a route into home ownership, but difficulties may arise for some disabled people. As Goodridge (2004, p 14) states: 'Shared Ownership leases are only recognised by Housing Benefit administrators when issued by a Local Authority or RSL; parents who share ownership with their offspring (say adults with learning difficulties) are therefore unable to claim HB to cover the rented portion.' There is also considerable debate about the effectiveness of shared ownership for the recipients (Ford and Quilgars, 2001; Caldicott, 2005; Collinson, 2005). There are some schemes, however, that have been specifically introduced for particular groups. A pilot scheme currently under way, for example, offers shared ownership to people labelled with learning difficulties. The scheme, run by Wrexham Council, the Ling Trust and Clwyd Alyn Housing Association, involves a 75 per cent interest-only mortgage for the buyer (paid for by the Department for Work and Pensions), with 25 per cent owned by the housing association (which also undertakes repairs and maintenance) that the buyer pays rent to (BBC, 2010).

Various schemes exist to help owner-occupiers experiencing problems to continue with their mortgage payments and maintain their home, some of which even involve the householder temporarily becoming a tenant. Arrangements include making lower monthly payments for a short period of time through Income Support for Mortgage Interest or the Homeowner Mortgage Support Scheme (assistance with mortgage interest payments). For more 'vulnerable' households, the safety net of the Mortgage Rescue Scheme enables the home to be sold, totally or partially, to, for example, an RSL, with the borrower becoming a tenant. The property can then be bought back if their situation improves. This support is not available to everyone, however, as many '... borrowers from unscrupulous sub-prime lenders are ineligible for help' (Marshall and Rashleigh, 2009, p 18), being regarded instead as 'intentionally homeless'. Nonetheless, in situations of this type, local authorities are required to provide temporary accommodation for those deemed to be priority need for a short period of time, a label that includes many disabled people.

Addressing financial barriers to housing

Approaches to tackling some of the more general financial barriers that disabled people encounter (relating to income and employment) have been in place for many years, and include the DDA and the New Deal for Disabled People and Access to Work schemes. In addition, there has been some recognition of the need to involve disabled people in the development of employment policy (PMSU, 2005). There is no space to discuss these initiatives here, but more information can be found in Roulstone and Barnes' (2005b) *Working Futures*. Despite some advances, recent public spending cut announcements have included significant changes to ESA and the withdrawal of support for employment (Disability Alliance, 2010a), measures that are likely to have a substantial impact on many disabled people's ability to acquire and remain in employment (as well as affecting levels of income). Such moves arguably overlook the numerous barriers to employment for disabled people (see the beginning of this chapter). Most disability employment policy has focused on supply-side restrictions to employment, and has thus aimed to make the individual more employable, despite the overwhelming evidence pointing to the negative effect of barriers within the workplace (demand-side constraints) (Roulstone and Barnes, 2005a; Piggott and Grover, 2009). It is extremely important that policymakers both acknowledge and develop strategies for tackling such barriers. Furthermore, it is worth remembering that '... policy developments in the employment field can have only a limited impact on the employment problems of disabled people' (Barnes and Roulstone, 2005, p 319). Broader social, cultural and environmental issues must therefore be considered, including barriers that arise within transport, education and support systems. Furthermore, while addressing employment barriers is essential to enabling disabled people to participate as economic actors within paid employment, Roulstone and Barnes (2005c) suggest that one way forward might be to question '... whether paid work is the only legitimate source of social citizenship and inclusion' (p 10). For them, disabled people's roles as employers of personal assistants, and the unpaid contributions made to user involvement, should be considered of social value.

More specifically in relation to income barriers to the owner-occupied sector, and in addition to the anti-discrimination legislation already in place, the introduction of initiatives such as the removal of stamp duty for disabled people who are '... purchasing a property that will require substantial alteration to meet their needs, in order to offset the additional cost of adaptation' (DRC, 2007a, p 8) may be a way forward. This may go some way to alleviating the costs associated with making a property accessible. In addition, factors relating to the source of income accepted for a mortgage application need to be tackled. Improving the perception of state benefits as income could considerably increase the opportunities of some disabled people to access the owner-occupied sector. Many disabled people are reliant on benefits for long-term income and it is therefore important to include this in affordability calculations or income multiples (Burns, 2002). A more consistent approach is needed so that either all benefits, or at least certain benefits (such as DLA), are accepted as income. For this to be achieved, government intervention may be necessary, perhaps through offering guarantees that particular benefits will remain in place (Burns, 2002). Nonetheless, underwriters are likely to remain cautious in order to lend 'responsibly' (in line with industry regulations), particularly with the transitory nature of elected governments. Perhaps, then, it is the *guidelines* or information provided to lenders about DLA and other types of benefits that need to be changed, making it clear to lenders that benefits such as DLA can be spent at the recipients' discretion (see also Chapter Six).

Another possible approach to the issue of benefits, perhaps representing a more immediate solution, might be for a more useable information system to be employed between lenders and brokers. As one industry informant from the current author's research argued, finding a lender that accepts benefits as income can be a lengthy process. He believed that future developments could include lenders improving the ways in which they publish information for mortgage brokers on how "... income is broken down ... so therefore when we key in that they have got this income and that income, and these two benefits, which lender is actually going to accept it on that basis comes up". It may be, then, that the principal search engines used by brokers (including Trigold, Mortgage Brain and EMoneyfacts) could contain more comprehensive information provided by lenders with regard to their acceptance of state benefits and allowances, for affordability calculation purposes. This may assist in locating a suitable lender for the applicant more promptly. In addition, establishing lenders that specialise in the provision of mortgages for disabled people might help to improve the situation for some, although separating the needs of disabled people from their non-disabled peers is unlikely to be the answer.

Conclusion

The interaction between disabled people's socio-economic circumstances, institutional practices and housing options demonstrates just how significant financial barriers can be in affecting housing choices and opportunities. Disabled people have long been disadvantaged as a result of the operations of the market, with the principles of marketisation arguably responding little to impairment and undermining the basis of independent living. Disabled people's disadvantaged position within the labour market can mean limited available funds for exercising choice in housing. Access to the owner-occupied sector is particularly restricted, and there is an increased likelihood of disabled people experiencing financial difficulties once in the owner-occupied sector. Consequently, disabled people may find themselves in a riskier situation than their non-disabled peers, in which the chances of mortgage arrears are increased (particularly in the current economic climate).

In addition, access to home ownership may be affected by risk assessment procedures. While it may seem that aspects of 'difference' do not feature in systems predominantly reliant on available financial resources, it appears that particular groups may be considered as higher risk. As we have seen, for example, financial institutions may perceive disabled people in a more negative light when it comes to examining applicants' eligibility for loans, especially in terms of income and employment. With the recent economic crisis, disabled people may find that the situation gets worse before it gets better, with those considered higher risk being even less likely to secure mortgage loans. The story of risk assessment is continued in the next chapter, which looks more closely at whether or not (and to what extent) certain impairments are assessed as 'higher risk'. The chapter also explores the impact that attitudes, assumptions, practices and limited understandings of disability may have on disabled people's opportunities for accessing housing across all tenures.

Summary of key issues
- The difficulties that disabled people encounter in exercising choice within housing relate to general disadvantage in the labour market (resulting in poor employment opportunities and often low incomes) and additional costs or outgoings relating to impairments and disabling environments.
- Further barriers arise in relation to risk assessment practices, with disabled people's income and employment situations often being

viewed negatively in relation to risk, which in turn affects disabled people's chances of becoming owner-occupiers.

- The 'credit crunch' has had a detrimental impact on housing for everyone, with implications for housing supply and funds for owner-occupation. For disabled people, however, it may be that housing opportunities have been further reduced, especially in relation to access to the owner-occupied sector, as mortgage lenders become even more risk averse.

Recommended further reading

FSA (Financial Services Authority) (2000) 'In or out? Financial exclusion: a literature and research review', www.fsa.gov.uk/pubs/consumer-research/crpr03.pdf

Garnett, D. and Perry, J. (2005) *Housing Finance*, Coventry: Chartered Institute of Housing.

Hagner, D. and Klein, J. (2005) 'Homeownership for individuals with disabilities: factors in mortgage decisions', *Journal of Disability Policy Studies*, vol 15, no 4, pp 194-200.

JRF (Joseph Rowntree Foundation) (2004) 'Disabled people's costs of living', *JRF Findings*, 054, www.jrf.org.uk/sites/files/jrf/054.pdf.

PMSU (Prime Minister's Strategy Unit) (2005) *Improving the Life Chances of Disabled People: Final Report*, London: Cabinet Office.

SIX

Attitudinal constraints: assumptions and institutional practices

Attitudes and assumptions held by housing providers and institutions can be just as 'disabling' as the physical and economic environment, and it is these that form the focus of this chapter. While the 'disabling' nature of attitudes in general have been discussed elsewhere in detail (Wolfensberger, 1972; Finkelstein, 1980; Barnes, 1991; Swain and Lawrence, 1994), here we consider the impact that attitudinal factors can have on disabled people's opportunities within housing. These attitudinal considerations are taken in a broad sense to include the attitudes, assumptions and stereotypes held by a range of different 'actors' about disabled people and their needs, encompassing individual perspectives as well as institutions at a wider level. Thus, the label refers loosely to the role played by individuals within housing services and organisations, as well as to the regulations and policies that guide individuals' actions towards disabled people.

While attitudes would seem to reflect individual biases and prejudice (and thus are an effect of 'agency'), they are often influenced and formed by structural factors or social processes and cultures. Housing policymakers, providers and professionals' ideas, knowledge and understanding of disability are influenced by the assumptions and stereotypes held by society in general, as are institutional practices. As a result, the policy discourse of community care (Clapham, 2005) and the dominant perception of disability play a significant role. As we have seen, the latter has largely reflected a more individual or 'medical' interpretation of disability. Here, disabled people have been cast in the role of passive recipients of services; as dependent and in need of care; as disadvantaged by their impairment, rather than wider social processes; and as different, with needs that can be considered 'special' and thus requiring separate forms of provision to the rest of the population. People with particular impairments, such as people labelled with learning difficulties, also have to contend with assumptions made in relation to their capacity to make decisions about their housing (Morris, 2004; McGlaughlin et al, 2004; Bowey et al, 2005).

At the same time, attitudes are complex and so a strong feeling about something or someone does not necessarily result in us taking action relating to it (Swain and Lawrence, 1994). In addition, while attitudes and assumptions may affect professional and practitioner behaviours towards disabled people, they are not the only influences to consider. Likely to be just as important to the actions of those working in the housing field as understandings of disability are the rules and regulations of the organisations that they work for. So, for example, anti-discrimination legislation may influence actions. This chapter therefore examines the ways in which the attitudes and assumptions held, and the practices in place among public and private sector housing providers, affect housing opportunities for disabled people. We see how attitudinal factors affect the availability of accessible dwellings, the allocation of social rented housing, the provision of private rented housing and access to the owner-occupied sector. In effect, we see how different actors work as 'gatekeepers' to various forms of housing for disabled people.

The house-building and construction industries

We saw, in Chapter Four, the ways in which disabled people experience barriers in the physical environment. This partly relates to the role of the house-building industry in constructing 'disabling' environments. Indeed, as Hanson (2004) states, '... one of the most powerful disincentives for the inclusive design of the built environment is professional attitudes and assumptions encapsulated in the distinction between general and special needs' (pp 11-12). The values, assumptions and knowledge of professionals (such as planning regulators, property developers and house builders) about disabled people are therefore extremely important in the availability of accessible housing. This is especially so in private sector housing. Research into the perceptions held by house builders has shown that understandings of barrier-free housing can be limited and that disabled people's housing needs are rarely understood or considered. This may mean that disabled people are viewed as a 'minority' group, or as the 'other'; as a group with 'special' housing needs to be met elsewhere (primarily in the social sector); as the 'expert' in the design process; or as the 'annoying consumer' (Herd, 1999; Imrie and Hall, 2001; Imrie, 2003, 2006b; Burns, 2004). One informant from the current author's research was distinctive in that she lived in New Zealand, but her experience in dealing with land agents is useful here:

'During my visits to open homes I met land agents who often rang me when they thought they had something that might suit me. None seemed to understand the needs of a person with a little sight but using a guide dog and took me to unsuitable homes. I felt they wanted me to be hidden away, to live somewhere where people would not notice me, and also felt they classed me in with older people. This is an interesting statement as the townhouse I have purchased is on a rear section with six other townhouses of various sizes, all I think with older people living in them.' (Anne)

The physical environment as it is today has therefore been built on a more individual understanding of disability, where the physical environment is deemed to suit the majority of people, and the apparent 'minority' considered to be outside of the 'norm' are required to adjust to it. Problems with accessibility are seen to stem from individual failure to adapt to the environment, rather than a social responsibility to create a physical environment that caters for bodily diversity. House builders' assumptions about the types of bodies that occupy properties therefore draw on dominant discourses of 'normal bodies' (and thus reflect wider social ideas about disabled people) (Burns, 2004). Where disabled people have been considered, it is argued that assumptions have been based on a limited conception relating to mobility impairments (Imrie, 2003; Burns, 2004).

While individual values and assumptions relating to disabled people are important, behaviours within the building and construction industry meanwhile are affected by regulations and institutional priorities such as competition, profit maximisation and risk minimisation (Rowe, 1990; Harrison with Davis, 2001; Imrie, 2003). It has been suggested that the '... limited financial impact of disabled people' (Harrison with Davis, 2001, p 119), and the fact that disabled people's housing needs are rarely heard, have contributed to the fact that disabled people are not regarded as part of the target market by the house-building and construction industries (Imrie, 2006a). With builders' priorities resting on meeting the needs and preferences of the general population, the assumption is that accessible designs or features that meet disabled people's needs might be rejected or disregarded, or perceived as 'clinical' (Cooper and Walton, 1995). As Imrie (2003) states, 'Builders assume that disability and good design are seen by consumers as antithetical ...' (p 391). Together, these factors mean that relatively few accessible properties are built in the private sector.

With the introduction of accessibility guidelines in the building regulations, there have been some improvements in the availability of properties that meet some access standards (as discussed in Chapters Two and Four). Nonetheless, research into the attitudes of builders and developers towards Part M of the English building regulations has shown that while not all builders are averse to building properties that meet more diverse needs, the regulations are generally seen simply as a means of meeting the needs of a minority (Burns, 2004), as a financial burden (Imrie and Hall, 2001) or as a way of reducing the stock of affordable housing available on the market that is needed for first-time buyers and those on low incomes (including disabled people) (Imrie, 2003). This latter point is also reflected in the views of the Home Builders Federation in relation to Lifetime Homes standards (HBF, 2008). This seems to overlook the fact that some disabled first-time buyers may require housing that is both affordable *and* accessible (see Holly's statement in Chapter Five). Overall, Imrie (2003) argues that 'Part M does little to challenge, and indeed reaffirms, the reductive conceptions of disability held by most builders' (p 402), regarding the market for accessible housing as a minority issue. The built environment, then, reinforces the exclusionary and '... normative values in our society about bodies and the spaces in which they reside' (Burns, 2004, p 768).

Rented accommodation: allocation procedures and exclusion

We focus here on housing allocation systems within renting where various assumptions about disabled people and their housing needs, as well as organisational and regulatory practices, play important roles in disabled people's housing opportunities. As we saw in Chapter Five, many disabled people lack the financial resources necessary to purchase the housing and support of their choice. As a result, many rely on social rented accommodation, which offers more affordable housing and for which assessments are carried out by local authority social services departments (England and Wales), social work departments (Scotland) or health and social service trusts (Northern Ireland) (Prideaux et al, 2008). This means that disabled people – like other individuals considered 'vulnerable' or in 'priority need' – are subject to various assessment processes in order for their eligibility or entitlement to housing to be evaluated. Disabled people may also be subject to assessments of need relating to applications for adaptations or other community care services. As Smith and Mallinson (1997) point out, people with 'health problems' and 'mobility needs' have historically been treated as 'deserving', particularly when housing stock is limited. It may be, then, that systems of support that employ processes of categorisation and measurement actually prioritise disabled people (as with some women; see Cramer, 2005). Perhaps this highlights the need for care when thinking about barriers and oppression. Nonetheless, allocation processes tend to be influenced by medical assessments reinforcing a 'medical' understanding of disability (DTZ Pieda, 2003), perhaps resulting from local authority schemes resting on ideas of achieving an improvement in health through rehousing. As we will see later, such medical assumptions can be problematic for disabled people.

In relation to applications for social housing, local authorities and housing associations use housing registers to store the details of eligible applicants. Tenants are then selected from these registers using various criteria, often through the allocation of points for particular household characteristics, with housing being offered to those with the greatest number of points and thus considered the highest priority. This 'needs-based' system replaced an allocation approach that focused on those deemed to be 'deserving' (Fitzpatrick and Pawson, 2007), moving instead towards a method that prioritised particular groups. These groups include pregnant women and families with dependent children; people living in temporary or insecure housing; people requiring housing on medical or welfare grounds; households that cannot secure settled accommodation (due to social and economic circumstances); and homeless households (Fitzpatrick and Pawson, 2007).

Some housing associations use a 'matching system' to allocate more suitable dwellings to people with particular impairments. These Accessible Housing Registers – or Disability Housing Registers as they are sometimes called – are advocated by many as a means for more effectively meeting the housing needs of disabled people and making more appropriate use of the accessible housing available (Herd, 1999; Stirling with Lloyd, 2004). These registers identify disabled people seeking accessible housing, locate accessible properties and match disabled people to suitable housing (Disability Wales, 2009). The use of matching systems has been criticised, however, for preventing disabled people from being able to exercise choice in terms of location and type of property. It merely perpetuates the notion that disabled people do not have opinions about their requirements, and regards them as a 'unit' to be fitted into a particular type of housing (Hamer, 2005b). This can be problematic as people rarely fit into neat categories of impairment or social situation, and so classification of people in this way is unlikely to yield accurate results (Means, 1996). Furthermore, it has been found that decisions on acceptance of accommodation have to be made very quickly (which can cause particular strain for mental health service users; see Goodridge, 2004 and ODPM, 2004), and where people have declined a match through such a system, they have been moved to the bottom of the waiting list. These issues tend to arise when matching systems are combined with more traditional housing registers, but they can also be used within choice-based letting (CBL) schemes (ODPM, 2006). As the Office for Disability Issues (ODI, 2008) states, Communities and Local Government (CLG):

> ... has set a target for all local authorities to have adopted Choice-Based Lettings by 2010 and is also encouraging local authorities and housing associations to make information available on the accessibility of the social housing stock through the National Register of Social Housing (NROSH). CLG will continue to encourage the adoption of Accessible Housing Registers through, for example, forthcoming statutory guidance on Choice-Based Lettings. (p 44)

Thus, as of 2010, it was expected that social housing providers would be using CBL to allocate housing, although not all local authorities solely use CBL. Some, for example, use CBL for selected properties, such as those in lower demand. CBL is a system intended to provide more information and potential choice to people seeking tenancies (although the extent of real choice over property and areas is determined by supply and weight of demand). Properties are identified and advertised in a visible way (similar to the approach taken by estate agents in the private sector) and tenants who are on the housing register may 'bid' for the properties they would like to be considered for. Property particulars, location and accessibility of the dwelling, if shown, can then be taken into account by the potential tenant, albeit within constraints of available stock (see Leeds Homes for an example: www.leedshomes.org.uk). There is some evidence that customers prefer CBL to the traditional points-based system (Brown and King, 2005) and it has been noted that the '... absence of penalties for "refusals" under CBL', relating mainly to the requirement to 'bid' for properties, is a considerable benefit (although the inability to wait may disadvantage certain households) (Fitzpatrick and Pawson, 2007, p 175). Nonetheless, as well as constraints relating to supply and demand within CBL, the '... high level of personal motivation, ability and assertion to compete' for the more accessible, well-located, desirable properties can cause difficulties for some (Goodridge, 2004, p 15). The eligibility and assessment criteria used by different authorities may also still affect disabled people's opportunities for housing.

Under the CBL system, certain requirements must be met in order for an applicant to secure a property. As Brown and King (2005) explain, the applicant must be deemed to be eligible, the landlord must perceive the property to be a suitable match for the applicant's needs (which is determined by the landlord) and the landlord must consider the applicant a priority over other applicants. As they point out, the '... landlord will also have a mechanism allowing vulnerable households to override the normal bidding system', whereby priority cases are determined '... according to statutory requirements, national guidelines and local policies' (p 64). These include the 1996 Housing Act, amended by the 2002 Homelessness Act, which makes it a requirement to give preference to certain groups (see Chapter Two). Assessment of priority cases may relate to time spent on the waiting list; points achieved through existing points-based systems; and, in some authorities, the use of 'priority cards' that give priority to statutory homeless households (Fitzpatrick and Pawson, 2007). Local authority websites offer details on their allocation procedures and often on their priority needs bands. These can include four or five different bands to which applicants are allocated according to their circumstances (for example, if they are homeless, if they live in overcrowded housing or if they have medical grounds for needing to be rehoused). Those who are successful in the bids are those who have previously been placed in the highest priority band. For two applicants in the same band, further criteria might be involved, such as local connections to the area or length of time spent on the waiting list. It may be, in some cases, that despite the presence of a CBL approach, the landlord's priority need system is the principal means for securing housing, which may be very similar to allocation policies in place prior to CBL (Brown and King, 2005; Cowan and Marsh, 2005). While eligibility criteria tend to vary among different authorities, as do the assessment procedures used, it is important to be aware of the implications of landlords' assessments of priority cases for disabled people.

As mentioned earlier, medical assessments are sometimes used within housing allocation to determine priority need cases. There are two key issues that arise here. First, criteria and goals of rehousing on medical grounds can contrast to the goal of supporting or enforcing independent living. Harrison with Davis (2001, p 121) explain, for example, that '... being disabled and in ill-health are not the same', and so assessments that use medical criteria may focus on whether an individual's impairment or 'condition' is made worse rather than whether the dwelling restricts them. Thus, professional judgement of the severity of a person's impairment determines how successful an application for housing will be, rather than housing experiences such as inaccessible dwellings, neighbourhood harassment or poor support systems (Crowther, 2000). In this way:

> ... somebody who is registered blind, and living in relatively appropriate accommodation, may be afforded higher priority than somebody who is partially sighted who is living in accommodation which is thoroughly inaccessible to them. (Derbyshire, 1998, pp 61-2)

In a similar way, it has been shown that occasional wheelchair users can be disadvantaged in allocation processes (Nocon and Pleace, 1998), and that a single disabled person living in the parental home is rarely considered a priority (Fitzpatrick, 2002). There is a tendency, therefore, for eligibility criteria to rest on questions of dependency such as '... "what is wrong *with* this person?" rather than "what is wrong *for* this person"' (Morris, 2004, p 432). Hence, while under the 1995 DDA qualifications for eligibility should not be discriminatory, Derbyshire (1998) points out that such assessments, often made by occupational therapists or social workers, are based on subjective judgements about '... the severity of one's individual situation as against another's, based purely on their "medical condition"' (p 62) and hence may contravene the legislation.

Second, such medical assessments can be problematic as while many local authorities will accept evidence provided by the applicant to determine whether someone is 'vulnerable' or in 'priority need', it has been suggested that the majority of local authorities '... seek to provide their own medical evidence' (Hunter, 2007, p 22). In such situations, they may consult a professional medical service that offers advice to housing organisations to ascertain an applicant's status. One such example is NowMedical, sometimes used by housing officers to provide a more consistent decision-making framework (Hunter, 2007). Hunter (2007) argues that such agencies generally have no contact with the applicant '... and simply give an opinion based on the written evidence that the authority has' (p 24). As such, they are based on predetermined, professionally defined categories of impairment. There are clearly problems with using such arm's-length services to inform assessment processes rather than relying on consultation with disabled people. As we will also see later in relation to risk assessment for owner-occupation, the use of such predetermined classifications can be detrimental to housing opportunities for certain impairment groups.

In addition to assumptions and practices relating to 'need' in allocation processes, notions of risk can be significant in housing entitlement. Housing providers may be influenced, for example, by assumptions relating to risk and capacity (Morris, 2004). Furthermore, similar to the way in which some disabled people are excluded from home ownership on the basis of risk assessments, Cobb (2006) notes how within rented accommodation '...justifications for exclusion, grounded in rationalities of risk and responsibility, are applied to the paradigm of the mentally disordered tenant' (p 239). Under the 1996 Housing Act, social landlords were made responsible for undertaking policies that reduce antisocial behaviour, which has been shown to have implications for some mental health service users. Antisocial behaviour has been defined by Cobb (2006) as '... low-level disorder affecting the quality of life of residents in their neighbourhoods' (p 241). The 'introductory tenancy', which is a low-security tenancy, has also had an impact here. Following greater powers for local authorities in the control of antisocial behaviour through their housing (for instance, restricting access on grounds of behaviour or granting applicants lower priority on waiting lists):

> Risk assessments are employed within allocation decision making, enabling exclusion of individuals on application. Introductory tenancies extend the operation of these processes by providing a further opportunity to assess risk in situ, while retaining the power to evict an occupant easily if that risk materialises. (Cobb, 2006, p 245)

It has been previously shown that mental health service users and people labelled with learning difficulties might disproportionately experience antisocial behaviour orders (ASBOs) which are civil orders issued against those considered to be causing distress or harrassment to others (Hunter et al, 2007). In fact, the number of people labelled with learning difficulties receiving ASBOs is so great that '... advocacy groups such as the National Autistic Society have signed up to *ASBO Concern*' (Harrison and Sanders, 2006, p 161; emphasis in original). This seems to cause some tension between the obligation for social housing landlords to control antisocial behaviour and the requirement to grant priority-need status to certain groups (including people labelled with learning difficulties and mental health service users) in the allocation of housing (Cobb, 2006).

Further issues relating to assessments of individuals relate to cases in which people living in residential care accommodation face difficulties in finding housing that enables them to live more independently. It may be, for instance, that they do not meet the allocation criteria for social rented housing, as they are regarded as being suitably housed (PMSU, 2005) and thus there is no need to explore alternative options. It has also been suggested that some people may be forced into residential care homes in different ways. For example, young disabled people may be moved into residential care in the transition from residential educational institutions, and the 2003 Community Care (Delayed Discharge) Act could potentially '... make things worse because there will be greater pressure to move people out of hospital quickly, and thus less time to explore and put in place alternatives to residential care' (Morris, 2004, p 436). Moreover, because of various rules in place, local authorities may be discouraged from supporting a disabled person to move out of residential care and live independently because of financial disincentives that can arise for the local authority in which the care home is situated (see Clements, 2007). The financial basis on which assessment processes rely has been criticised by Clements (2007), who states that:

> The base line for 'eligibility' for support is primarily a determination based upon the resources a local authority is prepared to put into the social services budget... It is at least arguable that as a society we count the cost of that which we do not value. That by constantly stressing the cost impact of supporting disabled people, the government is articulating and advancing a deeply offensive question – namely whether we can afford to allow disabled people to live independently – whether indeed the sum total of disabled people's experiences can be expressed in financial terms. (p 11)

Thus, as Morris (2004) argues, assessments of disabled people for services are mostly 'resource-led' rather than 'needs-led'. This means that even if people are eligible for support or services, at a different time or in a different local authority they may no longer be eligible if fewer resources are available.

These latter issues illustrate the conflicting demands placed on housing providers, which can affect the services offered to disabled people. Local authorities have a duty under the 1970 Chronically Sick and Disabled Persons Act and the 1986 Disabled Persons (Services, Consultation and Representation) Act to meet the housing needs of disabled people and to advertise their services (although some local authorities lack awareness of these obligations; see Herd, 1999). It has been suggested, however, that '... informal systems of discouraging applications' (Heywood with Smart, 1996, p 3) can occur due to fear of not being able to meet expressed need, as demonstrated in the current author's research by Ellen's experience of the adaptations process:

> '... it was hopeless, I couldn't open any of the windows, the kitchen was completely inaccessible, the bathroom was just manageable. I lived there for seven years after having some adaptations done. But at that time I had very little knowledge of the aids and adaptations process, and I would say that local authorities, at that time and is still the case, are very reluctant for whatever reason, to be open about what the aids and adaptations process is. So there is a great deal of having to find out for yourself.'

Local authorities can also be under pressure to let accommodation quickly, which can conflict with the sometimes lengthy processes involved in arranging adaptations or support packages for people prior to them moving into a dwelling. Again, such applications may be discouraged, or not treated as a priority in these cases (Hudson et al, 1996).

There is some suggestion that differential experiences of social renting on account of the treatment of attributes of individuals may also occur, for instance, in relation to impairment label and ethnicity (see Begum, 1992). Harrison (2003, p 56) describes a study on housing and mental health care in which 'Asian mental health service users experienced problems of inappropriate housing, difficulties with neighbours, burglaries, racist attacks or harassment, and fears for their personal safety', with little cultural sensitivity or appropriate support provided. It is possible that cultural insensitivity within service provision could represent an additional barrier to some disabled people from non-white cultural backgrounds. It has been suggested, too, that the housing offered to certain groups might be too small to accommodate all family members in some Pakistani and Indian households, or that it might be located outside of their local area with its essential ties and support networks (Molloy et al, 2003). Accordingly, accessible housing could be turned down for its unsuitability in other ways. Moreover, many disabled people are at risk of ending up in less desirable parts of social renting, just as other groups are. Experiences may then be made worse by antisocial behaviour and local estate deterioration.

Material on private landlord attitudes and practices is limited, but some brief notes are made here on available literature. In relation to securing privately rented accommodation, whether directly via the landlord who owns the property or via the letting agent, there is some suggestion that disabled people can be subject to negative attitudes and practices that fail to prioritise their needs. It would seem that disabled people's needs are rarely perceived as a priority when balanced against the accumulation of profit for the landlord in this sector. There is a tendency for private landlords to lack knowledge of disabled people's housing needs and their obligations under the DDA (Aston et al, 2007) or to employ practices that may exclude some disabled people (such as refusing tenancies to benefit claimants; see Herd, 1999). A report for the Department for Work and Pensions by Aston and colleagues (2007) looked at how landlords had been responding to the requirements laid out by the DDA and the more recent duties of 2006. They found that, in some cases, disabled people's requests for adaptations, repairs or maintenance had not been met by the private landlords. This failure to respond to adaptations requests is also supported by earlier research (see Goodridge, 2004). When interviewing private sector landlords, however, Aston and colleagues (2007) found that many claimed to have '… been able to respond to adjustment requests from tenants, although there had been some instances where they had had tenants they felt they could no longer house, usually as a result of worsening dementia or mental illness' (p 5). This might indicate some exclusion of mental health service users within private renting, but further evidence is needed here. Furthermore, Aston and colleagues (2007) point to the limited awareness among private landlords of the range of different impairments covered by the DDA, with most referring simply to issues faced by people with mobility or visual impairments. It has also been shown that many private landlords hold limited information about their disabled tenants compared with social sector landlords, although this is partly due to landlords feeling that requesting this type of information might be intrusive (Aston et al, 2007). It is important to recognise, however, that private sector landlords operate in a very different system to social landlords, with profit and financial gain, as opposed to service provision, being the primary motive. As such, '… it is understandable that the social housing sector has been proactive in the area of disability, to the extent that it is ahead of the newest legislation, while the private sector has tended to lag behind in terms of both awareness, policy and practice' (Aston et al, 2007, p 99).

Owner-occupation and risk assessment

Various studies have highlighted the impact of assumptions, values and practices of 'gatekeepers' in relation to owner-occupation (such as estate agents and financial services employees) on disabled people's access to home ownership. It has particularly been noted that those in the industry often fail to regard disabled people as customers of the sector (Burns, 2002; DTZ Pieda, 2003; Thomas, P., 2004; Hamer, 2005c, 2005d). This section draws mainly on findings from the current author's research to provide further evidence of this, demonstrating how the mortgage industry can play a role in restricting access to the owner-occupied sector for disabled people.

Looking at the role of impairments within the mortgage application process, one aim of the current author's research was to identify how different impairments are perceived within the industry, particularly whether certain impairments are regarded as higher risk than others. Earlier research provided some suggestion that impairment may be considered in relation to risk in the mortgage-lending decision. The claims of an underwriter from a large lending institution, for instance, suggested that while information on a person's impairment does not affect the decision, it is apparently 'nice to know' (Hemingway, 2004a). One could question why the provision of such personal information is necessary if it is not to be used in the decision to lend. Furthermore, the same informant also stated that if the condition was made known to them, they might be required to further investigate it, particularly in relation to whether it would affect a client's ability to meet mortgage payments. In addition, in an American study addressing underwriters' assessments of disabled people during mortgage applications, it was shown that distinctions between impairments might be made. Hagner and Klein (2005) found that a person with a physical impairment might be more successful in their application than a person with a 'developmental' impairment (which seemed to include autism). The assessment process can be especially unfavourable for disabled people if the institution has a limited understanding of disability (such as an unqualified version of the 'medical' model). An evaluation from such a narrow understanding of disability may perceive disabled people to be more of a risk than might otherwise be the case, and lead to an inability to secure insurance or a mortgage. This was illustrated in Hemingway (2004a) by the example of one informant who had not been to hospital since birth (where she had been born without limbs) but was unable to secure life insurance as she was believed to be too high a risk. For her, as a healthy non-smoker, such a situation was very frustrating, especially when she had more knowledge about her own body than an 'expert' using 'scientific' calculations.

It was important to begin the investigation by ascertaining whether a lender would know that a person had an impairment during the mortgage application. If they did not, it would be unlikely to affect the decision. Hemingway (2004a) showed, however, that it would be possible for lenders to find out this type of information in a range of ways, for example through direct questioning, or via details provided on the mortgage application form (such as source of income, especially Disability Living Allowance) or life insurance, if this was a condition of the mortgage. Moreover, at the beginning of the current author's study, contact was made with an informant from a large lending institution (a bank). This informant explained that the institution she worked for did ask about health, and so they would be aware of someone having either muscular dystrophy or multiple sclerosis, or being a mental health service user (her examples). She also stated that all of the lender's mortgage applications were dealt with face-to-face, so employees would be able to see if someone had an impairment (assuming it was a visible impairment). In addition, Chris's experiences implied that some disabled people might be required to 'declare' their impairment for their bank account records. Speaking of his telephone contact with a member of staff at the bank, he stated:

> '... she said that because of the way that I was speaking, she could tell that I had problems and then I said what do you mean by that, and she said, "Well, you're not normal, are you?" ... The inference because of the way that I was speaking that she assumed that I had all of these "problems" with the rest of my body was extremely offensive. I'm quite confident in speaking, I'm quite assured and people never comment on it...'

Chris was understandably upset not only about the negative assumptions he had experienced during the conversation, but also about the fact that he should apparently have informed the bank about his impairment. As he stated:

> '... the woman who I spoke to, the supervisor, also told me that there should be a record of the fact that I had "problems" on my bank account. This is extremely important because I do not see why my speech impairment and a difficulty with writing documents should be on my

bank account. She told me that "people with problems" had to have this sort of thing marked on their bank account when they set up the account, then she told me that the reason that I was having problems was because the bank hadn't got the record and therefore their banking services could not be accessible to me. I made the point that if I had erectile dysfunction, then why should that personal fact be at the bank? When I started banking with them when I was 11, I had only just been diagnosed as dyslexic and dyspraxic and it wasn't suggested to me and my parents that this should go on my bank record. Obviously, I could have been diagnosed as dyspraxic after this, but at the point of entry to the bank it was assumed that I should have told them this to put on record.'

Chris's experiences therefore indicate that some disabled people may be expected to 'declare' their impairment so that it can be noted on the banks records (presumably so that access needs can be met). If this is standard procedure, and the customer were then to apply for a mortgage with the same institution, the bank would clearly have impairment-specific information about that person. One cannot be certain, therefore, that this information would not then be used in the underwriting process or for other purposes, which raises questions about the right to keep such personal information from being stored, used and potentially shared by such large institutions. There are therefore several instances in which it may become apparent that a client is a disabled person and while this is not necessarily the case for all applications (and the information may not be used), it provides some indication that it could be considered.

The independent financial advisers (IFAs), mortgage brokers and lender representatives interviewed for the current author's research were asked directly whether certain impairments might be considered higher risk during risk assessment for a mortgage or whether distinctions might be made between impairments in risk assessment. While the majority of informants stated that income was the most important element to securing a mortgage, and impairment would have no bearing on the lender's decision, some differences in the treatment of impairments emerged that had the potential at worst to prevent an individual from securing a mortgage, or at best to make the process more difficult. A couple of responses suggested that the risk attributed to a person with an impairment during risk assessment was dependent on the 'degree of disability' or, as one informant from a small, independent lending institution stated, "... obviously the severity of the disablement will impinge on whatever somebody would lend, which is logical for anybody". Overall, several particular impairments stood out within the conversations as potentially being regarded as higher risk. These included 'cognitive impairments' (or 'learning difficulties'), 'mental impairments' and impairments or conditions often referred to as 'progressive', 'deteriorating' or 'degenerative'. Physical or sensory impairments were generally not discussed, which may imply that they would not be considered in the risk assessment process. We take a closer look now at some of the responses that emerged (see also Hemingway, 2010).

It would seem that people labelled with learning difficulties might face difficulties resulting from lender concerns around their ability to understand the mortgage contract. As one informant explained:

> 'Learning difficulties for us, as a financial services organisation, is probably the most difficult barrier to overcome, because how can you possibly understand how much an individual understands about the process, of whether they are mentally capable of entering into a contract?'

She stated that if the lending institution she worked for felt that someone had 'profound learning difficulties', it would be likely to refuse the mortgage. It was suggested by several other informants, however, that such concerns might be resolved by arranging a mortgage with a power of attorney. Among the underwriters interviewed, there seemed to be some inconsistency as to how to approach the issue of determining whether a potential customer has the capacity to understand the contract they are entering into. There was some consensus that it was not the role of the lender to investigate this, unless approached directly by the mortgage applicant. The responsibility apparently rests with the financial adviser, broker or solicitor in their function as intermediaries. It would therefore appear that capacity is not an aspect that is usually considered by an underwriter in relation to the application, unless raised by an agent during the mortgage assessment process.

Concerns around lending to mental health service users seemed to closely relate to what is deemed 'responsible' lending, especially in light of Financial Services Authority (FSA) regulations. One informant suggested, for instance, that if presented with someone who was a mental health service user, even if their income was sufficient, it would be necessary for the institution he worked for to assess whether they understood the responsibility they were taking on. It would appear in this case that income is not the only consideration, and so in such an example, industry perceptions of impairment quite evidently play a role in the decision to lend. The comments of the other informants who raised 'mental impairments' as a concern seemed to revolve more around legal matters, with some informants suggesting that it might actually be illegal to lend in this situation. As one informant (who worked for a large lending institution) stated: "I have never encountered the problem but the law states lenders cannot lend to individuals with mental health problems." Another informant (a mortgage broker) seemed to voice the same concerns, although he did not appear to be as confident in his claims as the previous informant:

> 'People with mental impairments, I wouldn't have thought legally, and I've got no proof of this, wouldn't legally be allowed to be party to a mortgage because they have, or if they are judged not sound of mind to be responsible for an awful lot of debt, I don't think that is going to happen. I don't think any solicitor in the world would allow that to happen.'

This uncertainty around legal implications is a concern, for it may be that applications from mental health service users are avoided at the financial intermediary level.

With regard to what the informants referred to as 'progressive' impairments – which, according to Diversus (2005) tend to include conditions such as multiple sclerosis, muscular dystrophy and cancer – or 'degenerative' or 'deteriorating' conditions, concerns were raised either in relation to presumed shorter life expectancy or the potential loss of income. Some informants believed that this could affect the loan risk and therefore present difficulties for clients with impairments classified in this way. Informants' interpretations of these classifications differed, however, with one informant describing MS and myalgic encephalomyelitis (ME) as 'degenerative diseases'. This could be construed as inaccurate, as the term 'degenerative diseases' is more commonly applied to conditions such as Alzheimer's disease, Parkinson's disease and osteoporosis. It was therefore sometimes unclear as to what impairments the informants were referring to. In terms of perceived loss of income, then, it was suggested that the lender might query the future security of the loan during the assessment process. An underwriter for a small building society explained his concerns in relation to 'responsible lending' and FSA regulations. He suggested, for instance, that higher risk might be attributed in the case of:

> '... a deteriorating disability where the level of income is
> likely to fall. Please bear in mind that I have a responsibility
> under MCOB 11 [FSA rules] to lend responsibly and
> it might be construed as being irresponsible to lend to
> someone whose financial circumstances are highly likely to
> deteriorate. I would, however, suggest that this is no different
> than lending to a person who is anticipating retirement and
> who is facing a subsequent drop in salary, as this would also
> be considered to carry a potentially unacceptable level of
> risk. In simple terms I can with a clear conscience state
> that each case is considered absolutely on its individual
> merits and irrespective of any form of discrimination and
> will be agreed primarily because we think that the loan
> will be affordable for its term based upon the foreseen
> circumstances.'

On the other hand, there was also some suggestion that progressive
impairments may not necessarily be regarded as higher risk, or at least
not be considered in this way in the loan assessment. One underwriting
informant for a large building society pointed out that while he
understood that some lenders would find this type of case difficult to
assess, his lending institution would have no problem with it, as the
loan would be secured on the property. In this way:

> '... if a situation arose where the mortgage defaulted, then
> we would ultimately repossess the property in order to
> recover the loan (whilst this may sound insensitive, this is
> the reality of the situation).'

Another informant, an underwriter for a large bank, supported this
claim. For some lending institutions, therefore, in cases where the risk
focuses mainly on the property, it may seem less important for the
individual to be assessed in relation to their impairment. It should be
noted, however, that the interviews were conducted in 2006, before
the economic downturn, so there may be less of a tendency today
to rely on a property to secure a loan. Although not the case for all
institutions, it seems that there is a general understanding that people
with particular impairments may encounter additional difficulties,
or barriers, especially on account of two different factors: first, the
assumed ability to earn (particularly in relation to perceived progressive
conditions) and second, the assumed ability to understand the contract.
It also appears that perceived additional risk might be attributed to the

alleged reduced life expectancy of people with certain conditions or impairments, albeit again in relation to the client's income.

Concerns were also raised over the classification of impairments, with evidence of some confusion between learning difficulties/cognitive impairments and 'mental' impairments or mental health service users, as the following two examples demonstrate:

> 'I think it's awful that they use the term learning difficulties to refer to someone who is mentally handicapped' (IFA)

> '... mental disability does have an effect on lending criteria in the sense that mental disability ... people who are thick, people with an IQ in say, the 70s, 80s, and people with an IQ in the 50s, 60s normally would be under care any how, they never would be working, and they're extremely likely not to have a mortgage. So lenders will not lend to that, end of story.' (IFA)

This latter quotation also highlights some of the negative assumptions made about disabled people. Such lack of distinction between 'cognitive' impairments (also referred to as learning difficulties) and 'mental' impairments is evident in the DDA, which may have implications for the ways in which people with particular impairments are treated by lending institutions and by other industry employees. The same is true of attitudes towards, and understandings of, progressive impairments. This lack of understanding of the labels applied to particular clients is an important finding in itself, and suggests that the categories used within the industry may in fact be inaccurate. Uncertainty around the labelling of specific conditions may have important implications for their use within financial services, whether used within mortgage appraisals or life insurance (as also shown in Chapter Two in relation to the DDA). The responses of several of the disabled people interviewed also showed how the use of computer software that is incapable of distinguishing sufficiently between impairments can have negative consequences in some mortgage applications, effectively 'screening out' people with particular impairments. As Carol recalled:

> 'It was actually through [bank name concealed] that I applied for this a couple of years back. Then they go through the health questions, and I answer them and they said, "Oh, you've got multiple sclerosis then," and I said, "Excuse me, I've not." They then said, "Well, our computer says that if

you've got a visual impairment that you've described as optic neuropathy, then our computer says you've got multiple sclerosis." I told them they could go and do the other thing basically! So, I was anticipating those kind of problems because unfortunately, too many financial institutions do have all this actuarial data just on a computer that can't make a sensible commonsense decision.'

One informant from a Nottinghamshire-based organisation for disabled people explained his thoughts on this:

'I think that is more about lack of understanding and lack of knowledge and is about attitude, because attitude has a heck of a lot to do with it. That is an old one of "computer says …"! "Oh well, the computer told me," [laughs], well hang on a minute, there must have been a human who put the information in there at some point!'

The findings suggest that some institutions consider impairment within the mortgage application, particularly in relation to perceptions about the applicant's capacity to understand the contract or commitment, and the assumed effect on employment circumstances (or ability to earn). It was difficult to determine a 'hierarchy' of impairments because of the inconsistency in institutional practices (and this may not be desirable anyway), but it was evident that certain impairments were both perceived and treated differently by some institutions, which could have a negative effect on some disabled people's applications for a mortgage. It therefore appears that while impairment is not formally considered in risk assessment, distinctions are sometimes made between disabled people, and these may have some effect on the underwriting decision to ensure that money is lent responsibly.

Addressing attitudinal barriers to housing

As we have seen, housing practitioners, providers and professionals across all tenures act as potential 'gate keepers' to housing and related services for disabled people. As such, the assumptions they hold about disabled people and their understanding about what disability actually is can be crucial to the housing options and pathways of disabled people. Challenging negative stereotypes and limited knowledge is, then, extremely important. While attitudes are a product of wider social discrimination, and the aim should be to address these as a whole and at an early stage, there are some more specific measures that, if applied, may assist more swiftly in the reduction of barriers created by the housing, building and financial industries. Addressing attitudinal barriers requires an approach that prioritises greater involvement of disabled people in decision making and in the planning, management and delivery of services; implements training for housing providers, practitioners and policymakers; and challenges rules, regulations and codes of practice within institutions. In terms of greater involvement of disabled people, it has long been suggested that disabled people need to be more involved in housing planning, management and provision (MacFarlane and Laurie, 1996), and, as we will see later in relation to housing need, user involvement is essential to ensuring that disabled people's housing needs are met. Service providers must, therefore, understand the importance of consultation, and involvement, with disabled people and the development of user-led services should be encouraged within local authorities. We are yet to see if substantial developments have been made in this respect by the Disability Equality Duty (DED) in relation to housing.

Research has shown that knowledge of the DDA and duties under the Act tends to be limited among landlords in the private sector (Aston et al, 2007) and among financial services and estate agent staff (Hemingway, 2008), although it would be reasonable to expect a better level of understanding given the most recent changes to the legislation. It has also been shown that architects, builders and planners lack understanding of the needs of disabled people and barrier-free design (Herd, 1999) and that social housing provider staff sometimes lack understanding of disabled people's needs (Molloy et al, 2003). There would therefore appear to be a strong case for informing providers, practitioners and policymakers within the housing field via specific measures such as disability equality training (DET), although legislation may be required to ensure its enforcement (for more information on DET, see Gillespie-Sells and Campbell, 1991; French, 1992; Swain and Lawrence, 1994). There may also be scope for introducing DET into existing mandatory qualification assessments in the financial sector. Training may also be required in the use of communication equipment (such as hearing loops) and in communicating with, and assisting, different groups.

Challenging rules, regulations and codes of practice within institutions is also necessary if we are to see a reduction in the types of constraint mentioned above. The allocation procedures used within social renting, for instance, highlight some important issues around defining need. As we have seen, housing providers have begun to take more account of diversity when assessing need and distributing resources, with the emergence of 'priority' and 'special needs' categories. These have tended, however, to be based on stereotyped assumptions and individual or 'medical model' understandings about disability, as well as being predominantly professionally defined (which can contrast with the needs and wishes of the householders). This has often resulted in separate provision in specially designed properties. Such an approach, aside from being largely exclusionary, fails to acknowledge that disabled people's needs might involve more than physical accessibility. It may be, for instance, that the physical design of the dwelling is less important to the disabled person than having the same housing options as their non-disabled peers or, for instance, choosing the location of the property, especially in relation to work, schools or particular amenities (for some useful illustrative examples, see Bull and Watts, 1998, pp 14-16). Furthermore, fundamental human needs – relating to the norms and values of society – are often neglected by professional definitions in favour of classifying need according to 'functional' necessities (feeding, bathing and going to the toilet) (Heywood with Smart, 1996).

Issues of relativity are also important to discussions about housing need, as not only does the 'home' mean different things to different people, but people also require different things of it, and so housing policy needs to take account of such diversity. Difference may relate, for instance, to gender, with different housing needs for men and women. There may also be variations in terms of age, as children, young people, working-age adults, and older people tend to have differing needs and preferences. For example, community care policies that provide services to help disabled people remain in their own homes may not be suitable for all. As Means (1996) points out, '... the achievement of citizenship for many younger physically disabled people requires them to leave the parental home in order to achieve independent lifestyles. Staying put is not the route to independence for everyone' (p 228). Approaches to addressing housing need should also take account of diversity in relation to ethnicity, relationships, sexuality, culture, religion and impairment, while issues of 'simultaneous oppression' (see Chapter One) highlight the need to consider different aspects of people's identities – such as age and impairment – together (see the report by Oldman and Beresford, 2000, on disabled children). Thus, assessing housing need is complex, and housing practitioners and providers should avoid simple associations between need and specific impairment. Consideration must be given to social, financial and environmental needs, as well as to housing quality for the disabled person and their family (as need can operate within family contexts). In addition, more inclusive approaches to defining housing need that take account of human needs should be developed (as shown earlier).

The complexities inherent in defining housing should also underline the importance of involving disabled people (including disabled children) in assessments and the provisions made, but this has not always been part of the decision-making process. The experience of Rebecca from the current author's research is useful here. Rebecca, a wheelchair user, claimed that a perfectly accessible kitchen had been ripped out when she first moved into her social rented property, only to be replaced by an inaccessible one. She even stated that the landlords failed to put any kitchen drawers into the kitchen and when she enquired as to why, "... they said well, you're an invalid, and invalids don't eat with cutlery, they use their hands! I said well what about my child and my husband? Again I got, well you're an invalid, you get meals on wheels don't you?" Such derogatory attitudes seem to have been commonplace in Rebecca's experience, and while this is clearly an extreme example of poor treatment, it highlights the impact that negative attitudes and poor consultation can have on disabled people's housing circumstances. It seems clear that the negative experience reported by Rebecca (relating to the creation of an inaccessible kitchen), and the unnecessary expense incurred, could have been avoided if the council had actually discussed the adaptations they were carrying out with her and considered what she required from her dwelling. It has been suggested, therefore, that the assessment process, and housing services for disabled people in general, should be more 'user led' (Means, 1996; Clements, 2007), with greater involvement of disabled people in public service decision making. This has been increasingly reflected in legislation over the years (such as the 1989 White Paper on community care and the DED, which actively promotes the involvement of disabled people within public services) and has resulted in the emergence of more 'needs-led' assessment, 'user-led' services and greater 'user involvement'.

User involvement takes many forms and is achieved in different ways but, regardless of the approach used, it benefits the user through enabling them to take control of their own needs, have their say and ultimately challenge the balance of power. Within the field of disability service development, user involvement is basically seen as active engagement or participation of service users in shaping public sector services. Thus, rather than just being consulted, disabled people should be involved in decision making, planning and delivery of the services that affect their lives. Nonetheless, the level at which this is achieved within different organisations and institutions varies significantly, and levels of involvement can be constrained in different ways for different groups. Access or communication issues can exclude some people (Crowther, 2000), for instance, or, as the Joseph Rowntree Foundation (JRF, 2001) found, discrimination and lack of – or insecure – funding can prevent participation. In addition, while various agencies may wish to implement greater user involvement to inform their service provision, they may find that '... the absence of effective structures for involvement' (Cooper, 2005, p 75) and limited resources (Means, 1996) prevent their effectiveness. Indeed, as Cooper (2005, p 75) states, '... there would appear to be a chronic tension at the heart of community care policy between two contradictory objectives – the containment of public spending and the stated aim of offering needs-led provision'. Overall, there has certainly been a positive drive to deliver services that are better informed by the actual users, especially with the DED, but the way in which this is achieved requires further assessment, monitoring and development if significant changes are to be witnessed here. Moreover, the DED does not apply to the private sector, despite the fact that important changes could be made here. Furthermore, public expenditure cuts may result in a decline in support for consultation and involvement of disabled people, as we have seen in relation to the recent abolition of the Disabled Passengers Transport Advisory Committee.

Specifically within financial institutions, more account needs to be taken of the dangers of risk evaluation. At the same time, lending institutions must protect themselves against genuine risk and so a balance needs to be established between risk minimisation and fair lending. It is important to recognise that these organisations are a product of their time and conditions. The structure of society, based on a capitalistic or market-led economy in which businesses are primarily profit driven, is one of the underlying explanations for the development of processes of risk management. Institutions are driven by profit, but also, as Harrison (1979) highlights, by growth and security, and these factors combine to inform the practices and perspectives of the industry. Nonetheless, the discriminatory processes of the present period need to be understood and challenged, if equality of opportunity for all members of society is to be achieved. Addressing barriers in risk assessment therefore requires a combination of institutional action, education and government intervention. Training (as mentioned earlier) and the provision of information and guidelines for financial services staff, in relation to 'disabling' and discriminatory practices, specific impairments and income from state benefits to be used within risk assessment, would be beneficial here. At present within the industry the use of classifications could be more accurate but perhaps financial institutions should not be allowed to categorise in the first place. With change to practices, much will rest on available financial resources to accommodate it. Individual institutions may feel that the cost of implementing change, such as the training of all staff, is too great and thus is not possible. The government could play a role in encouraging and funding the kinds of change that need to be made (via targets to provide motivation and impetus), particularly in terms of improving disability equality. Regulatory changes and the introduction of initiatives such as Treating Customers Fairly (TCF) have proved to be important developments for promoting good practice in financial service provision, although the effectiveness of the latter has been limited to date. While representing positive progress, TCF principles need to be developed further if they are to really make a difference to the opportunities of excluded groups.

Shared examples of good practice offer the potential for housing providers in both the public and private sectors to learn from each other, to transfer good practice from one context to another and to provide ideas and workable guidelines for practitioners and policymakers. Research by Aston and colleagues (2007, p 101), for instance, suggests that sharing good practice examples among landlords could improve provision for disabled people, which could be encouraged via:

> ... local forums or other networking opportunities which would appeal to the private as well as the social sector or through online discussion sites, where good practice examples could be provided, and the relative costs and benefits of making adjustments could be discussed.

Various good practice guides have been written on housing provision for disabled people over the years, and these have offered important insights, recommended procedures and good practice examples (see for instance, Fiedler, 1988; Morris, 1990; Laurie, 1991; Derbyshire, 1998; Crowther, 2000; Bevan, 2002; Goodridge, 2004). Laurie (1991) discusses public and private sector good practice, Crowther (2000) offers advice to social landlords (including a disability discrimination check list), Shelter provides various good practice downloads via its website and Goodridge (2004) offers an extensive list of sources on good practice. (See also some of the websites listed in the References at the end of the book that offer links to specific organisations, agencies and good practice examples.) Sharing of good practice is useful not just nationally, but also internationally, and we have a lot to gain from exploring the approaches and policies pursued in other countries (see Chapter Two).

There are, then, some potential strategies for improving attitudes and practices within housing provision. As mentioned earlier, however, such targeted approaches to attitudes should not be at the expense of addressing negative attitudes and institutional discrimination against disabled people on a broader social level. As such, disabling structures and individual actions must continue to be challenged to promote more inclusive practices for disabled people at all levels of society.

Conclusion

We have seen how the social model of disability can be used to highlight possible restrictions that arise from the assumptions and practices of individual actors and of institutions. Disabled people are subject to negative assumptions and stereotypes about their preferences, needs and capacity to make decisions across all areas of housing. Notions of dependency, 'care' and personal tragedy, and limited conceptions of human bodies, have had a profound effect here. The words of one of the informants from the current author's research highlight the effects that such assumptions can have on disabled people:

> 'We are not the problem, but however much you believe that in your heart of hearts, the having to face it every single day ... it's like being the celebrity but without the money, in that wherever you go, for those of us with visible impairments, you walk into a room and everybody notices you ... you can't walk anywhere without people looking at you with curiosity, disgust, whatever. Its difference, but it's how they react to difference, because lots of people react to difference positively, but with impairment I think without exception it's a negative reaction. A lot of disabled people don't have the energy to battle with that every single day.... Because it's all about having to go over, to overcompensate for everybody all of the time. Somehow, we are expected to be able to make someone feel comfortable about our impairment, which is outrageous!... All of this impacts on why finding housing is difficult, because people would rather that we didn't exist, that we were something that people didn't have to think about.' (Ellen)

Thus, negative or limited attitudes or assumptions about disabled people lead to problems relating to inaccessible housing, housing allocation processes, eligibility for privately rented accommodation and risk assessment in access to owner–occupation. In addition, we have seen again how the concept of risk is used by housing and finance providers to mark out particular groups as more 'vulnerable' or 'risky', which can lead to greater disadvantage for some.

It has been shown that perceptions of disabled people across all housing tenures appear to imply an individual or 'medical' model understanding of disability. This could potentially affect practices and behaviours, which may disadvantage disabled people both in their encounters with housing staff and their applications for housing (whether for a tenancy or a mortgage). Disablist attitudes and practices can also interact with other oppressions such as racism and sexism (hence reflecting what is often referred to as simultaneous oppression). It may be, then, that dominant social perceptions of disabled people affect the provision of services, but it is also likely that housing and finance providers are influenced in their practices and decisions by the rules and regulations of their organisation or their job (particularly with the DDA legislation in place). Thus, the attitudes, assumptions and practices of housing and mortgage providers are crucial in disabled people's housing opportunities, and service providers therefore need to recognise the 'gate-keeper' role that they play in access to resources for disabled people (Begum, 1992). We take a look now at the impact that the factors raised in relation to physical, communication, financial and attitudinal matters can have on the meanings attributed to 'home', and summarise key findings presented throughout the book.

Summary of key issues
- Attitudes and assumptions held by service providers within the housing field about disabled people can be just as disabling as the physical and financial environment. Stereotypes relating to dependency, personal tragedy, care, minority and 'special' needs, as well as 'medical' model assumptions, can be important here, as can assumptions relating to capacity and risk.
- Attitudes and assumptions are not the only factors affecting behaviour, as the rules and regulations governing the practices of organisations and institutions are also significant.
- There is a need for an improved understanding of the social basis of disablement, and greater level of consultation with disabled people about their needs, while at the same time working towards the greater involvement of disabled people in service delivery and decision-making processes.

Recommended further reading

Aston, J., Hill, D. and Williams, C. (2007) *Landlords' Responses to the Disability Discrimination Act*, Leeds: Department for Work and Pensions.

Crowther, N. (2000) *Overcoming Disability Discrimination: A Guide for Registered Social Landlords*, London: RNIB and the Housing Corporation.

Harrison, M. with Davis, C. (2001) *Housing, Social Policy and Difference: Disability, Ethnicity, Gender and Housing*, Bristol: The Policy Press.

Herd, D. (1999) *A New Threshold for Disabled People? A Report by the Housing Reference Group for Scotland*, Scotland: Disability Rights Task Force.

Stirling, T. with Lloyd, D. (2004) *'There's More to it Than Wide Doors': The Case for a Disabled Persons Housing Service in South East Wales*, Wales: Disability Wales.

Swain, J. and Lawrence, P. (1994) 'Learning about disability: changing attitudes or challenging understanding?', in S. French (ed) *On Equal Terms: Working with Disabled People*, Oxford: Butterworth Heinemann, pp 87-102.

SEVEN

Creating the 'home' in a society of barriers

The holistic nature of the disability and housing relationship has often been overlooked in favour of prioritising physical matters, but this book has drawn attention to the many interlocking and overlapping variables that affect disabled people's housing choices and opportunities. As we have seen, UK governments have acknowledged aspects of the housing problems facing disabled people, but there is much work still to be done. While some of these issues, such as financial constraints, may be shared by other low-income groups, there are various physical and attitudinal barriers that are distinctive to disabled people. There are also some groups who experience particular disadvantage. This chapter takes a look at some of the themes addressed throughout the book and summarises key messages, beginning with an overview of what the social approach to disability has shown us about choices, opportunities and barriers within housing for disabled people. It then examines the impact that factors discussed in earlier chapters (relating to inaccessible environments, labour market positions and attitudinal constraints) can have on a person's sense of 'home'. It shows how these factors affect disabled people not just in terms of housing choices, opportunities and pathways, but also in terms of their *experiences* of housing or *meanings* of home. Finally, it summarises key issues to provide an accessible overview for practitioners, policymakers and researchers within the housing and disability fields.

Disabled people's access to housing: a social model perspective

The emergence of the social model of disability during the 1970s and 1980s was a crucial development in disabled people's lives, and although subject to critique over recent years, it arguably remains an extremely important tool with which to assess the social exclusion of disabled people. It is hoped that this book has made evident the significance of the social model in the case of housing, demonstrating the ways in which systematic processes and perspectives affect disabled people's housing opportunities, and how barriers arise within important decision-making contexts. We have seen, for instance, that while the social rented sector provides affordable, accessible housing, and often confers disabled people with priority need status, the limited housing stock, high demand and resource-led allocation and adaptations procedures may mean that very few disabled people have access to housing adequately suited to their needs. Furthermore, housing provision can be inconsistent across different local authorities, and particular groups can be subject to limited assumptions that affect the support or services they receive (for example, in relation to impairment label or ethnicity). The private rented sector may offer greater choice and flexibility in general than social renting, but options for some disabled people can be limited. There are few accessible properties in the sector and despite increased responsibilities on private landlords to make reasonable adjustments through the 1995 Disability Discrimination Act, adaptations may still be constrained by landlord restrictions, property types and locations, and tenant concerns in requesting them. Furthermore, meeting higher private sector rents on lower incomes may prove difficult, and some benefit claimants may find that they are barred from private renting by certain landlords. Similarly, while owner-occupied housing tends to be associated with greater control, security, investment and choice, and is the aspiration of many, disabled people may encounter barriers that restrict access to the tenure. These include limited accessible properties, poor affordability and processes of risk assessment that may affect ability to secure a mortgage. It would seem, then, that the public sector provides greater opportunities for access to housing, partly relating to better monitoring and regulation. It may be that disabled people's housing options within the private sector could be improved with similar regulatory pressures and closer monitoring, but it is difficult to see how this would be balanced against profit maximisation.

Disabled people and their families therefore encounter difficulties within housing at all levels, within all tenures and across constraints that we can categorise as physical, financial, attitudinal and related to communication (although these overlap). There may be additional barriers, too, relating to lack of support that may prevent some people, particularly young disabled people, from accessing more independent living options (see French and Swain, 2006). Perhaps there is another barrier here that needs to be mentioned – that of 'internalised oppression' (Mason, 1990; Rieser, 1990; Barnes et al, 1999) or 'felt stigma' (Barnes, 2006), described as '... the cumulative emotional and psychological implications of social exclusion ...' (Barnes, 2006, p 18). It is important to recognise that this is not a barrier created by disabled people, but rather is a consequence of social exclusion and disadvantage experienced by disabled people. The effect of such 'internalised oppression' may be that disabled people are less likely to challenge the discrimination or exclusion encountered, and in the case of housing, this may prevent their attempts to enter the housing tenure of their choice through fear of being rejected by, for instance, a mortgage lender (even though this may not be actual or based on experience) (see Molloy et al, 2003). In a similar way, French (1994) argues that disabled people living in institutional accommodation may – through a 'self-fulfilling prophecy' whereby people live up to others' expectations of them – sustain staff assumptions and thus reinforce '... erroneous stereotypes and prejudices which justify the institution's existence' (p 122). As a consequence of these many different barriers, disabled people may have restricted access to the opportunities and services that are readily available to non-disabled people, not merely because of actions by specific agents and institutions, but also because of underlying assumptions and practices that are difficult to change in the short term.

When we look at structure, we therefore look at social barriers. The material in this book has shown the extent of the constraints that disabled people may encounter through focusing on these social elements, and thus confronting the established restrictions within the institutional mainstream. We have seen how a focus on structure, and the 'barriers' approach, can present a more accurate picture of the many disabling processes and practices at work within housing (in contrast to approaches focusing on individual causes of disadvantage), but there is also some need for caution. Focusing too tightly on barriers can prevent identification of the ways in which structural factors can provide opportunities and choices, and so a broad approach is required that acknowledges positive effects. Socio-economic environments can be 'enabling' and supportive and can offer opportunities (an examination of differential treatment can provide important insights here). In addition, the full implications of structural factors are not necessarily evident from simply talking about collective oppression or commonalities of outcomes for individuals, as disabled people's experiences may vary, as a result of institutional practices and mechanisms. Inconsistency of treatment was particularly evident in disabled people's dealings with the financial services industry, especially for people with certain impairment labels (and it is here that notions of risk also play an important role). It was shown, for instance, that risk assessment procedures might involve processes whereby perceptions of impairments become the foundation for disablement. There has been much debate within disability studies with regard to the importance of considering individual impairment within the social model, but this book has shown that it is possible to identify impairment-specific issues using a social model approach, by focusing on the external reactions to a person's impairment rather than those restrictions associated with the impairment itself. Therefore, the 'disabling' consequences of *perceptions* and *classifications* of impairments should be acknowledged.

It is argued, then, that the social model – despite its many challenges – is a valuable tool for action within policy. A focus on structural barriers has helped to shift understandings of disability away from the individual, to demonstrate how disability results from social and economic disadvantage. This provides important insights into welfare systems and policy provision. Practitioners and policymakers would benefit from assessing institutionalised practices from this perspective, in addition to understanding the importance of utilising experiential information (consulting and involving disabled people) to inform developments in policies, practices and processes. As Clapham (2005) argues, policymakers need to provide households with greater choice and control over their housing pathways, and to consider people's lifestyles, identity, meanings of home and self-esteem in housing policy. In this way, disabled people's own voices and experiences should be central to informing service provision. As well as identifying both the positive and negative practices that a social model approach may uncover, this book has shown why there is a need for a more detailed exploration of existing barriers. Such an approach helps to emphasise the mechanisms and institutional practices at work that may result in the different treatment of individuals, and thus offers further insights into welfare provision. The social approach to disability, then, arguably continues to provide a valuable way to challenge social inequality.

Experiences of housing: meanings of 'home' for disabled people

As we have seen, the difficulties that disabled people encounter in relation to inaccessible environments, income, labour market position, attitudes, assumptions and institutional practices, many of which non-disabled people do not encounter, have a negative impact on opportunities for accessing housing. These factors affect not just housing opportunities and pathways, but can also have a direct impact on feelings of 'home'. In relation to the physical environment, for example, it may be that inadequately designed houses, poorly implemented adaptations and inaccessible neighbourhoods and transport systems affect relationships, independence, autonomy and control that are central to a person's sense of home. It has been suggested that disabled people's experiences have been neglected in previous research into the meanings of home, although several recent studies have introduced important findings in this area (see Tamm, 1999; Hanson et al, 2002; Tipper, 2003; Borg et al, 2005; Heywood, 2005; Imrie, 2006a; French and Swain, 2006). These studies have pointed to factors such as the role of accessibility, safety and professional intervention in disabled people's sense of home. It has also been suggested that meanings of home may be affected by its '... relative significance ... in terms of daily time spent there' (Harrison, 2004b, p 61). This is important for disabled people because, as Hamer (2005a, p 5) suggests, '... low incomes, low rate of employment and lack of mobility mean they are likely to spend more time at home than non-disabled people'. As we saw earlier, the home is also important for older people for the same reason (see also Wahl et al, 2009). Furthermore, the dwelling may be the only place where disabled people can escape from perceptions of themselves as the 'other' (although it may also reinforce a sense of 'otherness'; see later) (Burns, 2004). Here, we explore some of the material from the existing literature, supplemented by findings that have emerged from the current author's interviews with 20 disabled people. We focus now on the impact of four key elements: the physical environment, attitudinal factors, affordability (relating to tenure) and impairment-related issues.

The physical environment

We saw in Chapter Four the importance of the physical design of housing in disabled people's opportunities to access accommodation, but it can also play a hugely significant role in the meaning ascribed to home. This is because the '... emotions connected to the home are intimately bound up to housing design' (McKechnie, 2006, p 4) and as such, the house is '... more than just a neutral physical location' (Clapham, 2005, p 138). As two informants in the current author's research stated:

> '... a property where I can be one hundred per cent independent is just about everything... I suppose that's what having the home that I've got now means to me, in that it allows me to be the person that I want to be because I'm not having to rely on other people, I'm not having to ask people to do things for me, I can do everything that I need to do, whereas for the first 20 years of my life, my life was the absolute opposite to that. Everything had to

be done by other people because things were inaccessible, always having to ask, always having to be grateful, always having to seek permission. But in a property where I have everything at the right level, I can, in a sense, have choice and control.' (Ellen)

'To me it has got to be accessibility, it has got to be a place where I can do things without having to ask people, and where I know where everything is as well ... home, it's in an environment that I can exist, that negates the effect of disability as much as possible.' (Steven)

This desire for an accessible environment that facilitates independence is something a non-disabled person would be less likely to mention in their feelings of 'home', and reflects the impact of a disabling society on people with impairments. If living in an accessible dwelling (or a suitably adapted house; see Heywood, 2005), with inaccessible environments everywhere else (including the houses of families and friends), the home may constitute the one place in which independence can be exercised. As Ellen put it, "... I think for many of us, when the outside world can be hostile and can be deeply inaccessible and discriminatory, the one place I know isn't, is here." This may also mean, however, that disabled people become socially isolated and restricted to the dwelling, and consequently the opposite effect might be had; where the dwelling fails to constitute 'home' for the inhabitant. As Imrie (2006a) found among some of his respondents in his study of accessible housing, '... the home had become the place of confinement and, far from being a haven, was, in part, a signifier of a life that had been lost' (p 101).

As we have seen, there are limited accessible properties available within all tenures. Disabled people may therefore be forced to live in inaccessible dwellings, which may have a considerable impact on the sense of home that can be achieved. Inaccessible housing may compromise independence and affect common associations with home, such as security, safety and comfort (Heywood, 2005), autonomy or spontaneity (especially for disabled children; see Allen et al, 2002), and sanctuary and privacy. It may be, for instance, that day-to-day activities that prepare people for the outside world (such as washing, using the toilet and dressing) are restricted or prevented by inadequately designed environments. Imrie (2006a) highlighted the experience of one respondent, Ann, who was '... constrained in using her downstairs WC because there is no guarantee that she can use it without being seen by another family member' (p 102). Similar cases are discussed by

Heywood (2005) where adaptations to properties have proved either inadequate or requests for adaptations have been declined, resulting in reliance on family and friends to assist with 'intimate personal tasks'. As Heywood (2005, p 543) explains, '... a young middle-aged woman, desperately distressed at being denied bathing adaptations said she "did not expect her children to wash her", meaning that she did not want them to; did not want to turn roles on their head'. Another woman felt that she had to ask a neighbour to empty her commode prior to visits from her grandchildren:

> Few people would want to ask a neighbour to empty a commode, because such a task might alter the relationship with the neighbour and set up an unacceptable degree of obligation. But it seems this woman made this hard choice as a price worth paying in order to preserve the even more precious relationships with her children and grandchildren. (Heywood, 2005, p 543)

Standardised housing that fails to cater for diversity in the human body can therefore result in some disabled people experiencing '... the home as a series of "disembodied spaces" or places that are designed in ways that are rarely attentive to their physiological and bodily needs and functions' (Imrie, 2006a, p 94). This could also mean that parts of the house remain unused.

While adapted properties can restore many positive associations with home, Heywood (2005) found that this might not occur if the occupant is not adequately consulted in the adaptations process. In such cases, adaptations may fail to fully address the needs of the occupant or their family (such as the need for space), and thus have a negative effect on relationships and meanings of the home (Heywood, 2005). Adaptations may also have a negative impact on the 'feel' of certain spaces within the home (Clapham, 2005). Furthermore, the aesthetic qualities of the dwelling (such as decor, possessions and cleanliness) can be important in creating a sense of home, but may be compromised for some disabled people by the design of healthcare devices and equipment. As Angus and colleagues (2005, p 171) state: 'Objects associated with healthcare are not decorative. They are constructed from materials that are durable, easy to clean and maintain. Their uses are concerned with bodily functions, which are usually secluded from sight, and they link the user with illness, infirmity and indignity'. Similarly, it has been argued by Imrie (2006a) that aspects of the design of housing could '... amplify and draw attention' to impairments (p 99) (see also Freund,

2001), which might reinforce a sense of 'otherness' (Burns, 2004). A person's possessions, and the placing of these, may also be important to feelings of 'home'. It may be, for example, that in addition to associations with memories, possessions contribute '... to the personalisation of space in that they can enhance our feeling of being in control of our environment, increase our self-confidence, provide us with feelings of security' (Clapham, 2005, p 139). It has been suggested that for some people, particularly those with visual impairments, the awareness of possessions, along with the familiarity of their positioning, is especially important in feeling at home, which has implications for the activities of support workers in the dwelling (Angus et al, 2005).

The immediate neighbourhood or local residential environment can be just as important as the dwelling itself in meanings of home, as shown in the responses of informants in the current author's research (see also Chapter Four). This is particularly so with regard to the general accessibility of the physical environment, which can enhance feelings of safety, security, independence and inclusion in the community. In poorer areas, however, feelings of safety and security may be particularly difficult to achieve for some. It has been suggested, for instance, that processes of residualisation and subsequent limited housing stock mean that disabled people can be located on the poorer, less desirable, 'run-down' estates (Harrison with Davis, 2001), which may pose particular problems for some disabled people (Oldman and Beresford, 2000). The availability of shops, amenities and services can also be important. Robert stated that these factors were central to the meaning of 'home' for him and his partner, especially as they both have visual impairments. He stated that the place where he lives "... is still a village, even though we are bordered by all the motorways, and its still got a village feel about it ... we've got a local shop, a supermarket, butchers, bakers, post office and everybody knows us. It's all together; pubs, clubs ... it's all in a small area." The matter of transport, in terms of being in close proximity to a main bus route, was also raised by several informants in the current author's research who had visual impairments. As Shahina stated "... that's what is important to me, the access, transport access is very important". Physical factors that affect meanings of home are therefore about more than just the dwelling itself, and may include the accessibility of the local environment, the availability of accessible public services and amenities and the proximity of good transport links.

Attitudes and practices

Interactions with professionals, providers of support and neighbours may also affect meanings of home for disabled people. This may be because support from assistants or professionals allows disabled people to achieve a greater sense of home, or it may be because interactions with such personnel have a negative effect on issues of control, privacy or safety. With people's homes increasingly becoming the site for 'care' and support (Dyck et al, 2005), the relationship an individual has with the home may be affected when 'professionals', support workers or other employees visit. This may affect the association of home with notions of 'retreat' or the private sphere. As Dyck and colleagues (2005, p 181) state, 'Somewhat ironically, when the home becomes increasingly important as the core site of everyday life for those whose mobility and activities are constrained, it also becomes its most "public"'. This lack of privacy may affect both disabled people and their families, and in such situations members of the household have to '... adjust to the working hours of the professionals' and find themselves '... exposed to the gaze of many' (Tamm, 1999, p 52). A similar situation may arise for many homeless people (a large proportion of whom are mental health service users), with privacy being affected by constant surveillance in homelessness shelters. Homeless people's sense of home may be further affected by short stays in shelters and temporary accommodation and lack of continuity in day-to-day routines (Padgett, 2007). The presence of carers, professionals and support workers affects not only the privacy that can be achieved in the dwelling, but also control over the arrangement of the home environment. This may be detrimental where the ability to control the home environment and create boundaries between personal and 'caring' spaces is crucial to maintaining a sense of home (Dyck et al, 2005).

Interactions with professionals may affect meanings of home in other ways as a result of poor consultation, the treatment of disabled people according to perceptions of personal attributes (such as ethnicity or sexuality) and restrictions placed on support workers. French and Swain (2006) discuss, for instance, how poor communication on the part of occupational therapists, and their failure to consult with disabled people may lead to inadequate adaptations and hence, inaccessible environments (which, as we saw earlier, may affect meanings of home). It may also be that attitudes of staff towards other aspects of disabled people's identity affect disabled people's ability to 'be themselves' in their own home. As Smailes (1994) found, disabled lesbians face particular barriers relating to perceptions of their sexuality, whether in residential care, supported accommodation or owner-occupied housing. She argues, for instance, that there '... is rarely a choice of carers....Agencies supposedly facilitating independent living may not acknowledge lesbian relationships' (p 154). There may be a similar failure to consider the relationships of gay men, people labelled with learning difficulties and older people, although such issues remain under-researched. Finally, household cleanliness and order is often an important aspect of home, but as research by Angus and colleagues (2005) has shown, restrictions on staff employed to clean disabled people's dwellings – relating to health and safety regulations or lack of available hours, for example – may result in the deterioration of the accommodation and a subsequent negative impact on the householder'sfeelings of home.

Disabled people living in residential care homes may also find that the attitudes and practices of the institution and its staff affect common associations with home. There has been much criticism of the conditions inside this form of accommodation (Goffman, 1961; Barnes, 1990; Finkelstein, 1991; French, 1994; Means, 1996; Morris, 1999; Carvel, 2007), and in particular of the lack of control that inhabitants can exercise over their own lives. Hunt (1981, p 38), a former resident of a residential home, describes the kind of liberties he and the other residents fought for, including the freedom '... to choose our own bedtimes, drink alcohol if we chose, freedom for the sexes to relate without interference, freedom to leave the building without having to notify the authorities'. These are basic rights that are often taken for granted. Without control over such basic personal choices, alongside the limited privacy within such institutions (Means, 1996), it is difficult to see how such accommodation could ever truly represent a 'home' for the residents. Thus, we can see that the very phrase 'care home' may represent a contradiction of terms, if 'home' is believed to be about control, power and self-management.

We looked earlier at how the accessibility of a neighbourhood can be important to meanings of 'home', but it is also significant in terms of the sense of inclusion that can be achieved in the neighbourhood and local community. For one of the current author's research informants (Reg), being actively involved in the community was important and he believed that being on good terms with neighbours gave him an added feeling of safety. Such a sense of inclusion may be affected, however, by '...hostilities locally to those who are perceived as "different"' (Harrison, 2004b, p 61), or by 'nimbyism' (not in my back yard). This may arise as a result of negative perceptions of particular individuals (especially mental health service users) living in a neighbourhood (Herd, 1999) or opposition to proposals for shared or supported housing units to be located within the community (Goodridge, 2004). Research has shown that disabled people can be subject to abuse, harassment and more subtle social exclusion or social isolation within the communities in which their dwellings are located (Fyson et al, 2007), particularly mental health service users (Read and Baker, 1996). Mental health service users may also be some of the most common recipients of anti-social behaviour orders (ASBOs), as their behaviour can be perceived as threatening or as '... negatively affect[ing] the quality of life of neighbours' (Cobb, 2006, p 241).

Research into the experiences of disabled children has shown how they, and their siblings, are often subject to verbal and physical abuse from other children in the neighbourhood (Chamba et al, 1999; Oldman and Beresford, 2000). Some disabled people have even avoided having adaptations made to their homes, such as ramps installed, for fear of drawing attention to themselves as different (Imrie, 2006a). This is illustrated by the recent case of Fiona Pilkington, who took her own life and that of her disabled daughter after being harassed by local teenagers over a number of years. As one press commentary stated: 'An inquest has been told that the ever-changing gang of around 16 local youngsters seemed unable to leave the family in peace because they were perceived as different and vulnerable, and fair game' (Walker, 2009, p 1). Rehousing is often offered as a solution to the problems disabled people and their families encounter within particular neighbourhoods (if support is offered at all) (Oldman and Beresford, 2000), but this does nothing to challenge these negative assumptions and behaviours. It is perhaps even more damaging as it can reinforce the perceived vulnerability and dependency of disabled people.

Affordability and tenure

The role of tenure in meanings of home is significant, for as we have seen, disabled people may be more reliant on social renting than non-disabled people. With changes to housing tenure occurring since the 1950s (the growth of home ownership and decline of social renting), the significance of tenure in the meaning assigned to home has gained greater attention (Mallett, 2004) and has been the subject of much dispute (Saunders and Williams, 1988; Saunders, 1989; Gurney, 1990; Kearns et al, 2000). There is a tendency, for instance, to perceive certain benefits as accruing from owner-occupation (rather than renting), which strongly relates to positive associations with home. Some have suggested that owner-occupation is associated with greater status and control than social renting (with the latter being increasingly stigmatised) (Saunders and Williams, 1988; Dupuis and Thorns, 1996). The element of control apparently offered by owner-occupation certainly seemed important for several of the disabled informants from the current author's research:

> 'I believe that it can't truly be your home if you don't own it. You are always governed by someone else with either the choices you make, tenancy length and even colour schemes in some places!' (Jenny)

> 'Well, it's about control. That is one of the things I hated about living in the rented sector. If you comply with everything that is in the tenancy agreement, you can't even put a nail in the wall to hang a picture up, let alone decorate it as you want to have it. So it's about that but also when you buy it gives you the choice of exactly where you want to be. That was the main issue for me, because public transport was the big thing.' (Carol)

> 'I enjoy the sense of having the possession of the house. Not from its value point of view, but from the point of view that it's somewhere I can go away from and come back to, knowing that it's there, it's mine. I haven't got to worry about someone saying, "I'm sorry, you can't come back here"...' (Reg)

As far as can be judged from these perspectives, not only does ownership appear to be important as a consequence of control over the property internally and externally, and greater choice of location (albeit subject to financial restrictions), but the perceived security of the tenure also seems to influence the meaning applied to home. It was, however, difficult to set aside the role of additional variables (such as age and household composition) within interpretations. Context can also be significant to perceptions of tenure. As Dupuis and Thorns (1996) point out, in New Zealand home ownership is perceived '... as the normal, taken-for-granted tenure' (p 486) and as such, is considered to be of great importance. Indeed, for many of the people interviewed in the study, '... home was synonymous with home ownership' (Dupuis and Thorns, 1996, p 486).

Looking at differences between tenant and owner-occupier perspectives of home, Saunders (1989, 1990) (using a survey across three towns in England) claimed that renting was criticised by tenants for the lack of autonomy and the waste of money it represented. The tenants in this study mentioned the neighbourhood and family more often than owners, who tended to focus attention on possessions and 'home comforts'. Saunders (1989) explained this division as being the result of tenants lacking a sense of belonging, which then leads to a search for security through other means, such as the family and neighbourhood (thus suggesting that personal relationships could be more central to tenants' perceptions of home). Saunders' (1989, 1990) work has, however, received considerable critique in terms of its methods, terminology and assumptions (Somerville, 1992; Darke, 1994; Hamnett, 1999; Heywood, 2005) and for minimising '... the anxieties and difficulties associated with owner occupation especially for those on low incomes' (Gurney and Means, 1993, p 122). Kearns and colleagues (2000) conducted a study involving adults in eight local authority districts of West Central Scotland. Their work focused on the psycho-social benefits of home and found no significant division between tenures in the benefits acquired from the home. Furthermore, Forrest and colleagues (1990) point out that the supposed autonomy achieved by owners is not unavailable to tenants, and is '... more likely to reflect the wider life experience and to be a product of work, family and community situation as well as housing' (p 95). In addition, research by the current author showed that family and relationships were raised as important by only a quarter of the tenants, compared with just over half (seven) of the owners, which suggests that owner-occupiers are more likely to associate family with home (albeit that numbers here are small). It was also probable, however, that this reflected alternative factors. Of the seven owners who mentioned family, for instance, only Jessie lives on her own, with the other six living with either a partner and/or children. Over half of the tenants, on the other hand, live on their own, only one of whom cited family as significant. It could be argued, therefore, that these differences reflect household composition rather than tenure.

While the extent to which tenants can achieve a sense of 'home' remains contested, there seems to be some agreement in the literature that owner-occupation is the superior tenure in achieving a sense of 'ontological security' (Giddens, 1984) or belonging, although this is contingent on a number of factors such as the conditions of the period. Ontological security has been defined as '... the feeling of well-being that arises from a sense of constancy in one's social and material environment which, in turn, provides a secure platform for identity development and self-actualization' (Padgett, 2007, p 1926). Gurney (1990) notes the importance of distinguishing ontological security from physical security, stating that '... *ontological security is more to do with meaninglessness than powerlessness*' (p 4; emphasis in original). This 'ontological security' is reflected in the positive perceptions of home recalled by owners, including pride, autonomy, control, security, retreat from the social gaze, the element of choice exercised in location of the dwelling, and the pleasure some gain from making improvements to the property (Rakoff, 1977; Saunders and Williams, 1988; Lewin, 2001). Owner-occupation, in this way, is the tenure most associated with 'actualising' positive notions of home (see Rakoff, 1977). This can be problematic for disabled people because of financial barriers (discussed earlier as including disadvantaged labour market positions, generally lower incomes and risk assessment practices) that may mean that fewer choices are available to disabled people in terms of tenure. As such, disabled people's reliance on social renting may affect sense of home if, as some suggest, greater feelings of home are to be achieved by owning one's dwelling.

There is, however, opposition to the supposed link between tenure and positive meanings of home, or more specifically, ontological security. Tomas and Dittmar (1995, p 496), for instance, claim that '... a series of extended (and welcome) stays with friends could provide a person with a sense of home and a measure of ontological security – a positive experience of housing which involves neither residential stability nor ownership or renting a property'. In general, we may expect experiences to differ *within* ownership, and Gurney (1990) maintains that there are three key areas of potential difference, first, through mortgage repayments (with distinctions between wealthier home owners and those who struggle to meet payments); second, through the amount of control exercised (particularly in relation to differences between first-time buyers and experienced buyers, those with a mortgage and outright owners); and third, through the type of accommodation inhabited (including the design of the dwelling). For Gurney (1990) then, more important than the distinction between tenants and owners are the differential experiences of owners. These may be a consequence of the variants within the owner-occupied sector itself, for example, leaseholds, flats, shared ownership, equity and so forth, which are likely to expose different experiences of ownership. The benefits achieved from home ownership may also vary among different households in terms of gender, ethnicity and so forth. Furthermore, owner-occupation is not devoid of problems and insecurity, which may affect the 'ontological security' that is achieved, especially for low-income owners (Kearns et al, 2000). Thus, it appears that particular conditions or circumstances affect the level of 'ontological security' achieved. It is also worth noting that owner-occupation is set in historically specific circumstances. Strong and reliable associations have not always existed, for instance, between home ownership and feelings of independence, control and relative autonomy (see Stevenson, 1984; Craig, 1986; McCulloch, 1990; Hamnett, 1999; Hemingway, 2008). The apparent security offered by home ownership is also questionable in light of the recent economic crisis.

Issues relating to specific impairments

While physical, attitudinal and financial factors are significant to meanings of 'home', it is difficult to overlook aspects described by disabled people as relating to their impairment. It may be that experiences of pain affect the way in which disabled people use, and feel about, their homes (Dyck et al, 2005), for example, and others have referred to the importance of home for notions of 'recovery' and rehabilitation. Borg and colleagues (2005, p 243) looked at the role of home in the '... processes of recovery from severe mental illness' across four different countries (Italy, Norway, Sweden and the US). Participants in the study identified key aspects in relation to the significance of home for them, with reference to control, finding a balance between social lives and privacy (which related more to professional interventions) and, for all informants, '... the importance of having a secure base from which to launch efforts towards recovery' (p 243). It was also suggested that control could be particularly significant for those '... who had experienced homelessness or spent months in psychiatric institutional settings' (p 248), perhaps demonstrating the emotional or psychological security that 'home' can provide.

Research by the current author also suggested that a person's sense of home could be mediated through their understanding of their impairment, as shown in the experiences of two informants. For Alan, having agoraphobia has meant that there have been times when it has been difficult for him to leave the home, or even a particular room. Although he has worked hard to deal with this, he still feels that he has some difficulties in this respect. So for him, home represents "... a kind of physiological safe place", but at the same time, issues of isolation and loneliness are particularly difficult, and so just as essential to his concept of home are the people he lives with – his family. Furthermore, Chris felt that the meaning of home, for him, was partly affected by his impairment, or at least 'mediated' through his impairment:

'... one of the things about the home for me is that it is a space which I can gear to the actual way that I need to live my life. Because shared housing means I can't govern the space, I don't mean aesthetically, I mean in the way that things are organised ... it's difficult. That is something which I really desire, which I can sort of make conducive to the way in which I want to live my life, which I think is partially to do with my impairment but also something which everyone has to an extent. So for me I don't think it is peculiar to people with dyspraxia, but I do think that my relation to the home is mediated through my relationship to my specific impairment, so through my relationship essentially to my body, and I think that is really important.'

So for Chris, the control of space within the home is of particular significance, and is something that he feels he cannot achieve in his current housing situation. Living in a shared property stems from the high cost of him and his partner renting the whole property, something they feel unable to afford at this stage. So, it is arguably not just about his actual impairment, but also the design or space he inhabits. Perhaps then, this highlights an example of the difficulties of finding accessible (and affordable) properties for people with a range of impairments (rather than simply mobility impairments).

Another important aspect of home highlighted by Chris, and something that he attributed to having dyslexia and dyspraxia, was the need for continuity. He held that a home would only be home for him if there were continuity in his living arrangements. So, having moved six times within five years, he did not feel that his accommodation constituted home. This need for continuity has been highlighted by Harrison (2004a, p 704), who, referring to the work of Freeman (1984), underlines how '... the importance of cultural continuity for a sense of security' is evident when looking at mental health and the environment. This issue of continuity may also be significant for other types of households, especially if tied up with memories (Harrison, 2004a).

It would seem, then, that while both disabled and non-disabled people may have similar perceptions of meanings of home, disabled people may be disproportionately affected by issues of access, support, professional intervention and limited financial resources. Moreover, feelings of home may be mediated through a person's experience of their impairment. Wider social disadvantage and disabled people's relationships with housing, therefore, have a substantial effect on notions of home, and so tackling this disadvantage remains an important priority. Housing providers would benefit from developing a deeper understanding about the significance of the broad range of factors that affect housing for disabled people. Thus, when considering housing options, provision and need, it is important not to neglect the meanings that a 'home' provides for its inhabitants, since these may be central to their experiences of the dwelling.

Key conclusions

This book has endeavoured to address the role that structural factors play in shaping housing choices and opportunities for disabled people. It has shown that the choices disabled people are able to make in relation to their housing are restricted by limited options (relating to housing supply, financial position and assumptions and practices of housing and finance providers) or a lack of awareness of their options (due to limited information). It appears, too, that institutional outlooks and practices can lead to differentiation between impairment, which can result in diverse housing experiences for people with different impairments. Programmes for action therefore need to tackle general barriers, at the same time as acknowledging difference. While this book has investigated key aspects of the disability and housing relationship, there is scope for further research in the field to provide more detailed evidence on specific elements of disadvantage and discrimination. Most research into disabled people's experiences of housing is small in scale, and so larger projects that provide more detailed insights into general housing would be beneficial here. More specifically, there are aspects of the disability and housing relationship that require further attention, such as homelessness, housing for disabled students, and comparative work on disability and housing. Research could also investigate the potential effects of 'simultaneous oppression' within institutional practices and perceptions (so that, in addition to disability and impairment, responses to gender, age, ethnicity and sexuality might be considered).

It should be recognised that disabled people's relationship with housing is a product, not just of their relationship with services, but also more generally with the state and with society as a whole. Housing is just one element of society in which disabled people encounter exclusion. Thus, while targeting initiatives and policies at specific housing issues may improve the situation for some, it is important to tackle economic and social inequality as a whole to reduce disadvantage and '... usher in a further stage in the ongoing struggle for a truly equitable and inclusive society' (Barnes, 2004, p 13). There needs to be greater effort to change the wider social perceptions and cultural representations of disabled people from an individualistic, medical understanding to one that recognises social and environmental constraints experienced by people with impairments. While positive progress has been made in many areas, there is still some way to go, with disabled people's rights to choice and independence constituting a crucial struggle and continued focus of the disabled people's movement. It is therefore essential that disabling structures and individual actions continue to be challenged to promote a more inclusive society and one in which disabled people can exercise the same rights, choices and opportunities as those available to non-disabled people. We end now with a review of the main issues presented throughout the book.

- Disabled people constitute a large proportion of the population, and as such, their housing needs should not be deemed a minority issue. This is particularly so in an ageing society, where many of the problems posed by physical access issues urgently need addressing. While UK governments have introduced various policies engaging with disabled people's housing needs, including generic anti-discrimination legislation and specific housing policies, there is much room for progress. In addition, the recent change of government and subsequent public spending cuts mean that we are likely to witness a withdrawal of support that may have a negative effect on housing options for disabled people.
- The individual model of disability has dominated housing policy and provision for disabled people. Impairment has been seen as the cause of disadvantage and thus a 'personal' tragedy for the individual, leading to the assumption that disabled people are dependent and must be cared for. This means that disabled people's actual needs within housing have either been neglected or have focused on specific, specialised provision that has been useful in some individual cases, but has on the whole been exclusionary. The shift to the social model of disability has led to greater recognition of the ways in which social, environmental and cultural barriers cause disability. Despite some critique of the social model in recent years, the social model's inherent emphasis on 'structure' remains central to understanding the disadvantage (and opportunities) experienced by disabled people within housing. Further exploration of specific actions and processes may also provide additional detail on differential experiences.
- While experiences of housing differ widely among disabled people, and not all experiences are negative, it is clear that disabled people encounter numerous difficulties within access to housing of various types. Barriers to housing are wide-ranging and include a

variety of constraints that can be grouped into several overlapping considerations, including physical, communication, financial and attitudinal barriers. The disadvantage that disabled people experience within housing therefore relates to the limited supply of accessible housing, lack of information and advice (including in accessible form), the poor financial positioning of disabled people, and the attitudes and practices of housing providers, practitioners and policymakers (with underlying assumptions of disabled people's housing needs as homogeneous, 'special' and separate from the rest of the population). This has resulted in a reliance on social renting (for which high demand means restrictive allocation procedures), with limited provision from the private sector and exclusionary practices within the owner-occupied sector. Such factors affect access to particular housing and limit choice.

- The difficulties that disabled people encounter in relation to inaccessible environments, financial disadvantage and the assumptions and institutional practices of housing and support providers affect not only opportunities to acquire or secure housing, but also experiences of housing or meanings of home. The meanings that a home provides for inhabitants are therefore important considerations within housing provision and definitions of need.

- Throughout, we have looked at some of the ways in which current housing provision and mortgage practice might be improved to facilitate disabled people's housing options, highlighting important areas for change to policymakers and practitioners. Developing improvements in disabled people's access to different tenures is likely to entail a complex process involving a combination of simple measures and large-scale structural changes. Addressing barriers requires institutional action, education, legislation and continuous monitoring to ensure that discriminatory or exclusionary practices are highlighted. Using evidence to underline these constraints is the first step, something this book has endeavoured to do. It is important to remember that wider social barriers also need to be challenged. From the point of view of disabled people, and of a fair society, policies need to be constantly reviewed and contested.

- Parts of this book have focused explicitly on UK policy and practice, but it is hoped that the points raised can be applied in different countries. UK researchers need to learn from disability experiences elsewhere and there is developing international interest in these issues. So far, however, there has been little bridge building among housing investigators and practitioners on disability issues. This book hopes to offer some starting points for international debate.

Recommended further reading

Dupuis, A and Thorns, D. (1996) 'Meanings of home for older home owners', *Housing Studies*, vol 11, no 4, pp 485-501.

Gurney, C. (1990) *The Meaning of Home in the Decade of Owner Occupation:Towards an Experiential Perspective*, Working Paper 88, Bristol: University of Bristol, School for Advanced Urban Studies.

Harrison, M. (2004) 'Defining housing quality and environment: disability, standards and social factors', *Housing Studies*, vol 19, no 5, pp 691-708.

Heywood, F. (2005) 'Adaptation: altering the house to restore the home', *Housing Studies*, vol 20, no 4, pp 531-47.

Smailes, J. (1994) '"The struggle has never been simply about bricks and mortar": lesbians' experience of housing', in R. Gilroy. and R. Woods (eds) *Housing Women*, London and New York, NY: Routledge.

References

Aalbers, M.B. (2005) '"The quantified customer", or how financial institutions value risk', in P. Boelhouwer, J. Doling and M. Elsinga (eds) *Home Ownership: Getting In and Falling Out*, Delft: Delft University Press.

Abberley, P. (1990) *Handicapped by Numbers: A Critique of the OPCS Disability Surveys*, Bristol: Bristol Polytechnic.

Abberley, P. (1992) 'Counting us out: a discussion of the OPCS disability surveys', *Disability, Handicap and Society*, vol 7, no 2, pp 139-55.

Abberley, P. (1999) 'The significance of work for the citizenship of disabled people', Disability Archive UK, www.leeds.ac.uk/disability-studies/archiveuk/archframe.htm

Abberley, P. (2002) 'Work, disability, disabled people and European social theory', in C. Barnes, M. Oliver and L. Barton (eds) *Disability Studies Today*, Cambridge: Polity Press.

ABI (Association of British Insurers) (2003) 'An insurer's guide to the Disability Discrimination Act 1995, www.abi.org.uk/Display/file/364/DisabilityGuide2.pdf

Ainscow, M. (2007) 'From special education to effective schools for all: a review of progress so far', in L. Florian (ed) *The Sage Handbook of Special Education*, London, Thousand Oaks, CA, New Delhi: Sage Publications.

Albrecht, G.L. (1992) *The Disability Business: Rehabilitation in America*, Newbury Park, CA: Sage Publications.

Allen, C. (1999) 'Towards a comparative sociology of residence and disablement – Britain and Sweden in interventionist welfare regime perspective', *Housing, Theory and Society*, vol 16, no 2, pp 49-66.

Allen, C., Milner, J. and Price, D. (2002) *Home is Where the Start is: The Housing and Urban Experiences of Visually Impaired Children*, Bristol: The Policy Press.

Allen, S., Resnik, L. and Roy, J. (2006) 'Promoting independence for wheelchair users: the role of home accommodations', *The Gerontologist*, vol 46, no 1, pp 115-23.

Altman, I. (1993) 'Homes, housing, and the 21st century: prospects and challenges', in E.G. Arias (ed) *The Meaning and Use of Housing: International Perspectives, Approaches and their Applications*, Aldershot: Avebury.

Andreeva, G., Ansell, J. and Crook, J. (2004) 'Impact of anti-discrimination laws on credit scoring', *Journal of Financial Services Marketing*, vol 9, no 1, pp 22-33.

Angus, J., Kontos, P., Dyck, I., McKeever, P. and Poland, B. (2005) 'The personal significance of home: habitus and the experience of receiving long-term home care', *Sociology of Health Illness*, vol 27, no 2, pp 161-87.

Arthur, S. and Zarb, G. (1995) 'Measuring disablement in society. Working paper 4: barriers to employment for disabled people', Disability Archive UK, www.leeds.ac.uk/disability-studies/archiveuk/archframe.htm

Association for Payment Clearing Services, British Bankers Association, Building Societies Association, Consumer Credit Trade Association, Council of Mortgage Lenders, Credit Card Research Group, Finance and Leasing Association, Institute of Credit Management and Mail Order Traders Association (2000) 'Guide to credit scoring', www.bba.org.uk/content/1/c4/66/11/Guide_to_Credit_Scoring_2000.pdf

Aston, J., Hill, D. and Williams, C. (2007) *Landlords' Responses to the Disability Discrimination Act*, Leeds: Department for Work and Pensions.

Barlow, J. and Venables, T. (2004) 'Will technological innovation create the true Lifetime Home?', *Housing Studies*, vol 19, no 5, pp 795-810.

Barnes, C. (1990) *'Cabbage Syndrome': The Social Construction of Dependence*, London: Falmer Press.

Barnes, C. (1991) *Disabled People in Britain and Discrimination: A Case for Anti-discrimination Legislation*, London: Hurst and Company.

Barnes, C. (1999) 'A working social model? Disability and work in the 21st century', Disability Archive UK, www.leeds.ac.uk/disability-studies/archiveuk/archframe.htm

Barnes, C. (2003) 'What a difference a decade makes: reflections on doing "emancipatory" disability research', *Disability and Society*, vol 18, no 1, pp 3-17.

Barnes, C. (2004) 'Independent living, politics and implications', Disability Archive UK, www.leeds.ac.uk/disability-studies/archiveuk/archframe.htm

Barnes, C. (2005) 'Disability activism and the price of success: a British experience', Background notes to a verbal presentation, Institute of Advanced Studies, University of Western Australia, Perth, 31 August.

Barnes, C. (2006) 'Independent futures: policies, practices and the illusion of inclusion', Background notes to a verbal presentation to the European Network for Independent Living, Disability Archive UK, www.leeds.ac.uk/disability-studies/archiveuk/archframe.htm

Barnes, C. and Mercer, G. (2003) *Disability*, Cambridge: Polity Press.

Barnes, C. and Roulstone, A. (2005) '"Work" is a four-letter word: disability, work and welfare', in A. Roulstone and C. Barnes (eds) *Working Futures? Disabled People, Policy and Social Inclusion*, Bristol: The Policy Press.

Barnes, C., Mercer, G. and Shakespeare, T. (1999) *Exploring Disability: A Sociological Introduction*, Cambridge: Polity Press.

Barton, L. (1997) 'The politics of special educational needs', in L. Barton and M. Oliver (eds) *Disability Studies: Past, Present and Future*, Leeds: Disability Press.

Baylies, C. (2002) 'Disability in the context of development – questions of rights and capabilities', *Disability and Society*, vol 17, no 7, pp 725-39.

BBC (British Broadcasting Corporation) (2009) The Love of Money: The Age of Risk, BBC Two, 17 September.

BBC (2010) 'Pilot scheme helps disabled house buyer in Wrexham', BBC News, http://news.bbc.co.uk/1/hi/wales/north_east/8515962. stm

Beazley, S., Moore, M. and Benzie, D. (1997) 'Involving disabled people in research: a study of inclusion in environmental activities', in C. Barnes and G. Mercer (eds) *Doing Disability Research*, Leeds: Disability Press.

Beck, U. (1992) *Risk Society: Towards a New Modernity*, London, Newbury Park, CA, New Delhi: Sage Publications.

Begum, N. (1992) '... Something to be Proud of ...': The Lives of Asian Disabled People and Carers in Waltham Forest*, London: Waltham Forest Race Relations Unit.

Begum, N. (1993) 'Independent living, personal assistance and disabled black people', in C. Barnes (ed) *Making our Own Choices: Independent Living, Personal Assistance and Disabled People*, London: BCODP.

Begum, N., Hill, M. and Stevens, A. (eds) (1994) *Reflections: The Views of Black Disabled People on the Lives and Community Care*, London: Central Council for Education and Training in Social Work.

Beresford, B. and Rhodes, D. (2008) *Housing and Disabled Children: Round-up, Reviewing the Evidence*, York: Joseph Rowntree Foundation.

Beresford, P. (2000) *Our Voice in Our Future: Mental Health Issues*, London: Shaping Our Lives/National Institute for Social Work.

Beresford, P. and Wallcraft, J. (1997) 'Psychiatric system survivors and emancipatory research: issues, overlaps and differences', in C. Barnes and G. Mercer (eds) *Doing Disability Research*, Leeds: Disability Press.

Bevan, M. (2002) *Housing and Disabled Children: Highlighting User-commended Services*, York: Centre for Housing Policy.

Birch, J. (2008) 'The big squeeze', *Roof*, May/June. http://www.roofmagazine.org.uk/features/the_big_squeeze/

Birch, J. (2010) 'The More Things Change', *Roof*, vol 35, no 4, pp 19-21.

Borg, M., Sells, D., Topor, A., Mezzina, R., Marin, I. and Davidson, L. (2005) 'What makes a house a home: the role of material resources in recovery from severe mental illness', *American Journal of Psychiatric Rehabilitation*, vol 8, no 3, pp 243-56.

Borsay, A. (1986) *Disabled People in the Community: A Study of Housing, Health and Welfare Services*, London: Bedford Square Press.

Bowey, L., McGlaughlin, A. and Saul, C. (2005) 'Assessing the barriers to achieving genuine housing choice for adults with a learning disability: the views of family carers and professionals', *British Journal of Social Work*, vol 35, no 1, pp 139-48.

Bowlby, S., Gregory, S. and McKie, L. (1997) '"Doing home": patriarchy, caring and space', *Women's Studies International Forum*, vol 20, no 3, pp 343-50.

Bradford, I. (1998) 'The adaptations process', in R. Bull (ed) *Housing Options for Disabled People*, Bristol: The Policy Press.

Bridges, S. (2005) 'Credit scoring', Experian Centre for Economic Modelling, www.nottingham.ac.uk/economics/ExCEM/issues/issues3.htm

Brisenden, S. (1986) 'Independent living and the medical model of disability', Disability Archive UK, www.leeds.ac.uk/disability-studies/archiveuk/archframe.htm

Brown, T. and King, P. (2005) 'The power to choose: effective choice and housing policy', *European Journal of Housing Policy*, vol 5, no 1, pp 59-75.

Brown, T. and Yates, N. (2005) 'Housing and community care: a comparative perspective', in M. Foord and P. Simic (eds) *Housing, Community Care and Supported Housing: Resolving Contradictions*, Coventry: Chartered Institute of Housing.

Bull, R. and Watts, V. (1998) 'The legislative and policy context', in R. Bull (ed) *Housing Options for Disabled People*, Bristol: The Policy Press, pp 13-39.

Burchardt, T. (2000) 'Enduring economic exclusion: disabled people, income and work', Joseph Rowntree Foundation Findings, www.jrf.org.uk/knowledge/findings/socialpolicy/060.asp

Burns, N. (2002) 'Access points and barriers to owner occupation for disabled people', Unpublished PhD thesis, University of Glasgow.

Burns, N. (2004) 'Negotiating difference: disabled people's experiences of housebuilders', *Housing Studies*, vol 19, no 5, pp 765-80.

Caldicott, H. (2005) 'Promoting shared ownership housing options for people with long-term mental health problems', *Housing, Care and Support*, vol 8, no 2, pp 10-12.

Carvel, J. (2007) 'Care homes criticised for restraints on residents', *The Guardian*, 18 December, www.guardian.co.uk/society/2007/dec/18/longtermcare.socialcare

CEBE (Centre for Education in the Built Environment) (n.d.) *Building and Sustaining a Learning Environment for Inclusive Design: A Framework for Teaching Inclusive Design within Built Environment Courses in the UK*, Cardiff: CEBE, www.cebe.heacademy.ac.uk/learning/sig/inclusive/full_report.pdf

Center for Universal Design (1997) 'The principles of universal design', www.design.ncsu.edu/cud/about_ud/udprinciplestext.htm

Center for Universal Design (2006) 'Universal design in housing', www.design.ncsu.edu/cud/pubs_p/docs/UDinHousing.pdf

Chamba, R., Ahmad, W., Hirst, M., Lawton, D. and Beresford, B. (1999) *On the Edge: Minority Ethnic Families Caring for a Severely Disabled Child*, Bristol: The Policy Press.

Chan, M., Campo, E., Esteve, D. and Fourniols, J. (2009) 'Smart homes – current features and future perspectives', *Maturitas*, vol 64, pp 90-7.

Clapham, D. (2005) *The Meaning of Housing: A Pathways Approach*, Bristol: The Policy Press.

Clark, L. and Marsh, S. (2002) 'Patriarchy in the UK: The language of disability', Disability Archive UK, www.leeds.ac.uk/disability-studies/archiveuk/archframe.htm

Clements, L. (2007) 'The need for new legislation', Briefing Paper, www.wyed.co.uk/lukeclements/downloads/PDF_Sep08_04.pdf

CLG (Communities and Local Government) (2007) 'Your Right to Buy your home: a guide for tenants of councils, new towns and registered social landlords including housing associations', www.communities.gov.uk/pub/286/YourRighttoBuyYourHome_id1151286.pdf

CLG (2008) *Lifetime Homes, Lifetime Neighbourhoods: A National Strategy for Housing in an Ageing Society*, http://www.communities.gov.uk/publications/housing/lifetimehomesneighbourhoods

CLG (2009) *Housing and the Credit Crunch: Third Report of the Session 2008-2009*, London: The Stationery Office.

CLG (2009a) *English House Condition Survey 2007: Annual Report*, London: CLG.

CLG (2009b) 'Help at every step to avoid repossessions', www.communities.gov.uk/news/corporate/1312583

CML (Council of Mortgage Lenders) (2009) 'Wholesale funding – where next?', *CML News and Views*, no 23, 24 Nov, www.cml.org.uk/cml/publications/newsandviews/53/183

CML (2010) 'Walking very slowly to catch up: housing supply and demand', *CML News and Views*, no 4, 2 March, www.cml.org.uk/cml/publications/newsandviews/59/213

Cobb, N. (2006) 'Patronising the mentally disordered? Social landlords and the control of "anti-social behaviour" under the Disability Discrimination Act 195', *Legal Studies*, vol 26, no 2, pp 238-66.

Collinson, P. (2005) 'Dream home? Come on, wake up', *The Guardian*, 29 January, http://society.guardian.co.uk/housing/story/0,7890,1400919,00.html

Condie, M. and Penney, N. (2009) 'Now you see it ...', *Roof*, vol 34, no 4, pp 22-23.

Cook, I. (2005) 'The rights way forward', *The Guardian Unlimited*, www.guardian.co.uk/extendingboundaries/story/0,,1654175,00.html

Cooper, C. (2005) 'Involving users and carers in housing and social care planning – the rhetoric of "user empowerment"', in M. Foord and P. Simic (eds) *Housing, Community Care and Supported Housing: Resolving Contradictions*, Coventry: Chartered Institute of Housing.

Cooper, C. and Walton, M. (1995) *Once in a Lifetime: An Evaluation of Lifetime Homes in Hull*, Hull: University of Humberside.

Corbett, J. (1994) 'A proud label: exploring the relationship between disability politics and gay pride', *Disability and Society*, vol 9, no 3, pp 343-57.

Cowan, D. and Marsh, A. (2005) 'From need to choice: welfarism to advanced liberalism', *Legal Studies*, vol 25, no 1, pp 22-48.

Craig, P. (1986) 'The house that Jerry built? Building societies, the state and the Politics of owner-occupation', *Housing Studies*, vol 1, no 2, pp 87-108.

Cramer, H. (2005) 'Informal and gendered practices in a homeless persons unit', *Housing Studies*, vol 20, no 5, pp 737-51.

Crawford, G. and Foord, M. (1997) 'Disabling by design', *Housing Review*, vol 46, no 5, pp 98-100.

Crosby, N. and Jackson, R. (2000) 'The seven needs and the social model of disability', Derbyshire Coalition for Inclusive Living, www.dcil.org.uk/Papers/7Needs.htm

Crow, L. (1992) 'Renewing the social model of disability', *Coalition*, July, pp 5-9.

Crow, L. (1996) 'Renewing the social model of disability', in C. Barnes and G. Mercer (eds) *Exploring the Divide: Illness and Disability*, Leeds: Disability Press.

Crowther, N. (2000) *Overcoming Disability Discrimination: A Guide for Registered Social Landlords*, London: Royal National Institute for the Blind and the Housing Corporation.

Cullingworth, B. (1969) *Council Housing Purposes, Procedures and Priorities*, London: Department of the Environment.

Czischke, D. (2007) 'Social housing in the European Union: overview of key approaches, rends and issues', in D. Czischke (ed) *Current Developments in Housing Policies and Housing Markets in Europe: Implications for the Social Housing Sector*, Belgium: European Social Housing Observatory, CECODHAS – HOUSING EUROPE.

Darke, J. (1994) 'Women and the meaning of home' in R. Gilroy and R. Woods (eds) *Housing Women*, London and New York, NY: Routledge.

Dartington, T., Miller, E.J. and Gwynne, G. (1981) *A Life Together*, London: Tavistock.

Davis, K. (1981) '28-38 Grove Road: accommodation and care in a community setting', in A. Brechin, P. Liddiard and J. Swain (eds) *Handicap in a Social World*, London: Hodder and Stoughton, pp 322-7.

Davis, K. (1990) 'A social barriers model of disability: theory into practice. The emergence of the "seven needs"', Paper prepared for the Derbyshire Coalition of Disabled People, Disability Archive UK, www.leeds.ac.uk/disability-studies/archiveuk/archframe.htm

Davis, L. (1995) *Enforcing Normalcy: Disability, Deafness and the Body*, London: Verso.

Department for Constitutional Affairs (2007) *Mental Capacity Act 2005: Code of Practice*, London: The Stationery Office.

Derbyshire, F. (1998) *Better Housing Management for Blind and Partially Sighted People: A Good Practice Guide*, London: Royal National Institute for the Blind.

Dewsbury, G., Rouncefield, M., Clarke, K. and Sommerville, I. (2004) 'Depending on digital design: extending inclusivity', *Housing Studies*, vol 19, no 5, pp 811-25.

DH (Department of Health) (1989) *Caring for People, Community Care in the Next Decade and Beyond*. Cm 849, London, Her Majesty's Stationery Office.

DH (2001a) *Valuing People: A New Strategy for Learning Disability for the 21st Century*, www.archive.official-documents.co.uk/document/cm50/5086/5086.pdf

DH (2001b) *Planning with People: Towards Person Centred Approaches – Guidance for Implementation Groups*, London: DH.

Directgov (2010a) 'Guide to financial support for disabled people', www.direct.gov.uk/en/DisabledPeople/FinancialSupport/Introductiontofinancialsupport/DG_10020535

Directgov (2010b) 'Buying your housing association home: the Right to Acquire scheme', www.direct.gov.uk/en/HomeAndCommunity/BuyingAndSellingYourHome/HomeBuyingSchemes/DG_066460

Disability Alliance (2010a) 'Triple-jeopardy in new government's welfare reform proposals puts disabled people at greater risk of poverty', www.disabilityalliance.org/welreform2.htm

Disability Alliance (2010b) 'Emergency Budget', www.disabilityalliance.org/emergency.htm

Disability Wales (2009) 'Accessible housing', www.disabilitywales.org/accessible-housing

Diversus (2005) 'Disability Discrimination Act 1995 – what about people who know their condition is going to get worse over time?', www.handsonaccess.com/xhtml/article.asp?PageName=99

DoE (Department of the Environment) (1974) *Housing for People who are Physically Handicapped*, London: Her Majesty's Stationery Office.

Doherty, K.A. (2006) 'Practitioner article: housing homeless disabled people', Shelter, http://scotland.shelter.org.uk/__data/assets/pdf_file/0005/23189/PN5Fdisabled5Fpeople.pdf

Donnison, D.V. (1967) *The Government of Housing*, London: Penguin Books.

DPI (Disabled People's International) (1981) *Proceedings of the First World Congress*, Singapore: Disabled People's International.

Drake, R. (1999) *Understanding Disability Policies*, Basingstoke: Palgrave Macmillan.

DRC (Disability Rights Commission) (2005a) 'Shaping the future of equality: discussion paper', www.equalityhumanrights.com/Documents/DRC/Policy/drc35.doc

DRC (2005b) 'What does the law say about service providers?', www.drc_gb.org/businessandservices/bizdetails.asp?print=true&id=189&title=bs

DRC (2007a) 'Meeting the future housing challenge in England and Wales: creating an alternative future', http://drc.uat.rroom.net/DisabilityDebate/docs/Meeting_the_future_housing_challenge_in_England_and_Wales.doc

DRC (2007b) 'Disability Rights Commission: disability briefing', www.leeds.ac.uk/disability-studies/archiveuk/archframe.htm

DTZ Pieda (2003) *Demonstration Project: Housing for Disabled People – Interim Report*, Edinburgh: Ownership Options and Margaret Blackwood Housing Association.

Dupuis, A. and Thorns, D. (1996) 'Meanings of home for older home owners', *Housing Studies*, vol 11, no 4, pp 485-501.

Dyck, I., Kontos, P., Angus, J. and McKeever, P. (2005) 'The home as a site for long-term care: meanings and management of bodies and spaces', *Health and Place*, vol 11, pp 173-85.

EC (European Commission) (2009) *Report of the Ad Hoc Expert Group on the Transition from Institutional to Community-based Care*, EC. http://ec.europa.eu/social/BlobServlet?docId=3992&langId=en

Essex Coalition of Disabled People (2010) 'Emergency Budget announces potentially worrying changes to DLA', www.ecdp.org.uk/home/2010/6/23/emergency-budget-announces-potentially-worrying-changes-to-d.html

Evans, S. (2007) 'Disability, skills and work: raising our ambitions', *SMF Foresight*, London: Social Market Foundation. http://www.smf.co.uk/assets/files/publications/Disability,%20skills%20and%20work.pdf

Fiedler, B. (1988) *Living Options Lottery: Housing and Support Services for People with Severe Physical Disabilities*, London: The Prince of Wales' Advisory Group on Disability.

Finch, P. (2010) 'The big squeeze', *Roof*, vol 35, no 3, p 9.

Finkelstein, V. (1980) *Attitudes and Disabled People: Issues for Discussion*, New York, NY: World Rehabilitation Fund.

Finkelstein, V. (1991) 'Disability: an administrative challenge? The health and welfare heritage', in M. Oliver (ed) *Social Work: Disabled People and Disabling Environments*, London: Jessica Kingsley.

Finkelstein, V. (1994) 'Getting there: non-disabling transport', Disability Archive UK, www.leeds.ac.uk/disability-studies/archiveuk/archframe.htm

Finkelstein, V. (1996) 'Outside, "inside out"', *Coalition*, Disability Archive UK, www.leeds.ac.uk/disability-studies/archiveuk/archframe.htm.

Finkelstein, V. (2001) 'The social model of disability repossessed', Manchester Coalition of Disabled People, Disability Archive UK, www.leeds.ac.uk/disability-studies/archiveuk/archframe.htm

Fisher, K.R., Parker, S. and Purcal, C. (2009) 'Measuring the effectiveness of new approaches to housing support policy for persons with disabilities', *Australian Journal of Public Administration*, vol 68, no 3, pp 319-32.

Fitzpatrick, J. (2002) *Mainstream Housing Options for People with Learning Difficulties: An Action-centred Report and Information Resource for PARENT PRESSURE*, Edinburgh: Communities Scotland.

Fitzpatrick, S. and Pawson, H. (2007) 'Welfare safety new or tenure of choice? The dilemma facing social housing policy in England', *Housing Studies*, vol 22, no 2, pp 163-82.

Fitzpatrick, S. and Stephens, M. (1999) 'Homelessness, need and desert in the allocation of council housing', *Housing Studies*, vol 14, no 4, pp 413-31.

Foord, M. (2005) 'Introduction: supported housing and community care – towards a new landscape of precariousness?', in M. Foord and P. Simic (eds) *Housing, Community Care and Supported Housing: Resolving Contradictions*, Coventry: Chartered Institute of Housing.

Foord, M. and Simic, P. (2005) (eds) *Housing, Community Care and Supported Housing: Resolving Contradictions*, Coventry: Chartered Institute of Housing.

Ford, J. (1998) *Risks: Home Ownership and Job Insecurity*, London: Shelter.

Ford, J. and Quilgars, D. (2001) 'Failing home owners? The effectiveness of public and private safety-nets', *Housing Studies*, vol 16, no 2, pp 147-62.

Forrest, R., Murie, A. and Williams, P. (1990) *Home Ownership: Differentiation and Fragmentation*, London: Unwin Hyman.

Foundations (2007) 'Policy bulletin 23rd January 2007: Disabled Facilities Grant (DFG) consultation', www.foundations.uk.com/Files/DFG_Review.pdf

Freeman, H. (1984) *Mental Health and the Environment,* London: Churchill.

French, S. (1992) 'Simulation exercises in disability awareness training: a critique', *Disability and Society*, vol 7, no 3, pp 257-66.

French, S. (1993) 'Disability, impairment or something in between?', in J. Swain, V. Finkelstein, S. French and M. Oliver (eds) *Disabling Barriers – Enabling Environments*, London: Sage Publications.

French, S. (1994) 'Institutional and community living', in S. French (ed) *On Equal Terms: Working with Disabled People*, Oxford: Butterworth-Heinemann.

French, S. and Swain, J. (2006) 'Housing: the users' perspective', Disability Archive UK, www.leeds.ac.uk/disability-studies/archiveuk/archframe.htm

Freund, P. (2001) 'Bodies, disability and spaces: the social model and disabling spatial organisations', *Disability and Society*, vol 16, no 5, pp 689-706.

Fyson, R., Tarleton, B. and Ward, L. (2007) 'The impact of the Supporting People programme on adults with learning disabilities', *JRF Findings*, 2106, http://www.jrf.org.uk/publications/impact-supporting-people-programme-adults-with-learning-disabilities

Garnett, D. and Perry, J. (2005) *Housing Finance*, Coventry: Chartered Institute of Housing.

Giddens, A. (1984) *The Constitution of Society: Outline of a Theory of Structuration,* Cambridge: Polity Press.

Gilbert, A., Lankshear, G. and Petersen, A. (2008) 'Older family-carers' views on the future accommodation needs of relatives who have an intellectual disability', *International Journal of Social Welfare*, vol 17, no 1, pp 54-64.

Gillen, S. (2007) 'Lost in the system: the missing learning disabilities "patients" on NHS campuses', www.communitycare.co.uk/Articles/2007/06/14/104785/Lost-in-the-system-the-missing-learning-disabilities-39patients39-on-NHS.htm

Gillespie-Sells, K. and Campbell, J. (1991) *Disability Equality Training: Trainers Guide*, London: Central Council for Education and Training in Social Work.

GLA (Greater London Authority) (2006) 'Capital homes: London housing strategy 2005-2016. Equality impact assessment: report of the analysis of housing needs surveys', www.london.gov.uk/gla/publications/housing/eqia-report.pdf

Gleeson, B.J. (1997) 'Disability studies: a historical materialist view', *Disability and Society*, vol 12, no 2, pp 179-202.

Goffman, E. (1961) *Asylums: Essays on the Social Situation of Mental Patients and Other Inmates*, New York, NY: Anchor Brooks.

Goldsmith, S. (1997) *Designing for the Disabled: The New Paradigm*, Oxford: Architectural Press.

Gooding, C. (1996) *Blackstone's Guide to the Disability Discrimination Act 1995*, London: Blackstone Press.

Goodridge, C. (2004) 'Housing: a contemporary view of disabled peoples' experience, provision and policy directions', www.drc-gb.org/docs/10_454_Housing%20Report.doc

Griffiths, R. (1988) *Community Care: An Agenda for Action*, London: HMSO.

Guardian, The (2010a) 'Mortgage aid cut will see disabled people lose homes', www.guardian.co.uk/society/2010/aug/09/mortgage-benefit-cuts-disabled-housing

Guardian, The (2010b) 'Budget 2010: tougher disability allowance test to reduce claimants', www.guardian.co.uk/uk/2010/jun/22/tougher-disability-allowance-test-budget

Guardian, The (2010c) 'Budget 2010: housing benefit reforms to deliver savings of £1.8bn a year', www.guardian.co.uk/uk/2010/jun/22/budget-housing

Guardian, The (2010d) 'Fund to help disabled people runs out of cash', www.guardian.co.uk/society/2010/jun/23/disability-fund-has-no-money

Gurney, C. (1990) *The Meaning of Home in the Decade of Owner Occupation: Towards an Experiential Perspective*, Working Paper 88, Bristol: University of Bristol. School for Advanced Urban Studies.

Gurney, C. and Means, R. (1993) 'The meaning of home in later life', in S. Arber and M. Evandrou (eds) *Ageing, Independence and the Life Course*, London: Jessica Kingsley.

Hagner, D. and Klein, J. (2005) 'Homeownership for individuals with disabilities: factors in mortgage decisions', *Journal of Disability Policy Studies*, vol 15, no 4, pp 194-200.

Hamer, R. (2005a) *House Hunting for All: Opening up Property Search Systems to Disabled People*, Edinburgh: Ownership Options in Scotland.

Hamer, R. (2005b) *Matching Systems for Disabled People and Accessible Houses*, Edinburgh: Ownership Options in Scotland.

Hamer, R. (2005c) *Discrimination against Disabled Homebuyers by Mortgage Lenders*, Edinburgh: Ownership Options in Scotland.

Hamer, R. (2005d) *Disabled People and Mortgages on Benefits*, Edinburgh: Ownership Options in Scotland.

Hamer, R. (2006) 'Review of homelessness and disabled people', www.ownershipoptions.org.uk/pdf/Homelessness%20and%20 disabled%20people.pdf

Hamnett, C. (1999) *Winners and Losers: Home Ownership in Modern Britain*, London and Philadelphia, PA: UCL Press.

Hanson, J. (2004) 'The inclusive city: delivering a more accessible urban environment through inclusive design', Paper presented atRICS Cobra 2004 International Construction Conference, Responding to Change, http://eprints.ucl.ac.uk/3351/1/3351.pdf

Hanson, J., Percival, J. and Zako, R. (2002) 'The housing and support needs of older people with visual impairment', *Thomas Pocklington Trust Research Findings*, Autumn, no 1, pp 1-12.

Harris, J., Sapey, B. and Stewart, J. (1997) 'Wheelchair housing and the estimation of need', Disability Archive UK, www.leeds.ac.uk/disability-studies/archiveuk/archframe.htm

Harrison, L. and Means, R. (1990) *Housing: The Essential Element in Community Care. The Role of 'Care and Repair' and 'Staying Put' projects*, Oxford: Anchor Housing Trust.

Harrison, M. (1979) 'Risk capital, equal opportunity, and urban issues', *Environment and Planning A*, vol 11, pp 585-96.

Harrison, M. (2003) *Housing and Black and Minority Ethnic Communities: Review of the Evidence Base*, London: Office of the Deputy Prime Minister.

Harrison, M. (2004a) 'Defining housing quality and environment: disability, standards and social factors', *Housing Studies*, vol 19, no 5, pp 691-708.

Harrison, M. (2004b) 'From Gans to Coleman to the social model of disability: physical environmental determinism revisited', in C. Barnes and G. Mercer (eds) *Disability Policy and Practice: Applying the Social Model*, Leeds: Disability Press.

Harrison, M. (2007) 'From the corporatist welfare state to the social model and disciplinary therapy: reminiscences of working with ideas and theories', Paper presented at the School of Sociology and Social Policy postgraduate and staff seminar, 2 May, School of Sociology and Social Policy, University of Leeds.

Harrison, M. and Hemingway, L. (2011) 'Understanding the significance of "difference" for housing scholarship, research and policy', *International Encyclopaedia of Housing and Home*, Oxford: Elsevier.

Harrison, M. and Sanders, T. (2006) 'Vulnerable people and the development of "regulatory therapy"', in A. Dearling, T. Newburn and P. Somerville (eds) *Supporting Safer Communities – Housing, Crime and Neighbourhoods*, Coventry: Chartered Institute of Housing.

Harrison, M. with Davis, C. (2001) *Housing, Social Policy and Difference: Disability, Ethnicity, Gender and Housing*, Bristol: The Policy Press.

Harrison, M., Hemingway, L., Sheldon, A., Pawson, R. and Barnes, C. (2009) *Provision and Support for Disabled Students in Higher Education*, Bristol: Higher Education Funding Council for England.

Hawtin, M. (2005) 'Housing and community care in its historical and political context', in M. Foord and P. Simic (eds) *Housing, Community Care and Supported Housing: Resolving Contradictions*, Coventry: Chartered Institute of Housing.

HBF (Home Builders Federation) (2008) 'Lifetime Homes "not a panacea"', www.hbf.co.uk

HCA (Homes and Communities Agency) (2010) 'H: further detail regarding proposed Lifetime Homes criteria', www.homesandcommunities.co.uk/public/documents/H_Lifetime_Homes.pdf

HCIL (Hampshire Coalition for Independent Living) (c1986) 'Project 81 – one step on', Disability Archive UK, www.leeds.ac.uk/disability-studies/archiveuk/HCIL/one%20step%20on.pdf

Hemingway, L. (2004a) 'Disability, home ownership and the mortgage industry, with particular reference to the situations faced by disabled people in securing finance for owner occupation', Disability Archive UK, www.leeds.ac.uk/disability-studies/archiveuk/archframe.htm

Hemingway, L. (2004b) 'Disability, home ownership and the mortgage industry: findings', Disability Archive UK, www.leeds.ac.uk/disability-studies/archiveuk/archframe.htm

Hemingway, L. (2008) 'Disability and housing: home, housing options and access to owner-occupation', Unpublished PhD thesis, University of Leeds.

Hemingway, L. (2010) 'Taking a risk? The mortgage industry and perceptions of disabled people', *Disability and Society*, vol 25, no 1, pp 75–87.

Herd, D. (1999) *A New Threshold for Disabled People? A Report by the Housing Reference Group for Scotland*, Scotland: Disability Rights Task Force.

Heywood, F. (2001) *Money Well Spent: The Effectiveness and Value of Housing Adaptations*, Bristol: The Policy Press.

Heywood, F. (2004) 'Understanding needs: a starting point for quality', *Housing Studies*, vol 1, no 5, pp 709–26.

Heywood, F. (2005) 'Adaptation: altering the house to restore the home', *Housing Studies*, vol 20, no 4, pp 531–47.

Heywood, F. with Smart, G. (1996) *Funding Adaptations: The Need to Cooperate*, Bristol: The Policy Press.

Hills, J. (2007) *Ends and Means: The Future Roles of Social Housing in England*, CASE Report 34, http://sticerd.lse.ac.uk/dps/case/cr/CASEreport34.pdf

HM Government (2010) *The Coalition: Our Programme for Government*, London: Cabinet Office.

Holmes, M. (2000) 'Disability, housing and homelessness' in J. Cooper (ed) *Law, Rights and Disability*, London and Philadelphia, PA: Jessica Kingsley, pp165–92.

Housing Development Directorate (1978) *Handicapped Children: Their Homes and Lifestyles.* Occasional Paper, 4/78 London: DoE.

Housing Development Directorate (1978) *Housing Services for Disabled People.* Occasional Paper, 3/78 London: DoE.

Housing Options (2004) 'Mortgages', Housing Options Fact Sheets, www.housingoptions.org.uk/factsheets/9-mortgages.htm

Hudson, J., Watson, L. and Allan, G. (1996) *Moving Obstacles: Housing Choices and Community Care*, Bristol: The Policy Press.

Hughes, B. (2005) 'What can Foucault contribute to the sociology of impairment?', in S. Tremain (ed) *Foucault and the Government of Disability*, Ann Arbor, MI: University of Michigan Press.

Hunt, P. (1966) 'A Critical Condition', in P. Hunt (ed) *Stigma: The Experience of Disability*, London: Geoffrey Chapman.

Hunt, P. (1981) 'Settling accounts with the parasite people: a critique of "A Life Apart" by E. J. Miller and O. V. Gwynne', *Disability Challenge*, 1 May, London: UPIAS.

Hunter, C. (2007) 'Denying the severity of mental health problems to deny rights to the homeless', *People, Place and Policy Online*, vol 2, no 1, pp 17-27.

Hunter, C., Hodge, N., Nixon, J., Parr, S. and Willis, B. (2007) 'Disabled people's experiences of anti-social behaviour and harassment in social housing: a critical review', Disability Rights Commission, Disability Archive UK, www.leeds.ac.uk/disability-studies/archiveuk/archframe.htm

Hurst, R. (2000) 'To revise or not to revise?' *Disability and Society*, vol 15, no 7, pp 1083-7.

Hyde, M. (2000) 'Disability', in G. Payne (ed) *Social Divisions*, Basingstoke: Palgrave Macmillan.

Imrie, R. (1996) *Disability and the City: International Perspectives*, London: Paul Chapman Publishing.

Imrie, R. (2003) 'Housing quality and the provision of accessible homes', *Housing Studies*, vol 18, no 3, pp 387-408.

Imrie, R. (2004) 'Disability, embodiment and the meaning of the home', *Housing Studies*, vol 19, no 5, pp 745-63.

Imrie, R. (2006a) *Accessible Housing: Quality, Disability and Design*, London and New York, NY: Routledge.

Imrie, R. (2006b) 'Independent lives and the relevance of lifetime homes', *Disability and Society*, vol 21, no 4, pp 359-74.

Imrie, R. and Hall, P. (2001) 'An exploration of disability and the development process', *Urban Studies*, vol 38, no 2, pp 333-50.

Imrie, R. and Kumar, M. (1998) 'Focusing on disability and access in the built environment', *Disability and Society*, vol 13, no 3, pp 357-74.

Jaegar, C.C., Renn, O., Rosa, E. and Webler, T. (2001) *Risk, Uncertainty and Rational Action*, London and Sterling, VA: Earthscan Publications Ltd.

JRF (Joseph Rowntree Foundation) (2000) 'The market potential for Smart Homes', *JRF Findings*, N40. http://www.jrf.org.uk/sites/files/jrf/n40.pdf

JRF (2001) 'Involving black disabled people in shaping services', *JRF Findings*, D61. http://www.jrf.org.uk/sites/files/jrf/d61.pdf

JRF (2002) 'Users' views of community care for Asian disabled people', *JRF Findings*, 752. http://www.jrf.org.uk/sites/files/jrf/752.pdf

JRF (2004) Disabled people's costs of living', *JRF Findings*, 054, www.jrf.org.uk/sites/files/jrf/054.pdf

JRHT (Joseph Rowntree Housing Trust) (2008) *The Garden Village of New Earswick*, York: JRHT.

Kearns, A., Hiscock, R., Ellaway, A. and Macintyre, S. (2000) '"Beyond four walls". The psycho-social benefits of home: evidence from West Central Scotland', *Housing Studies*, vol 15, no 3, pp 387-410.

Kloos, B and Shah, S. (2009) 'A social ecological approach to investigating relationships between housing and adaptive functioning for persons with serious mental illness', *American Journal of Community Psychology*, vol 44, pp 316-26.

Laurie, L. (1991) *Building our Lives: Housing, Independent Living and Disabled People*, London: Shelter.

Lewin, F.A. (2001) 'The meaning of home among elderly immigrants: directions for future research and theoretical development', *Housing Studies*, vol 16, no 3, pp 353-70.

Leyshon, A. and Thrift, N. (1999) 'Lists come alive: electronic systems of knowledge and the rise of credit-scoring in retail banking', *Economy and Society*, vol 28, no 3, pp 434-66.

Leyshon, A., Thrift, N. and Pratt, J. (1998) 'Reading financial services: texts, consumers, and financial literacy', *Environment and Planning D: Society and Space*, vol 16, pp 29-55.

Lobel, A. (2004) 'Spreading the net', *Money Marketing*, 30 September. http://www.moneymarketing.co.uk/analysis/spreading-the-net/50775.article

Lund, B. (1996) *Housing Problems and Housing Policy*, London and New York, NY: Longman.

Lund, B. (2006) *Understanding Housing Policy*, Bristol: The Policy Press.

MacErlean, N. (2003) 'Putting ownership within reach of disabled', *Observer,* 31 August, http://money.guardian.co.uk/print/0,,4743860-109001,00.html

MacFarlane, A. and Laurie, L. (1996) *Demolishing Special Needs: Fundamental Principles of Non-discriminatory Housing*, Derby: British Council of Organisations of Disabled People.

MacPherson, W. (1999) *The Stephen Lawrence Inquiry: Report of an Inquiry*, Cm 4262-I, London: The Stationery Office.

Madigan, R., Munro, M. and Smith, S.J. (1990) 'Gender and the meaning of the home', *International Journal of Urban and Regional Research*, vol 14, pp 625-47.

Mallett, S. (2004) 'Understanding home: A critical review of the literature', *The Sociological Review*, vol 52, no 1, pp 62-89.

Malpass, P. (2010) 'Sale of the century', *Roof*, vol 35, no 4, pp 26-7.

Mansell, J. and Beadle-Brown, J. (2009) 'Deinstitutionalisation and community living: position statement of the Comparative Policy and Practice Special Interest Research Group of the International Association for the Scientific Study of Intellectual Disabilities', Paper presented to IASSID Council Meeting, Singapore, 26 June.

Mansell, J., Knapp. M., Beadle-Brown, J. and Beecham, J. (2007) *Deinstitutionalisation and Community Living – Outcomes and Costs: Report of a European Study, Volume 2: Main Report*, Canterbury: University of Kent.

Marshall, T. (2009) 'Over the age limit', *Roof*, vol 34, no 6, pp 22-25.

Marshall, T. and Rashleigh, B. (2009) 'Sold out', *Roof*, vol 34, no 4, pp 18-21.

Martin, S., Nugent, C. and Porter-Armstrong, D.A. (2005) 'User perspectives: living and working within a "Smart Home" environment', *From Smart Homes to Smart Care*, vol 15, pp 33-41.

Mason, M. (1990) 'Internalized oppression', Disability Archive UK, www.leeds.ac.uk/disability-studies/archiveuk/archframe.htm

Matthews, B. (2002) 'The Disability Discrimination Act and developments in accessible public transport in the UK', *World Transport Policy and Practice*, vol 8, no 2, pp 42-9.

McCulloch, A. (1990) 'A millstone round your neck? Building societies in the 1930s and mortgage default', *Housing Studies*, vol 5, no 1, pp 43-58.

McGlaughlin, A. and Gorfin, L. with Saul, C. (2004) 'Enabling adults with learning disabilities to articulate their housing needs', *British Journal of Social Work*, vol 34, pp 709-26.

McKechnie, A. (2006) 'Changing rooms: exploring the meaning of the dwelling with reference to physical disability', Paper presented to the European Network for Housing Research Conference, Housing in an Expanding Europe: Theory, Policy, Participation and Implementation, Ljubljana, 2-5 July.

Means, R. (1996) 'From "special needs" housing to independent living?', *Housing Studies*, vol 11, no 2, pp 207-31.

Means, R. (1997) 'From the poor law to the marketplace', in J. Goodwin and C. Grant (eds) *Built to Last? Reflections on British Housing Policy* (2nd edn), London: *Roof* magazine.

Means, R. and Smith, R. (1996) *Community Care, Housing and Homelessness: Issues, Obstacles and Innovative Practice*, Bristol: The Policy Press.

Mencap (2010) 'Communicating with people with profound and multiple learning disabilities (PMLD)', www.mencap.org.uk/guides. asp?id=459

Mercer, G. and Barnes, C. (2004) 'Changing disability policies in Britain', in C. Barnes and G. Mercer (eds) *Disability Policy and Practice: Applying the Social Model*, Leeds: Disability Press.

MHA (Mental Health Alliance) (2009) 'Mental Health Act needs more monitoring as use of compulsory powers rises, says Alliance', www. mentalhealthalliance.org.uk/news/practanniversary.html

MHF (Mental Health Foundation) (2006) *Making the Link between Mental Health and Youth Homelessness: A Pan-London Study*, London: MHF.

Milner, J. (2005) 'Disability and inclusive housing design: towards a life-course perspective', in P. Somerville and N. Sprigings (eds) *Housing and Social Policy: Contemporary Themes and Critical Perspectives*, London and New York, NY: Routledge.

Milner, J. and Madigan, R. (2004) 'Regulation and innovation: rethinking "inclusive" housing design', *Housing Studies*, vol 19, no 5, pp 727-44.

Mind (2006) 'Legal briefing: disability discrimination', www.mind.org. uk/Information/Legal/Disab.htm

Mojtabai, R. (2005) 'Perceived reasons for loss of housing and continued homelessness among homeless persons with mental illness', *Psychiatric Services*, vol 56, no 2, pp 172-8.

Molloy, D., Knight, T. and Woodfield, K. (2003) *Diversity in Disability: Exploring the Interactions between Disability, Ethnicity, Age, Gender and Sexuality*, Department for Work and Pensions Research Report No. 188, Leeds: Centre for Disability Studies.

Moneyfacts (2005) 'Mortgage income multiples – credit scoring not good news for everybody', Press Release, 26 May, www.moneyfacts. co.uk

Monks, H. (2005) 'What a tangled web – if you are disabled', *Observer*, 6 February, http://money.guardian.co.uk/print/0,,5120469-112098,00. html

Moore, M., Beazley, S. and Maelzer, J. (1998) *Researching Disability Issues*, Buckingham and Philadelphia, PA: Open University Press.

Morris, J. (1990) *Our Homes, Our Rights: Housing, Independent Living, and Physically Disabled People*, London: Shelter.

Morris, J. (1991) *Pride against Prejudice: A Personal Politics of Disability*, London: Women's Press.

Morris, J. (1993a) *Community Care or Independent Living?*, York: Joseph Rowntree Foundation.

Morris, J. (1993b) *Independent Lives: Community Care and Disabled People*, Basingstoke: Palgrave Macmillan.

Morris, J. (1993c) 'Housing, independent living and physically disabled people', in J. Swain, V. Finkelstein, S. French and M. Oliver (eds) *Disabling Barriers – Enabling Environments*, London, Thousand Oaks, CA, New Delhi: Sage Publications.

Morris, J. (ed) (1996) *Encounters with Strangers: Feminism and Disability*, London: The Women's Press.

Morris, J. (1999) 'The meaning of independent living in the 3rd millennium', Disability Archive UK, www.leeds.ac.uk/disability-studies/archiveuk/archframe.htm

Morris, J. (2002) 'Moving into adulthood: young disabled people moving into adulthood', *JRF Findings*, ww.jrf.org.uk/knowledge/findings/foundations/512.asp

Morris, J (2004) 'Independent living and community care: a disempowering framework', *Disability and Society*, vol 19, no 5, pp 427-42.

Mullins, D. and Murie, A. with Leather, P., Lee, P., Riseborough, M. and Walker, B. (2006) *Housing Policy in the UK*, Basingstoke: Palgrave Macmillan.

Murie, A. (2007) 'Housing policy, housing tenure and the housing market', in K. Clarke, T. Maltby and P. Kennett (eds) *Social Policy Review 19*, Bristol: The Policy Press.

Muscular Dystrophy Campaign (2010) 'Concerns raised over Prime Minister's remarks on social housing tenancies', www.muscular-dystrophy.org/get_involved/campaigns/campaign_news/2575_concerns_raised_over_prime_ministers_remarks_on_social_housing_tenancies.

Myers, E.D. (1998) 'Workhouse or asylum: the nineteenth century battle for the care of the pauper insane', *Psychiatric Bulletin*, vol 22, pp 575-7.

Nocon, A. and Pleace, N. (1998) 'The housing needs of disabled people', *Health and Social Care in the Community*, vol 6, pp 361-9.

Nygren, C. Oswald, F., Iwarsson, S., Fange, A., Sixsmith, J., Schilling, O., Sixsmith, A., Szeman, Z., Tomsone, S and Wahl, H. (2007) 'Relationships between objective and perceived housing in very old age', *The Gerontologist*, vol 47, no 1, pp 85-95.

ODI (Office for Disability Issues) (2007) 'Independent living report. Summary: better outcomes, lower costs', www.officefordisability.gov.uk/docs/res/il/better-outcomes-summary.pdf

ODI (2008) 'Independent living: a cross-government strategy about independent living for disabled people', www.odi.gov.uk/docs/wor/ind/ilr-executive-report.pdf

ODI (2010) 'Key facts and figures: information covering key ODI-related themes', www.officefordisability.gov.uk/research/facts-and-figures.php#24

ODPM (Office for the Deputy Prime Minister) (2004) 'Mental health and social exclusion: Social Exclusion Unit Report', [online only] www.socialinclusion.org.uk/publications/SEU.pdf

ODPM (2006) 'Affordability and the supply of housing, session 2005-06: House of Commons', www.publications.parliament.uk/pa/cm200506/cmselect/cmodpm/703/703ii.pdf

OFT (Office of Fair Trading) (1999) 'Vulnerable consumers and financial services: the report of the Director General's inquiry', OFT 255, www.oft.gov.uk/NR/rdonlyres/7B904E77-3997-4693-A998-3174F1148B51/0/oft255.pdf

Oldman, C. (2002) 'Later life and the social model of disability: a comfortable partnership?' *Ageing and Society*, vol 22, pp 791-806.

Oldman, C. and Beresford, B. (1998) *Homes Unfit for Children*, Bristol: The Policy Press.

Oldman, C. and Beresford, B. (2000) 'Home sick home: using the housing experiences of disabled children to suggest a new theoretical framework', *Housing Studies*, vol 15, no 3, pp 429-42.

Oliver, M. (1983) *Social Work with Disabled People*, Basingstoke: Palgrave Macmillan.

Oliver, M. (1990a) 'The individual and social models of disability', Paper presented to a Joint Workshop of the Living Options Group and the Research Unit of the Royal College of Physicians on People with Established Locomotor Disabilities in Hospitals, 23 July, Disability Archive UK, www:leeds.ac.uk/disability-studies/archiveuk/archframe.htm

Oliver, M. (1990b) *The Politics of Disablement*, Basingstoke: Palgrave Macmillan.

Oliver, M. (1992) 'Changing the social relations of research production?', *Disability, Handicap and Society*, vol 7, no 2, pp 101-14.

Oliver, M. (1996a) *Understanding Disability: From Theory to Practice*, Basingstoke: Palgrave Macmillan.

Oliver, M. (1996b) 'Defining impairment and disability: issues at stake', in C. Barnes and G. Mercer (eds) *Exploring the Divide*, Leeds: Disability Press.

Oliver, M. (2004) 'If I had a hammer: the social model in action', in J. Swain, S. French, C. Barnes and C. Thomas (eds) *Disabling Barriers – Enabling Environments* (2nd edn), London, Thousand Oaks, CA, New Delhi: Sage Publications.

Oliver, M. and Barnes, C. (1998) *Disabled People and Social Policy: From Exclusion to Inclusion*, London: Longman.

OPCS (Office of Population, Censuses and Surveys) (1988) *The OPCS Surveys of Disability in Great Britain*, London: HMSO.

Padgett, D.K. (2007) 'There's no place like (a) home: ontological security among persons with serious mental illness in the United States', *Social Science and Medicine*, vol 64, pp 1925-36.

Parkinson, M., Ball, M., Blake, N. and Key, T. (2009) 'An independent report to the Department for Communities and Local Government', www.communities.gov.uk/documents/citiesandregions/pdf/1135143.pdf

Peck, S. (2010) 'Independent Living Fund to close', *DisabilityNow*, 14 Dec, www.disabilitynow.org.uk/latest-news2/independent-living-fund-to-close

Pfeiffer, D. (2000) 'The devils are in the details: the ICIDH2 and the disability movement', *Disability and Society*, vol 15, no 7, pp 1079-82.

Picking, C. (2000) 'Working in partnership with disabled people: new perspectives for professionals within the social model of disability', in J. Cooper (ed) *Law, Rights and Disability*, London and Philadelphia, PA: Jessica Kingsley, pp 11-32.

Piggott, L. and Grover, C. (2009) 'Retrenching Incapacity Benefit: Employment Support Allowance and paid work', *Social Policy and Society*, vol 8, no 2, pp 159-70.

Prideaux, S. (2006) *Good Practice for Providing Reasonable Access to the Physical Built Environment for Disabled People: An Analysis of the Legislative Structures and Technical Expressions of Discrimination and Disability in the Context of the Built Environment in six European and two non-European States*, Leeds: Disability Press.

Prideaux, S., Armer, B., Harris, J., Hemingway, L., Roulstone, A. and Priestley, M. (2008) 'Report on the social inclusion and social protection of disabled people in European countries: United Kingdom', Academic Network of European Disability Experts, www.disability-europe.net

Priestley, M. (1998) 'Constructions and creations: idealism, materialism and disability theory', *Disability and Society*, vol 13, no 1, 75-95.

Priestley, M. (1999) *Disability Politics and Community Care*, Cambridge: Polity Press.

PMSU (Prime Minister's Strategy Unit) (2005) *Improving the Life Chances of Disabled People: Final Report*, London: Cabinet Office, www.strategy.gov.uk/downloads/work_areas/disability/disability_report/index.htm

Race, D. (2005) 'Learning disability, housing and community care', in M. Foord and P. Simic (eds) *Housing, Community Care and Supported Housing: Resolving Contradictions*, Coventry: Chartered Institute of Housing.

Rae, A. (1996) 'Social model under attack', Disability Archive UK, www.leeds.ac.uk/disability-studies/archiveuk/archframe.htm

Rakoff, R.M. (1977) 'Ideology in everyday life: the meaning of the house', *Politics and Society*, vol 7, pp 85-104.

Ramesh, R. and Butler, P. (2010) 'Budget 2010 losers: women, disabled and families bear the brunt', *The Guardian*, www.guardian.co.uk/politics/2010/jun/23/budget-2010-losers-women-disabled

Randall, B. (2003) 'Integrated solutions', *Inside Housing*, pp 21-2, www.insidehousing.co.uk/journals/insidehousing/legacydata/uploads/pdfs/1072191568_IH.031114.020-022.pdf

Rapley, M. (2004) *The Social Construction of Intellectual Disability*, Cambridge: Cambridge University Press.

Ravetz, A. with Turkington, R. (1995) *The Place of Home: English Domestic Environments, 1914-2000*, London: E and FN SPON.

Read, J. and Baker, S. (1996) 'Not just sticks and stones: a survey of the stigma, taboos and discrimination experienced by people with mental health problems', Disability Archive UK, www.leeds.ac.uk/disability-studies/archiveuk/archframe.htm

Reeve, D. (2004) 'Psycho-emotional dimensions of disability and the social model', in C. Barnes and G. Mercer (eds) *Implementing the Social Model of Disability: Theory and Research*, Leeds: Disability Press, pp 83-100.

Rieser, R. (1990) 'Internalized oppression: how it seems to me', Disability Archive UK, www.leeds.ac.uk/disability-studies/archiveuk/archframe.htm

Roof News (2009) 'Most rough sleepers mentally ill', *Roof*, vol 34, no 4, p 4.

Roulstone, A. and Barnes, C. (2005a) 'The challenges of a work-first agenda for disabled people', in A. Roulstone and C. Barnes (eds) *Working Futures? Disabled People, Policy and Social Inclusion*, Bristol: The Policy Press.

Roulstone, A. and Barnes, C. (2005b) (eds) *Working Futures? Disabled People, Policy and Social Inclusion*, Bristol: The Policy Press.

Roulstone, A. and Barnes, C. (2005c) 'Working futures: disabled people, employment policy and social inclusion', in A. Roulstone and C. Barnes (eds) *Working Futures? Disabled People, Policy and Social Inclusion*, Bristol: The Policy Press.

Rowe, A. (ed) (1990) *Lifetime Homes: Flexible Housing for Successive Generations*, London: Helen Hamlyn Foundation.

Royal National Institute for the Blind (RNIB) (2009) 'UK law for websites', www.rnib.org.uk/professionals/webaccessibility/lawsandstandards/Pages/uk_law.aspx

Saunders, P. (1989) 'The meaning of "home" in contemporary culture', *Housing Studies*, vol 4, no 3, pp 177-92.

Saunders, P. (1990) *A Nation of Home Owners*, London: Unwin Hyman.

Saunders, P. and Williams, P. (1988) 'The constitution of the home: towards a research agenda', *Housing Studies*, vol 3, no 2, pp 81-93.

Sefton, T. with Baker, M. and Praat, A. (2005) 'Ethnic minorities, disability and the labour market: a review of the data', www.rnib.org.uk

Shakespeare, T. (1996) 'Rules of engagement: doing disability research', *Disability and Society*, vol 11, no 1, pp 115-19.

Shakespeare, T. (1997) 'Researching disabled sexuality', in C. Barnes and G. Mercer (eds) *Doing Disability Research*, Leeds: Disability Press, pp 177-89.

Shakespeare, T. (2000) 'Disabled sexuality: toward rights and recognition', *Sexuality and Disability*, vol 18, no 3, pp 159-66.

Shakespeare, T. (2006) *Disability Rights and Wrongs*, London: Routledge.

Shakespeare, T. and Watson, N. (2001) 'The social model of disability: an outmoded ideology', *Research in Social Science and Disability*, vol 2, pp 9-28.

Shelter (2006) 'Practitioner article: housing homeless disabled people', http://scotland.shelter.org.uk/files/seealsodocs/16783/PN%5Fdisabled%5Fpeople%2Epd

Shelter (2007) 'What is disability discrimination?', http://scotland.shelter.org.uk/advice/advice-4905.cfm

Shelter (2010) 'The accessibility barrier', http://england.shelter.org.uk/housing_issues/Improving_private_renting/the_accessibility_barrier#_ednref1

Shevlin, M., Kenny, M. and McNeela, E. (2004) 'Participation in higher education for students with disabilities: an Irish perspective', *Disability and Society*, vol 19, no 1, pp 15-30.

Simkiss, P. (2005) 'Work matters: visual impairment, disabling barriers and employment options', in A. Roulstone and C. Barnes (eds) *Working Futures? Disabled People, Policy and Social Inclusion*, Bristol: The Policy Press.

Simons, K. (1998) *Home, Work and Inclusion: The Social Policy Implications of Supported Living and Employment for People with Learning Disabilities*, York: York Publishing Services.

Smailes, J. (1994) '"The struggle has never been simply about bricks and mortar": lesbians' experience of housing', in R. Gilroy and R. Woods (eds) *Housing Women*, London and New York, NY: Routledge.

Smith, S. and Mallinson, S. (1997) 'Housing for health in a post-welfare state', *Housing Studies*, vol 12, no 2, pp 173-200.

Social Security Advisory Committee (1988) *Benefits for Disabled People: A Strategy for Change,* London: Her Majesty's Stationery Office.

Somerville, P. (1992) 'Homelessness and the meaning of home: rooflessness or rootlessness?', *International Journal of Urban and Regional Research*, vol 16, no 4, pp 529-39.

Somerville, P. (1997) 'The social construction of home', *Journal of Architecture and Planning Research*, vol 14, no 3, pp 226-45.

Stephens, M., Ford, J., Spencer, P., Wallace, A., Wilcox, S., and Williams, P. (2008) 'Housing market recessions and sustainable home ownership', Joseph Rowntree Foundation, Ref 2254 online report, www.jrf.org.uk/sites/files/jrf/2254.pdf

Stevenson, J. (1984) *British Society 1914-45*, London: Penguin Books.

Steven Winter Associates (1997) *Accessible Housing by Design: Universal Design Principles in Practice*, New York: McGraw-Hill Inc.

Stewart, J. (2004) 'Housing and independent living', in J. Swain, S. French, C. Barnes and C. Thomas (eds) *Disabling Barriers – Enabling Environments* (2nd edn), London, Thousand Oaks, CA, New Delhi: Sage Publications.

Stewart, J., Harris, J. and Sapey, B. (1999) 'Disability and dependency: origins and futures of "special needs" housing for disabled people', *Disability and Society*, vol 14, no 1, pp 5-20.

Stirling, T. with Lloyd, D. (2004) *'There's More to it Than Wide Doors': The Case for a Disabled Persons Housing Service in South East Wales*, Wales: Disability Wales.

Swain, J. and French, S. (2000) 'Towards an affirmation model of disability', *Disability and Society*, vol 15, no 4, pp 569-82.

Swain, J. and French, S. (2008a) 'Introduction', in J. Swain and S. French (eds) *Disability on Equal Terms*, London: Sage Publications.

Swain, J. and French, S. (2008b) 'Affirming identity', in J. Swain and S. French (eds) *Disability on Equal Terms*, London: Sage Publications.

Swain, J. and Lawrence, P. (1994) 'Learning about disability: changing attitudes or challenging understanding?', in S. French (ed) *On Equal Terms: Working with Disabled People*, Oxford: Butterworth Heinemann.

Swain, J., French, S. and Cameron, C. (2003) *Controversial Issues in a Disabling Society*, Buckingham: Open University Press.

Tamm, M. (1999) 'What does a home mean and when does it cease to be a home? Home as a setting for rehabilitation and care', *Disability and Rehabilitation*, vol 21, no 2, pp 49-55.

Thomas, C. (1999) *Female Forms: Experiencing and Understanding Disability*, Buckingham and Philadelphia, PA: Open University Press.

Thomas, C. (2002) 'Disability theory: key ideas, issues and thinkers', in C. Barnes, M. Oliver and L. Barton (eds) *Disability Studies Today*, Cambridge: Polity Press.

Thomas, C. (2004) 'Developing the social relational in the social model of disability: a theoretical agenda', in C. Barnes, and G. Mercer (eds) *Implementing the Social Model of Disability: Theory and Research*, Leeds: Disability Press.

Thomas, L.C. (2000) 'A survey of credit and behavioural scoring: forecasting financial risk of lending to consumers', *International Journal of Forecasting*, vol 16, pp 149-72.

Thomas, P. (2004) 'The experience of disabled people as customers in the owner occupation market', *Housing Studies*, vol 19, no 5, pp 781-94.

Thomas, P. and Ormerod, M. (2005) 'Adapting to life – are adaptations a remedy for disability?', in M. Foord and P. Simic (eds) *Housing, Community Care and Supported Housing: Resolving Contradictions*, Coventry: Chartered Institute of Housing.

Tipper, R. (2003) '"Home-making": negotiating the "meaning of home" in a residential home for people with learning difficulties', MA dissertation, University of Leeds, Disability Archive UK, www. leeds.ac.uk/disability-studies/archiveuk/archframe.htm

Titmuss, R.M. (1968) *Commitment to Welfare*, London: George Allen and Unwin.

Tomas, A. and Dittmar, H. (1995) 'The experience of homeless women: an exploration of housing histories and the meaning of home', *Housing Studies*, vol 10, no 4, pp 493-515.

Townsley, R. with Ward, L., Abbott, D and Williams, V. (2010) 'The implementation of policies supporting independent living for disabled people in Europe: synthesis report', www.disability-europe.net/content/pdf/ANED

Tregaskis, C. (2002) 'Social model theory: the story so far ...', *Disability and Society*, vol 17, no 4, pp 457-70.

Tremain, S. (2002) 'On the subject of impairment', in M. Corker and T. Shakespeare (eds) *Disability/Postmodernism*, London: Continuum.

Turner, M. and Beresford, P. (2005) *Contributing on Equal Terms: Service User Involvement and the Benefits System*, Bristol: The Policy Press.

UKDPC (United Kingdom's Disabled People's Council) (2005a) 'The social model of disability and emancipatory disability research – briefing document', www.bcodp.org.uk/about/research.shtml

UKDPC (2005b) '"Improving the Life Chances of Disabled People" – a response from the British Council of Disabled People', www.bcodp.org.uk/library/BCODP%20response%20to%20Improving%20Life%20Chances.doc

UN (United Nations) (2008) 'Article 19 – Living independently and being included in the community', *UN Enable: Rights and Dignity of Persons with Disabilities*, www.un.org/disabilities/default.asp?id=279

UPIAS (Union of the Physically Impaired Against Segregation) (1976) *Fundamental Principles of Disability*, London: UPIAS.

Van Dijk, R. and Garga, S. (2006) *UK Mortgage Underwriting*, London: Council of Mortgage Lenders.

Vernon, A. (1996) 'A stranger in many camps: the experience of disabled black and ethnic minority women', in J. Morris (ed) *Encounters with Feminism and Disability*, London: Women's Press.

Vernon, A. (1997) 'Fighting two different battles: unity is preferable to enmity', in L. Barton and M. Oliver (eds) *Disability Studies: Past, Present and Future*, Leeds: Disability Press.

Wagner Report (1988) *Residential Care: A Positive Choice*, London: Her Majesty's Stationery Office.

Wahl, H., Fange, A., Oswald, F., Gitlin, L. and Iwarsson, S. (2009) 'The home environment and disability-related outcomes in aging individuals: what is the empirical evidence?', *The Gerontologist*, vol 49, no 3, pp 355-67.

Walker, P. (2009) 'Incident diary reveals ordeal of mother who killed herself and daughter', *The Guardian*, 24 September, www.guardian.co.uk/uk/2009/sep/24/fiona-pilkington-incident-diary

Walsh, B.J. (2004) 'From housing to home making: worldviews and the shaping of home', Paper presented to the International Housing Research Conference, Adequate Affordable Housing for All: Reward, Policy and Practice, International Sociological Association, University of Toronto, June.

Whitaker, J. (2001) 'Segregated special schools must close', Disability Archive UK, www.leeds.ac.uk/disability-studies/archiveuk/archframe.htm

Williams, B., Copestake, P., Eversley, J. and Stafford, B. (2008) 'Experiences and expectations of disabled people: a research report for the Office for Disability Issues', www.odi.gov.uk/docs/res/eedp/eedp-full-report.pdf

Wolfensberger, W. (1972) *The Principle of Normalization in Human Services*, Toronto: National Institute on Mental Retardation.

Wollenberg, A. (2010) 'A question of fairness', *The Guardian*, 2 October, pp 1-2.

Wood, H. (2004) 'Sustaining disabled people in the community: does supported housing offer a real choice?', *Practice*, vol 16, no 3, pp 185-96.

Woodin, S., Priestley, M. and Prideaux, S. (2009) 'ANED country report on the implementation of policies supporting independent living for disabled people', www.disability-europe.net/content/pdf/UK-8-Request-07%20ANED%202009%20Task%205%20request%20template%20UK_to%20publish_to%20EC.pdf

Woolley, M.C. (2004) *Income and Expenditure of Families with a Severely Disabled Child*, York: Family Fund.

WHO (World Health Organization) (2002) *Towards a Common Language for Functioning. Disability and Health: ICF*, Geneva: WHO, www.who.int/classifications/icf/site/beginners/bg.pdf

Youreable.com (2006) 'Insurance, disability and discrimination', www.youreable.com/TwoShare/getPage/09Money/3Financial+products/Insurance+discrimination

Zarb, G. (2006) 'From paupers to citizens: independent living and human rights', Paper presented to Human Rights Transforming Services Conference, QEII Centre, London 27 March, www.drc.org.uk/library/drc_speeches/from_paupers_to_citizens_inde.aspx

Websites

Some websites can be consulted for further information. These are shown below as they were at the time of writing.

AbilityNet: www.abilitynet.org.uk

Accessible Property Register: http://accessible-property.org.uk

Action for Blind People: www.actionforblindpeople.org.uk

ANED (Academic Network of European Disability Experts): www.disability-europe.net/en/home

Association of Blind Asians: www.aba-uk.org

Australian Network for Universal Housing Design: www.anuhd.org

British Dyslexia Association: www.bdadyslexia.org.uk

BSHF (Building and Social Housing Federation): www.bshf.org/home.cfm?lang=00

Care and Repair England: www.careandrepair-england.org.uk

Care and Repair Scotland: www.careandrepairscotland.co.uk

CDS (Centre for Disability Studies): www.leeds.ac.uk/disability-studies

Center for Independent Living: www.cilberkeley.org

Center for Universal Design: www.design.ncsu.edu/cud

Centre for Accessible Environments: www.cae.org.uk

CIH (Chartered Institute of Housing): www.cih.org.uk

CLG (Communities and Local Government): www.communities.gov. uk/corporate

DAA (Disability Awareness in Action): www.daa.org.uk

Dial UK: www.dialuk.info/index.asp

Disability Archive UK: www.leeds.ac.uk/disability-studies/archiveuk

Disability Studies.net: www.disabilitystudies.net

Disabled People's International: www.dpi.org

DLF (Disabled Living Foundation): www.dlf.org.uk

DPTAC (Disabled Persons Transport Advisory Committee): www. dptac.gov.uk

EDF (European Disability Forum): www.edf-feph.org

EHRC (Equality Human Rights Commission): www.equality humanrights.com

ENHR (European Network of Housing Research): www.enhr.ibf. uu.se/index.html

European Urban Knowledge Network: www.eukn.org

Foundations: www.foundations.uk.com

Habinteg: www.habinteg.org.uk/main.cfm

HCA (Homes and Communities Agency): www.homesandcommunities. co.uk

Inside Housing: www.insidehousing.co.uk

JRF (Joseph Rowntree Foundation): www.jrf.org.uk

Margaret Blackwood Housing Association: www.mbha.org.uk

MHF (Mental Health Foundation): www.mentalhealth.org.uk/ welcome

Mind: www.mind.org.uk

National Housing Federation: www.housing.org.uk

NRAC (National Register of Access Consultants): www.nrac.org.uk

ODI (Office for Disability Issues): www.officefordisability.gov.uk

Ownership Options in Scotland: http://ownershipoptions.org.uk/

Property People: www.ppmagazine.co.uk

Ricability: www.ricability.org.uk

RNIB (Royal National Institute for the Blind): www.rnib.org.uk

RNID (Royal National Institute for Deaf People): www.rnid.org.uk

Scope: www.scope.org.uk

Sense: www.sense.org.uk

Shelter: http://england.shelter.org.uk and http://scotland.shelter.org.uk

SIA (Spinal Injuries Association): www.spinal.co.uk

Skill (National Bureau for Students with Disabilities): www.skill.org.uk

Speakability: www.speakability.org.uk

Tenant Services Authority: www.tenantservicesauthority.org

Thomas Pocklington Trust: www.pocklington-trust.org.uk

UKDPC (United Kingdom Disabled People's Council): www.ukdpc.net

Index